MERCHANTS, PILGRIMS AND HIGHWAYMEN

A History of Roads Through the Ages

HERMANN SCHREIBER

Merchants, Pilgrims and Highwaymen

A History of Roads Through the Ages

G. P. PUTNAM'S SONS
NEW YORK

FIRST AMERICAN EDITION 1962

Originally published in Germany under the title
Sinfonie der Strasse.

Library of Congress Catalog
Card Number: 61-15079

CONTENTS

ILLUSTRATIONS

Following Page 118

MAPS

MERCHANTS, PILGRIMS AND HIGHWAYMEN

A History of Roads Through the Ages

Chapter 1

THE AMBER ROUTES

Many centuries ago, when space became too restricted for wandering abroad, when the hunters came more and more into conflict with hostile tribes and the hunting-grounds had to be hotly contested, our forefathers resigned themselves, somewhat reluctantly, to a more settled way of life. The small kitchen-garden, in which the women had cultivated a few vegetables and herbs to cook with the game, suddenly acquired a new significance. The hunters became cattle-breeders and farmers.

Not all of those who lived in the dawn of European history, however, appear to have completely suppressed their wanderlust. Many a man, tormented by memories of freedom, devised some means whereby he could earn a livelihood without being condemned, like the womenfolk, to back-breaking work in the fields. You cannot be a wanderer and at the same time sow and reap; you must live by the labour of others.

It is only during the last few decades that archaeological research has revealed the full extent of overland travel in prehistoric times. We know now that flint implements of the Danish Ertböll culture —some four thousand years B.C.—were produced in large workshops and transported not only to Norway but also by long overland routes into the interior of Germany. In the third millenium B.C. there was a similar traffic in the blue-grey freestone of Spiennes in Belgium, which was hewn out of some two thousand shafts, some of them sixty feet deep, and sold as far away as the Ardennes. Production on this scale requires a steady market. So even then there must have been established trade connections and, above all, reliable means of communication. The tin which the Phoenicians brought in their ships from the tin-islands off Brittany, around the middle of the second millenium B.C., was also transported overland—at least for short distances.

There was, of course, no long-distance transport in bulk over these prehistoric roads. They were mostly rough tracks, sometimes even no more than narrow paths, about which one trader learned from another, or which he blazed for himself with small and frequently hidden signs. But if one were to reconstruct a road map of, for example, the Etruscan overland trade, it would bear a very close resemblance to a modern relief map of Europe. The travellers carrying their valuable loads had to take their bearings by certain landmarks and these were the rivers and the mountain ranges.

For hundreds, even thousands, of years traders used the same mountain passes and crossed the rivers by the same fords. At points of intersection and at the main river crossings arose settlements whose names still bear witness to their original purpose: from Bosphorus (Cowford) to Oxford, from Klagenfurt to Herford, from Stratford to Tiefurt. The Scythians named a whole river after a ford—Porata (Pruth)—and the ancient Persian word *poretus* (bridge) survives in the river Euphrates (the well-bridged).

If trading from prehistoric times right up to the Middle Ages was a hazardous business, the difficult roads, the flooded rivers and the landslides were not the only causes. The greatest hazard was always man himself. The traders tried to protect themselves against robbers by making treaties with the tribes. But all too often they had to defend their own lives and property. The old trade routes are lined with graves.

These graves have proved invaluable to the archaeologist in helping him to trace the course of the ancient roads. The richer the unfortunate trader, the more amber and gold, jewellery and implements were placed in his grave. Few places can boast such a collection of amber from the North and Etruscan filigree work from the South as Hallstatt in the Salzkammergut (Upper Austria) with its prehistoric graves. Hallstatt's salt mines made it one of the main trading centres of that early period.

We can safely assume that between the first traders in bell-shaped beakers and the last of the Etruscan traders about 1,500 years elapsed, roughly from 1900 to 300 B.C. During this period four trade routes ran across central and Eastern Europe, which were regularly used and which were named the 'amber roads' after the main commodity of those times. (Apart from its statuary and jewellery value, amber was an important ingredient in primitive and medieval medicines.) The first ran southwards from where Hamburg is today to the Rhine, then up-river to Basle, westwards to the Rhône, then down-river to the Mediterranean. There was an alternative route a little farther west, which crossed the Lower Rhine at Xanten and, passing through Metz, joined up with the first at Chalons. (The towns I have mentioned were not yet in existence; they are used here merely as location-points.)

The second, middle, road ran due south from the Baltic coast near Lübeck through Magdeburg, Halle, Hof, Regensburg and Hallstatt to the Brenner Pass.

The third is perhaps the most interesting. It began in the Samland on the East Prussian coast (where amber is still to be found), crossed the river Vistula, and reached the Danube through the Moravian Gate: in the Etruscan period it passed to the west of Vienna, in Roman times to the east at Carmuntum; from there it continued through Hungary to Aquileia (in the northern corner of the Adriatic).

The fourth road, the Baltic–Pontus amber road, followed for the most part the main eastern rivers, the Vistula, San, Sereth, Pruth, Bug and Dnieper.

These roads have been very accurately traced. J. N. von Sadowski, the Polish archaeologist, located each of the old crossing-points, each of the fords used by the amber traders on the rivers Oder, Vistula, Dnieper and Niemen. He associated all the amber deposits and Etruscan graves that were found in these areas with the early trade roads.

Of the roads themselves very little remains. One thing is certain: they were not roads in the modern sense of the word. Only where they approached settlements or where they intersected, for example near river fords or mountain passes, were efforts made to improve them. We know that some settlements played a prominent part in the old North–South trade as staging-points. Quite a few of them today are small, quiet places, of no importance so far as communications are concerned. One of these is the monastery town of Wilten, near Innsbruck, through which the middle amber road passed on its way to the Brenner Pass, from where it followed the line taken today by the railway from Innsbruck to Verona. Other places, however, have remained key-points up to the present day. One example is Bruck an der Mur, at which no less than three prehistoric trade routes met. The fords at Czarnikau and Kulm were also important junctions. Later, when Etruscan and Greek traders realized that the Samland was the main producer of amber and could be reached by

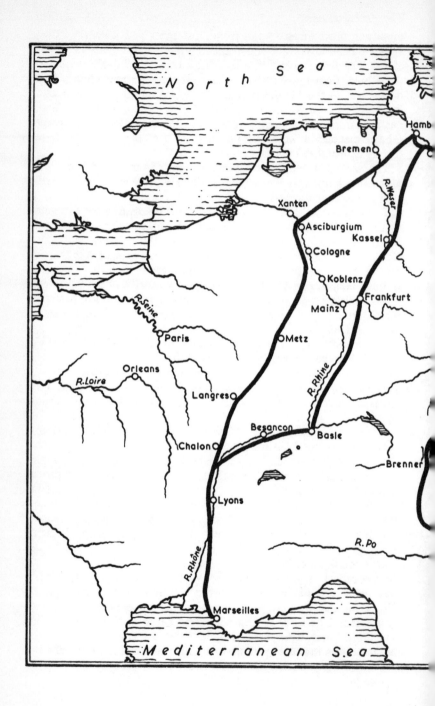

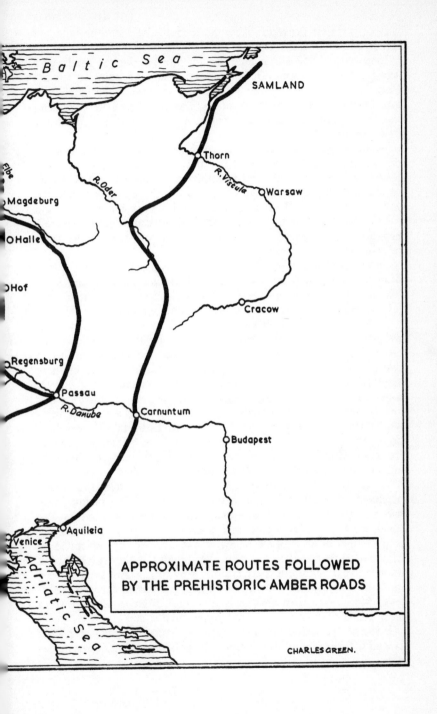

APPROXIMATE ROUTES FOLLOWED
BY THE PREHISTORIC AMBER ROADS

CHARLES GREEN.

way of the East Prussian lakes, the ford at Czarnikau became less important.

One of the few surviving relics of the old amber roads is a 'corduroy road', about fifteen hundred yards long, south of Elbing. Four layers of oak logs, lengthwise and crosswise alternately, enabled traffic to pass across the moors. The age of this stretch of road has been established from fragments of pottery dating back to the fifth century B.C.

Remains of the middle amber road were also discovered in the region of the Fern Pass between the Tyrolean towns Imst and Reutte. In the course of local blasting operations a ten-yard stretch of stone road with wheel grooves was discovered. These grooves, which are from pre-Roman times, are about six inches deep and roughly a yard apart. It is assumed that they were not merely produced by countless cart wheels, but were chiselled in the stone to give the wheels a firm hold.

At another spot in the same neighbourhood, where a swamp was drained, a corduroy road of alder trunks was found about three feet under the surface—yet another indication that even in pre-Roman times there were well-built roads across the Alps.

Although we cannot produce exact replicas of the amber roads, we possess an astonishing amount of evidence to show the volume and nature of the traffic that passed over them. Excavations in Silesia revealed not only large deposits of crude amber (one of these at Hartlieb, near Breslau, contained more than one and a quarter tons) but also manufacturing implements such as primitive cutting and boring machines, moulds for molten bronze, and other tools which had been brought north by road. Until fairly recently a dredging firm at Memel recovered enough pieces of wrought amber from the Gulf to prove beyond doubt that there was a thriving amber industry along that coast in prehistoric times.

There were also important amber centres in Switzerland, which occupied a special position as a transit country. The precious resin was transported up the Rhine and, before it continued on its way down the Rhône, Swiss craftsmen went to work on it, thus earning a substantial profit. Not all the Swiss lake-villages were inhabited by Etruscan amber-workers, as one over-zealous authority claimed a hundred years ago, but it is certainly true to say that even in very early times a veritable network of trade routes passed across Switzerland. More often than not the local inhabitants earned more from these roads than from their own unproductive soil.

Between the Baltic and the Mediterranean thousands of people earned their livelihood from amber, the gold of the sea. For centuries it was so highly valued that an amber statuette was worth an able-bodied slave.

Then, about 330 B.C., the peaceful trading of the Etruscans was seriously interrupted: a new people, the Romans, deprived them of town after town, cutting off the exchange of goods with the northern countries. In Massilia (Marseilles), too, the traders and craftsmen waited in vain for fresh supplies of amber. The expertise of the Etruscan barter-traders was not so easy to replace. By hook or by crook a new route to the amber countries had to be found—a route which did not require the specialized knowledge of the Etruscans. So it was decided to take to the sea.

Despite all the romantic accounts of early seafaring, despite the exciting picture of a prehistoric shuttle-service with rafts and canoes from one continent to another, the fact remains that without maps, compasses and a means of propulsion independent of the weather, ships were far from ideal as a means of transport. In the eyes of our forefathers, Europe—a continent without desert and liberally supplied with rivers and forests, a continent in which it was difficult to starve and even more difficult to die of thirst—compared favourably with the mist-shrouded North Sea, of which they knew very little.

In the scholarly *Historia Naturalis* of Pliny the Elder the following passage occurs:

> Pytheas reports that the Guinoni, a Germanic tribe, live on the sand flats by the sea called Metuonis, which stretches for six thousand stadia [nearly 690 miles]. From there it is said to be a day's sail to the island of Abalus. On its shores amber is washed up by the waves in spring, scum from the condensation of the sea. The inhabitants use it as fuel instead of wood and sell it to their Teuton neighbours.

The Pytheas quoted here as authority (about 330 B.C.) was regarded for more than two thousand years as possessing one of the liveliest imaginations in the history of seafaring; during the last few decades, however, scientific research—more particularly that of Professors M. Cary and Richard Hennig—has completely rehabilitated him. He was no mere spinner of seamen's yarns or glib commercial traveller; he was an unpretentious scholar, who noticed many things in Massilia that aroused his curiosity. He saw the absurdly small consignments of precious amber arriving from the North by road and realized why so many of the rich merchants looked at him thoughtfully when he spoke of the far countries in the North, which, he imagined, must also be accessible by sea. He

readily accepted the offer of a few of these wealthy merchants to fit
out a ship for him.

As a citizen of the ancient seafaring town of Massilia, Pytheas had
enough Greek and Phoenician blood in his veins to accept such a
challenge; he travelled farther north than any other seafarer of
ancient times that we know of, and he wrote an account of his voyage, in which he related such astonishing facts and observations
from northern Europe that his readers in Rome, Athens and Alexandria refused to believe them and accused him of lying. Unfortunately this account has only survived in quotations by other classical
authors, but this much is certain: Pytheas not only undertook an
extremely daring voyage of discovery but also made perhaps the
first serious attempt to replace the laborious and costly overland
method of transport by sea traffic.

The amber trade did not remain for long the monopoly of the
Etruscans and the seafaring men from Massilia; the adventurous
Greeks also made for the legendary amber country. In the course
of his excavations at Troy, Heinrich Schliemann, the German archaeologist, discovered a grave with four hundred amber beads which
date back to about 1850 B.C. In itself this was not conclusive proof
of independent amber trading by the Greeks, but, as is so often the
case, it was further proof of existing evidence.

In 1832 a Polish peasant was ploughing his field near the village
of Schubin, in the neighbourhood of Bromberg, when he unearthed
a hoard of old and highly improbable coins. There were thirty-nine
of them. The peasant thought little more about them till he
met a merchant who was on his way to Frankfurt-an-der-Oder and
handed them over to him. The merchant had no idea what they were,
but he knew that there were collectors in Berlin who would pay a
very tidy sum for such pieces. So he bought them from the peasant
and, next time he was in Berlin, took them to an antique-dealer.

On May 9th 1833, a certain Herr Levezow gave a lecture on the
Schubin discovery at the Berlin Academy of Sciences. He proved that
these were ancient Greek coins which by the symbols on them could
be identified as coins from Olbia, the Greek trading centre at the
mouth of the river Bug. Some had been minted there, others in
Athens, Aegina, and Cycicus, which had regular trade relations with
Olbia. But coins from Aegina were only in circulation until 431 B.C.,
the year in which the town was destroyed. So as early as the fifth
century B.C. a Greek trade route must have passed through Schubin;
and from Herr Schliemann's discovery it is a reasonable assumption that amber was one of the commodities which were carried on
the road.

For thousands of miles the great amber roads wound their way across rivers and mountains, through marshes, forests and plains. Very little remains of them today: a few coins, a bridge here, a fort there—and many graves. Yet at one time these busy roads brought the civilized peoples of the Mediterranean—the Etruscans and the Greeks—into contact with the tribes which they described contemptuously as 'barbarians'. Like our modern highways, these trade roads of ancient times were the arteries through which the life-blood (progress and development) of the various peoples flowed.

Chapter 2

THE ROYAL ROADS

The first established trade road we know of ran to the south of the Black Sea and of the amber rivers, which, many an ancient geographer believed, themselves secreted the amber in their beds, because they were the routes by which the traders returned from the Samland.

In Asia Minor the rivers are short and often tortuous (the Meander has become proverbial!), and periods of drought rob them of any value as means of communication. On the other hand, one of the major obstacles to road-building—applicable even today in Central and Eastern Europe—does not exist here; in the mountainous country of Anatolia there are virtually no marshy depressions. While there is not enough timber for corduroy roads, there is an ample supply of stones. One can understand the complaint made during one of the Crusades that this country had plenty of stones and very little bread.

Herodotus, who had so little reliable information about the peoples north of Olbia and apparently did not venture into the East European forests, seems to have acquired a great deal of first-hand information about Anatolia and Mesopotamia. But like so many other writers of travel-books he does not simply say: I was there and have seen this and that. His description of the royal roads of Persia, which are of such absorbing interest to us, is woven into a spirited account of the Spartan King Kleomenes I (about 500 B.C.). Yet the information he gives (and here he compares favourably with many later writers) is so detailed and so reliable that we know more about the main traffic routes in the kingdom of the Persian monarch, Darius I (521–485 B.C.), than about many of the roads in medieval Europe only 600 years ago. In the fifth book of his famous history, Herodotus writes:

> The entire way runs through populated and safe areas, and everywhere there are royal stations and excellent hostelries. On the way through Lydia [today, western Anatolia] and Phrygia [Inner Asia Minor], a stretch of ninety-four and a half parasangs, there are twenty stations.[1]
>
> From Phrygia one arrives at the Halys [a river which today is called the Kisil-Irmak], where there is a gate through which one must pass in order to cross the river, and it is guarded by a well-manned sentry-post. On the other side of the river one comes to Cappadocia [in the interior of eastern Asia Minor] on a road that stretches for a hundred and four parasangs to the border of Cilicia [country in the Taurus] through twenty-eight stations. Here at the border one must pass through two gates and two frontier-posts. When this is done, one enters on the road through Cilicia, a stretch of fifteen-and-a-half parasangs with three stations. . . .

So the principle is strictly observed along the entire length of the road that a resting-place must be provided at the end of each day's journey. Rivers have to be crossed by ferry. Along the whole stretch of road from Susa (the modern Schusch, which was the capital of the ancient Persian Empire) to Sardes (capital of Lydia) Herodotus records 111 stations, representing, by his reckoning, some three months on foot. A further three days took one from Sardes to Ephesus and so to the Mediterranean coast. This road, about 1,500 miles long, provides impressive evidence of the energy of the great Persian, King Darius I, who was determined to keep his immense empire under control and to be able to appear in person whenever and wherever necessary.

Darius I came to power in the year 521 B.C.; fragments of his royal road were doubtless already there, but mostly in a sad state of decay or neglect. The Persian royal road is, therefore, no older than the four amber roads—which, even as early as the sixth century B.C., were busy with commercial traffic—but it represents a different stage in road-building. It is, in fact, a *made-up* road, whereas the amber

---

[1] A parasang is an hour's journey—on foot over easy ground about 3½ miles, over difficult ground a shorter distance—so the road had twenty resting-places to about three hundred miles. This meant—and it is a principle we shall meet with elsewhere in Asia as well as in America—that each stage on the road was a good day's walk from the next.

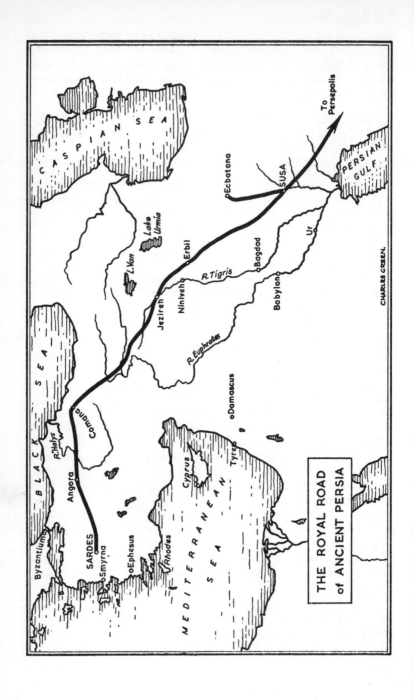

THE ROYAL ROAD of ANCIENT PERSIA

CHARLES GREEN.

roads were merely natural tracks which had been worked upon. Yet little more is left of it today than of the old European roads: in a valley east of the Tigris traces of a road were found which had been cut through sheer rock-face. Thanks to the precise distances given by Herodotus, who repeatedly mentions rivers and sentry-posts, it has been possible to follow the road with reasonable accuracy.

A striking feature of the Persian royal road is that it follows the shortest and technically most efficient route, even at the cost of by-passing some of the largest towns in the Empire. They are linked only indirectly with the main arterial road. So as long ago as the sixth century B.C. a basic principle of our modern highways was already being applied. But Darius I was not solely concerned with avoiding unnecessary traffic congestion; he had other motives too for building such an amazingly scientific road-system. The chief danger that threatened all Oriental potentates was of revolt, which might break out in any part of their vast empires. The densely-populated towns were naturally more prone to unrest than the open country, and one unruly town could disrupt the whole of the great highway, make it difficult or even impossible to bring up troops, and hold up dispatches.

Darius had built the road exclusively for the State, which in this case meant for himself and his government. It served to keep him informed, to transmit orders, and to transport the goods and chattels needed by the court. Darius had a road monopoly similar to that created 1,500 years later by the Mongol rulers through their famous postal service.

The ancient Persian road-builders were faced with many a technical problem that is still costing their modern colleagues a great deal of time and money. Owing to the sandy soil and frequent floods in the Tigris valley, the road from Susa had to be diverted through the Kercha and Kerind valleys to a mountain pass in the wild Zagros range (a mountain chain in western Iran). This meant a climb over a short stretch from about 500 feet above sea-level (Susa) to 5,000 feet. After negotiating the pass, the road again dropped more than 3,000 feet; the country to the north-west of the Zagros mountains is, on an average, only between 1,300 and 2,000 feet above sea-level. But there were also other natural obstacles: the narrow Tigris valley at Mosul, the 6,500-feet-high Karadja-Dagh, and the Taurus mountains.

The road was built entirely to meet the needs of the travellers: in hilly or mountainous country where the going was difficult the rest-houses were a mere twelve miles apart. This consideration shown to the civilian road-user contrasts to some extent with the official *raison d'être* of the road and suggests that it was not so exclusively reserved for the King and his couriers as the laws ordained.

The Persian royal road was clearly designed as *the* road in the Empire, the road *of* the Empire, and it was never intended as a replacement for other roads. The old trade routes and footpaths, mountain tracks and approaches to towns or oases all remained untouched and continued in use. The royal road was the first autonomous road, the first which can be described as having had a clearly defined life of its own within a national community, and for that reason it also had a special symbolic value for the Persian Empire and its people.

It became clear that no invader could make use of it. It did not lead to the main centres, to the important towns and fortresses which every military leader must subdue if he is to conquer a country. It was of no help to the Greeks, who under Cyrus fought against his elder brother, the Persian King Artaxerxes II, and who, after losing the battle of Kunaxa (in Babylonia), evacuated the country under Xenophon, the Greek historian (401 B.C.); Alexander the Great (356–323 B.C.) merely used it to avoid a few narrow passes, but otherwise found it impossible to follow; and it was of no use to the Romans (189 B.C.) in their campaign against the Seleucid rulers of Syria. It seemed almost as if only its creator, Darius himself, could wield this precious weapon. Under him it became the medium for Persia's much-admired communications system, the speed of which still arouses one's amazement. The horses for the royal couriers were kept in readiness in the shade of artificial oases, and the word that was used then to describe their progress, *angareion*, remained in use right up to the Middle Ages as the term for high speed. 'There is nothing in the world that could be faster than these couriers,' Herodotus exclaimed enthusiastically, and when we learn that a message was conveyed from Susa to Sardes—a distance of 1,500 miles—in ten days, then it is clear that achievements of this kind could only be surpassed by the railway and the motor-car.

The Persian royal road could not have been built anywhere else but in Asia Minor, which for thousands of years acted as a sort of watershed of human civilization, if not even as its source. At that time a Middle Kingdom (East Asia) had been in existence for many years, but little was known of it; and the city of Rome, to which, later, 'all roads' were to lead, was only a small provincial town in the early part of the first pre-Christian millenium, ruled by virtually unknown kings. Before Caesar (100–44 B.C.), all roads led to Damascus; ancient Greece was divided, a coastal kingdom without hinterland; ancient Egypt was created by her great river, on which she lived and on which there was increasing traffic. It was only in Syria that the Mediterranean washed against gates, not walls. The Syrian coastal towns were the terminal points of the caravan trails from distant Arabia and particularly from the great and mysterious countries of the East—India, Parthia and China. To the West the world ended at the 'Pillars of Hercules' and the Rock of Gibraltar; and those bold seafarers who escaped the Carthaginian pirates and ventured beyond were swallowed up in impenetrable mists. To the East the world was boundless; merchants and adventurers with brown faces and strange garments told haltingly of countries which had no equal throughout the whole Mediterranean in power and splendour and expanse.

We know today that these were no fairy-tales. The civilizations of Greece and Rome had so many precursors that we, unlike our grandfathers, no longer regard them as the first great empires but rather as the last of the great States in the ancient world: our knowledge of Ur, Babylon, and Assyria is far from new, but it is only in the last few decades that detailed information on the Hittites and the Thousand-Year Empire of the rulers of Mohendjo-Daro and Harappa has become available to us. Even smaller States such as Urartu, the centre of which was Lake Wan in eastern Anatolia, wielded great power for several centuries.

Looking back over thousands of years, we see vast areas of mountains and desert in Asia Minor teeming with life. Through gorges which even today are almost inaccessible, whole armies found their way; across deserts which only the aeroplane and the caterpillar tractor have opened up countless heavy-laden caravans travelled year in, year out, from the roof of the world—from Pamir to the Mediterranean, from the Mediterranean to Pamir. There were paths and roads without number and without age, and a nameless legion of men passed over them—in peace and in war, for good and for ill, as pilgrims or as plunderers. These words were dictated by King Sargon II of Assyria to his scribe Nabu-Shallim-shunu in the year 714 B.C. during a campaign against the mountain kingdom of Urartu and its vassals:

> With only one of my war chariots and a thousand of my fiery riders, archers, shield-bearers and lancers . . . I set out on the difficult road to Mussassir and gave my army its marching-orders from Arsiu, the mighty mountain which is as impossible to climb as a needle.
> I crossed the upper Zab [Zab el Kebir]; between the high mountains, the great heights, the inaccessible mountain peaks which defy description, between them there is no path for the

foot-soldiers. Mighty waterfalls rush down and the noise of their fall is like thunder . . . remote as Adad [the God of War]. They [the mountains] strike terror into those who penetrate them, where no ruler has yet set foot and whose paths no Prince who lived before me has ever seen. I felled the great tree trunks and had their tall tips cut through with bronze axes; I improved the narrow pass, through which the foot-soldiers had to force their way, and enabled the army to move on. I caused my war chariots to be hauled up with ropes and I took up my position on horseback at the head of my army, and my warriors moved forward slowly and in single file with their horses. . . .

The inconceivable hardships of these campaigns may explain the appalling savagery which followed the final victory. Sargon II had not spared his soldiers when they reached the wild and almost inaccessible mountains of Urartu in Asia Minor; he showed even less mercy to Urartu and the rich city of Mussassir, south of Lake Wan, and with triumph he counted the loot which he collected when his army finally emerged from the mountain passes and conquered the city:

> I caused the great thunder of my army to roll like Adad over this city. Old men and old women climbed on the roofs of their houses and complained bitterly. To save themselves they crept on all fours before me and wrung their hands . . . Victorious, I marched in and ordered the seals on the treasure-chambers to be broken. . . .

There were dozens, indeed hundreds, of other towns in Asia Minor which could boast just as much gold and silver as Mussassir when Sargon took it by storm, and just as many kings, generals and insurgents led their warlike armies in search of loot through the high valleys and gorges, across the mountain ridges and the empty plains. If for a few years the wars ceased—because all potential enemies had been subdued and forced to pay tribute—then the kings turned to building palaces and told the story of their epic deeds in reliefs of clay. Apart from the gold and silver treasures that were captured, there were other precious materials such as marble, cedar-wood and limestone, which were transported for long distances by prisoners of war. This could not be done without roads.

For centuries the Euphrates was forded by long-legged camels on their way to and from Syria, a country whose attraction was in no way diminished by the fact that it was not easy to reach. The towns of Syria were a constant source of dispute between Hittites, Egyptians, Urarteans, Assyrians, Medes and others; they were continually being fought for, conquered, sacked and rebuilt—ten, fifteen, twenty times; the walls and foundations of many Syrian towns tell their own story. And yet, thanks to the trade which survived each successive wave of destruction, they never ceased to flourish.

Within the network of trade routes in Asia Minor, the fortunes of the various towns changed considerably throughout the centuries. Tyre, Damascus, Antioch, Palmyra and others might at one point blossom forth, only to sink back into the shadows a few decades later. But even when one or other of them was in decline, it still retained a quality which it had acquired from its links with the mysterious hinterland—a cosmopolitan atmosphere reflected in the variety of tongues spoken by the merchants and in the mixture of races.

That even in those days the character of a town could be conditioned by something which today affects every town—long-distance roads—is best demonstrated in Ras Shamra. Situated about 120 miles north of Beirut, it was thoroughly explored by a French archaeologist, Claude Schaeffer, who in 1935 discovered and excavated the business quarter of the town, which dates back to the second millenium B.C. It was apparently inhabited by half a dozen different peoples, all of whom had their own separate residential areas and buried their dead under the houses rather than let them lie in 'foreign' soil. The scribes in this particular town commanded up to six languages, oral and written, and a dictionary existed to which in addition to six columns for the Oriental languages a seventh was later provided for Greek. . . .

There is no doubt that centuries before Alexander the Great not only present-day Iran but also her neighbours to the north, north-east and south-east were linked by efficient caravan routes with what was the the hub of the world, Syria. Of these trade routes the most important at one time ran from the Euphrates ford at Thapsakus to the river Tigris at Opis and from there on to Ekbatana in Medea (the north-western part of Iran), the seven-walled city with its splendid sun-temple. 'In all,' wrote Herodotus, 'there are seven rings, in the uppermost of which are the royal castle and the treasure-chamber. The largest ring is about the same circumference as the city of Athens. The breast-wall of the first ring is white, of the second black, of the third dark red, of the fourth dark blue, of the fifth bright red. Thus the breast-walls of these five rings are painted. Of the two uppermost, however, one is silver, the other gold.'

Farther on, the road touched the spot where the present capital of Iran, Teheran, stands. Then it continued eastwards between the Derja-Nemek Lake and the Caspian Sea till it turned in a north-easterly direction towards the town of Hekatolympos and the river Oxus (the Amu Darja in Turkistan). There it forked, one branch crossing the river to Samarkand, the other moving south-east along the river to the important trading centre of Baktra, which as early as the second millenium B.C. had been the capital of a mighty empire and was conquered by the Persians in the year 540 B.C.

Baktra and Samarkand were the towns in which traders from Asia Minor and eastern Asia came together; towns in which, two thousand years ago and even more, Syrian and Chinese traders met and negotiated. (See Chapter 3 on the Silk Roads.) But from Baktra there were also trade roads to India, a country which for some time had been trading by sea with Ethiopia, Rhodesia and southern Arabia. Compared with the sea routes, overland traffic was much more difficult. It was no simple matter to conduct hundreds of fully-laden camels over the mountains and bring them intact to Syria. The expert Indian seafaring man, on the other hand, was familiar with the changes in the monsoon and could rely on it to fill his sails for both the outward and the return voyage.

A glance at the map shows what formidable obstacles had to be overcome by the prehistoric overland traveller between Afghanistan and Pakistan: the 10,000-feet-high Shibar Pass between the Hindu Kush (25,000 feet) and the Kuh-i-Buba peak (16,700 feet), and, above all, the famous Khyber Pass on India's north-western frontier near Peshawar, which has always been an unruly area and one of the more costly burdens Britain had to bear while she was respon-sible for law and order in India. Traffic on the stretch between Baktra and Taxila uses the same gorges and passes today that were used by the prehistoric caravans. Only at Taxila could they comfort themselves with the knowledge that the arduous journey through the mountains was behind them.

Taxila lies between the Indus and Jhalum rivers in the Punjab not far from Rawalpindi. Two thousand years before Oxford, it had a famous university, which even princes attended: it is reported of Prasenajit, King of Kosala, that he studied there before making his historic visit to the Buddha (560–480 B.C.), which was the subject of a magnificent and still extant piece of sculpture. The caravan traveller, however, was doubtless less interested in the university than in the good roads in the Punjab. Kantilja—the chancellor of Chandragupta, the great Maurya king—in his *Arthashastra* (an old Indian political doctrine) described the system of government under the Maurya rulers about 320 B.C., and his account has been confirmed by Megasthenes, the Greek who about 310 B.C. served as a diplomat and official historian at Indian courts.

According to these reports, the roads linking the various settlements were carefully maintained and developed. As in Darius's Persian Empire it seems to have been generally recognized that the unity of great empires depends on the quality of their roads (the Maurya Empire stretched from the Indus to the Bramaputra and from the Himalayas to the Vindhya Range in the centre of India). Here, too, the main road was naturally the 'Great Royal Road', which Megasthenes regarded as one of the wonders of the world. It was the forerunner of the Grand Trunk Road which was built at such great expense in the eighteenth century (Panikkar). It began at the frontier of the Indian Empire, ran through Taxila and over the five streams of the Punjab, and then continued by way of Jumna to Prayag (now Allahabad), which was already an important city, both as a communications centre and as a military fortress. The road, which was altogether 1,500 miles long, finally reached the mouth of the Ganges by way of Pataliputra (which Megasthenes also visited). This extraordinary highway, built so early in history, was comparable both in length and in quality with the slightly older royal road in Persia. Its creator was Chandragupta (died 298 B.C.), the great organizer and unifier of India, who ruled for twenty-four years. He recruited the finest brains in his empire and made them his advisers and his friends. For the maintenance of his roads he had set up a special ministry which was responsible not only for milestones, rest-houses and road-safety, but above all for the smooth running of the many ferries; a road which had to cross such wide rivers would otherwise have been valueless. About the same time the custom seems to have started of planting trees at the roadside, a custom which is believed today to have had a religious origin.

Chandragupta's far-seeing government had also annexed the salt trade and declared it a State monopoly, which meant that one of the main trading commodities of those early centuries was under the direct control of the State and that therefore the State had a twofold interest in good roads. For they also contributed to the ingenious tax system of the Maurya Empire, which is still operative in India today (the British made only minor changes in it).

Like so many well-organized and powerful states, however, Chandragupta's empire (whose praises India's poets have never tired of singing) was also a power State. When we read in the *Rig Veda*:

'Send out thy spies, who can move around most quickly,
    Never allow thyself to be deceived . . .
    Obtain tidings of him whose mind is bent, both near
       and far, on intrigue',

then it is clear that the well-kept roads of the Empire were not used
solely by innocent traders and camel-drivers. The rulers knew that
a swift courier service was essential. . . . In the *Arthashastra* no less
than five categories of spy are mentioned, who moved about among
the travellers without arousing suspicion, but who would also visit
the towns and villages: men who read the stars or the lines in your
hand, men who lounged at street-corners or pretended to be simple-
minded. Some even played the ascetic, others were specially-trained
peasants and traders. The State also employed midwives, prostitutes,
female beggars and cooks as spies, so that, at least on the busy
royal road, all kinds of unsavoury characters must have spied on
one another.

Under Chandragupta's grandson Asoka, who ascended the throne
in 256 B.C., the entire traffic-system throughout the country was extended and improved. The congestion on the roads was relieved by
building canals and by encouraging inland water transport; and a
considerable number of new ferries were introduced to ease the
pressure of vehicles and caravans on the river crossings. Capital of
the Empire was Pataliputra, which was founded in the sixth century
B.C. The city lay on a loop of the Ganges, and the Sugangiya Palace,
seat of the Government, appears—to judge by Megasthenes's account—to have surpassed in splendour the palaces of Susa and
Ekbatana. Excavations have since borne this out. Although the
buildings themselves (for the most part of wood) have not survived,
the impressive ground plan of the settlement is in itself evidence of
its importance and of the size of its population.

In addition to literature and religion, technical subjects were also
taught at the high schools, and there was special technical training
in building and mining for the State service.

In later centuries weak princes lost their monopoly control over
roads and transport. Their place was taken by a nomadic tribe, the
so-called Brinsharas, who took over the whole transport system and,
from time to time, made their power felt on the roads. Like the
Camorra, who for a long time dominated Italy's markets and market
transport, they were not too particular about the means they employed and no outsider was able to break their monopoly.

The Brinsharas were described as bearded men, who wore yellow
loin-cloths; their womenfolk dressed in blue or white, painted their

faces, and wore flowers in their hair. The women and children of the tribe travelled with the men all over India; they took not only their families but also their domestic gods, their priests and skilled transport workers.

The foundations of this organization were probably laid at a time of general unrest, when small caravans could hardly expect to remain unmolested. The Brinsharas—like the early pioneers who centuries afterwards trekked through Red Indian territory—were in the habit of enclosing their caravan-camp each night in a ring of wagons, within which they pitched their tents. In the morning one of the priests would thank the cobra god, whose silver image they always carried with them, for a quiet night without incident.

It is apparently easier to found cities than to build roads, otherwise Alexander the Great (356–323 B.C.) would surely have left a road as a memorial to his greatness. Alexander, the most restless of all rulers in the ancient world, would undoubtedly have stood to gain more by a tremendous military road across Asia Minor than by the many widely scattered cities he founded.

But Alexander only had eleven years, and his victorious campaigns were conducted in such a way that he might almost have known his time was limited. This is not the place to enlarge on either the military or the historical significance of his conquests. It is enough to say that his gigantic achievements brought Asia and the Mediterranean countries closer together than at any subsequent period until the time of the Caliphs.

Like Napoleon, Alexander had conquered his enemies before they reached the field of battle; like the Corsican he knew how to move large armies, complete with their equipment, baggage and weapons, at an astonishing speed. We know that among his staff were specially chosen Greek and Macedonian road-builders. Today these men are called the Pioneer Corps, or military engineers, but Alexander's specialists had a much more difficult time than have their colleagues today: they had no detailed maps, no explosives and no reconnaissance aircraft at their disposal.

The first major achievement of the Alexandrine engineers was the lightning construction of a crossing over the Ossa mountains in Thessaly (north-west Greece). In the year 336 B.C. Alexander marched into Thessaly to find that the two main passes, the Tempe Pass and the Kallipeuke Pass, were already in the hands of the enemy. An attempt to take one or other by storm would have meant heavy bloodshed and would have aroused the bitter hostility of the Greeks, so creating a permanent enemy in the rear of his armies.

The decision to blaze a completely fresh trail across the mountains almost certainly had a decisive influence on Alexander's whole future. A nineteenth-century German historian, Johann Gustav Droysen, had this to say:

> To take them [the passes] by force of arms was impossible, and any attempt must be fraught with danger; Alexander chose to make another road of his own. To the south of the main pass tower the massive rocks of the Ossa, less steep towards the sea than on the side of Peneus; Alexander led his army to these less precipitous points and tried to climb, hewing steps in the rock where necessary. So, clambering up from rock to rock, he reached the plain of Thessaly in the rear of the Thessalian army. Without striking a blow he was master of a country which he had been anxious to win rather than subdue, so that he could enlist the excellent Thessalian horsemen for his war against the Persians. . . .

Alexander found himself in an equally difficult position before the island city of Tyre (in southern Lebanon), one of the most powerful of the Phoenician cities which barred the road to Egypt. As an attack from the sea without an adequate navy was foredoomed to failure, Alexander decided 'to restore the island city to the mainland' (Droysen) and built, under constant enemy fire, a causeway about half a mile long. The raw materials came from the houses in Old Tyre on the mainland, from which the inhabitants had fled, and there was more than enough wood in the land of the famous cedars. Long piles were driven into the soft sea-bed and stones poured in between them with a mixture of thick mud, which was pressed down to form a compact mass.

The Tyrenes realized with horror what this strange barbarian king was up to; on the landward side of the town they assembled every catapult and slinging device they could lay their hands on. Their projectiles wrought fearful havoc among the soldiers working on the open dam—till Alexander had two high towers built which gave enough protection for the work to be completed.

While Alexander's engineers were busy constructing the causeway across the arm of the sea, he occupied himself with other things in Syria. He got a fleet together in other ports, fought against Arab tribes, and freed the important caravan routes which led from the Orontes valley to the coast. Although these skirmishes lasted barely a fortnight, the causeway was sufficiently far advanced when he returned for him to use heavy siege-weapons against Tyre. In the crucial battle for the city—which was defended with great cunning and, for a commercial town, with remarkable courage—Alexander attacked from the sea and from the land. The engineers in the city and in Alexander's army (among them the famous Deimachos) vied with each other in ingenuity and inventiveness: Droysen's graphic account creates a vivid picture of one of the first great battles in world history in which the technician played a vital part, in which dams and special ships bearing siege-artillery, drawbridges, drag-chains, catapults and battering-rams were all employed. When a courier arrived by sea from Carthage to say that it could offer no help to the mother-city, the fate of proud Tyre was sealed. In the seven months it had taken him to conquer Tyre, Alexander must have realized the value of technical weapons and the importance of good approach-roads.

The detour across the Ossa mountains, the road which the Thra-cians had to build for Alexander's foot-soldiers in Pamphylia on the coast of southern Anatolia, the causeway at Tyre, and the high earth-rampart before Gaza—all these were essentially military crea-tions. If only because he had no time to spare, roads were of greater strategic importance to Alexander than any other factor. And Alexander's roads must have been very good: 90,000 men marched along them to India, reserves were frequently summoned from Macedonia, and, in addition, a large number of camp-followers moved with the army, on which they depended for their livelihood—prostitutes, jugglers, craftsmen, soothsayers and quacks, among others.

On an average eighteen to twenty miles were covered each day, but in forced marches that distance was sometimes doubled! This is no less astonishing than the conquest of mountain ranges which even today are still singled out by special expeditions. Alexander crossed the 11,500-feet-high Chawak Pass in the Hindu Kush and he reached the river Syr-Darja near the modern town of Chodchent. On the return march from India, Alexander crossed the land of Gedrosia or Gadrosia (Baluchistan), one of the least hospitable parts of Asia, in which his army suffered heavy losses.

It was not from ignorance of the hardships of the road that Alexander undertook this campaign, as Nearch [Greek admiral and friend of Alexander] alone maintains, but because he had heard that until then no one had succeeded in passing through here with an army. . . . The blazing heat, combined with short-age of water, is reputed to have been fatal to the greater part of the army and particularly to the pack animals. . . . If they completed the day's march before them by nightfall and came upon water in the morning, they were not in sore straits. But if, on account of the length of the march, the mounting sun

caught them still on the march, then they suffered doubly from
the searing heat and unquenchable thirst. . . . In great haste
the march went forward, and concern for the individual was
sacrificed to concern for the whole. . . . Many perished in the
sand as if they had been thrown overboard into a sea. . . .
When the army camped by a fairly small stream for the sake
of the water, about the time of the second night watch rain
which had fallen far away in the mountains unnoticed by the
army filled up the stream, which became so swollen that most
of the women and children who followed the army were
drowned and the whole of the King's field-equipment together
with the remaining sumpter-mules were lost. . . . Alexander left
most of the army behind, rode on with only five men and
found the sea. . . .

We see from this report—taken from *Arrabasis*, an account of
Alexander's campaigns by the Greek writer Arrian (A.D. 95–180)—
that, when Alexander marched in desert country, he followed the
practice of the old caravans, the same frugal method he also employed in the Tarim Basin, which has not changed to this day and
which opened up the deserts of Asia at least to the caravan routes.
Discontent in his own army had robbed Alexander of an encounter
with the Maurya Empire, the centre of which lay at that time on the
upper Ganges. Alexander failed to reach it. Had he marched on, had
he been able to remain only two years longer, the two greatest
princes of their time, Chandragupta and Alexander, would have met.
And the Eurasian fraternization festival, at which many of Alexander's soldiers contracted Macedonian-Asiatic marriages and received
costly gifts, would have taken place not at Susa but on the Ganges.

Nevertheless, a European wave had surged forward into the heart
of Asia (and penetrated still farther under several Greek governor-
princes after Alexander's time), into an area where the high mountains seem to be intertwined and where the roads too are closely
intertwined; where the ancient trade roads from India, China and
Asia Minor wind their way across the two or three mountain passes
and meet ineluctably and fatefully where the great rivers of Asia
rise.

Yet it was not war alone that created these great roads but also a
soft, gleaming fabric, which Alexander at his festival of universal
brotherhood spread over the ninety-two bridal couches of his
officers: silk.

Chapter 3

THE SILK ROADS

Many centuries before the 'Thousand-and-One-Nights' in which Scheherazade told her mysterious tales, the remote wonderland of the Orient was linked with the Western world by such a slender bond that this in itself can fairly be described as a fable of real life. Peoples who knew little or nothing of each other, who found great difficulty in understanding one another and could only communicate by gestures, passed great bales of silk from caravan to caravan. For it was so much coveted by Western women that their menfolk had to weigh it against gold. It came to them by the longest roads in the world—the silk roads.

Sven Hedin (1885–1952), the courageous and indefatigable explorer of Central Asia, was one of those scholars who found happiness in adventure. The river of his life was the Kuruk-darja, better known as the Tarim, a river which has been captivating historians and geographers for thousands of years. On the school maps which our fathers used, long stretches of it are undefined: its precise course was not known. Ancient Buddhist chronicles claim that the Tarim disappeared in the great salt-marsh in the Lop-nor (Chinese Turkistan) and flowed underground to re-emerge hundreds of miles farther to the East as the sacred river Hoang-ho. Ptolemy, the great astronomer and geographer of the ancient world, shared this view and on his map of the world he gave the upper course of the Hoang-ho and the river Tarim one and the same name: Oechardes.

The Tarim basin is a great stretch of wasteland between Tibet and Lake Balkash. This desert of sand and salt is nearly devoid of life; only on the river-banks, the occasional lake or oasis, can men exist and create settlements through which the long roads pass. If a river disappears or changes its course, then men and settlements also disappear, or move with the river to rebuild their villages and towns on its banks.

When Sven Hedin first went to Central Asia just before the turn of the century, the Tarim was flowing in its southern bed, and the old Lou-lan—the ruined town on the great salt-marsh which had once been an important staging-point on the busy trade route between China and Syria—lay far back from the river beyond the grim Lop desert.

On his second expedition to Turkistan in 1934 the Swedish explorer had a unique experience: the Tarim had suddenly and without any apparent reason changed its course, as it had done once—1,600 years—before. Hedin was thus given an opportunity such as few explorers have had: he was able to travel by river into the pre-history of a land which 1,600 years before had turned to desert when the river changed its course. With five boats Hedin travelled up the old bed of the Tarim, to which the river had returned, towards the mysterious city about which explorers had written such contradictory reports.

On May 6th, 1934, Sven Hedin's small fleet tied up near a high, reddish erosion-mound in order to explore the further course of the river, which was almost lost to sight among clumps of reeds. Some of Hedin's men found an old grave. He had obtained permission from the Chinese government to measure and explore, to take photographs and make drawings—but not to dig. Nevertheless he had brought one spade with him, and after hours of hard work he and his men succeeded in removing the rock-hard clay to reveal a mass grave containing skulls, leather slippers, a small basket and a number of vessels. The dead had not been laid in coffins, so they were presumably male or female servants. The mistress whom they had followed to the grave lay near by on a small hillock in a deep shaft, which was of exactly the same dimensions as the coffin, so that it could only be hauled up after one wall of the shaft had been removed. Over it, like a mute sentinel, rose a tall stake of tamarisk wood. Sven Hedin wrote:

> Tense with excitement, we waited to catch our first glimpse of the unknown, who had lain so long and undisturbed in death. But instead all that we found was a grey shroud, in which the body had been wrapped and which covered the

corpse completely from head to toe. This shroud was so brittle that it crumbled into dust at a mere touch of the hand. We removed the part covering the head—and at last we saw her, the sovereign lady of the desert, the Queen of Lou-Lan in all her beauty. . . .

On her head she wore a cap like a turban with a simple band round it. The upper half of her body was clothed in a shift of hemp, under which were similar garments in yellow silk. Her breast was covered by a square of red embroidered silk with a shift of blue material under it. The lower part of the body was wrapped in a double fold of silk, a kind of robe which was a continuation of the yellow silk garments and the shift. In the same way, a dress of white material completed the blue garment. Under it she wore a thin petticoat, drawers and embroidered slippers. Around her loins was a kind of lifebelt.

We took samples of all these garments with us: a few, such as the head-dress and the slippers, we removed entirely, together with a bag full of beautifully patterned pieces of silk in various colours. . . .

We know today why Sven Hedin was so moved by his discovery: in 1901 he had found the remains of an ancient city which, according to inscriptions discovered there, proved to be the long-sought capital of Lou-lan. It was conquered, though not for the first time, in 77 B.C.; thirty years before that, the Chinese general Chou-po-nu had taken the King of Lou-lan prisoner—perhaps the father or grandfather of the young queen whose grave Sven Hedin had uncovered. There is a significant sentence in the chronicles of the early Han period, which explains why the city suffered such an unhappy fate: 'Lou-lan, allied with Kushe, situated on the main highway. . . .'

This main highway proved fatal to the small kingdom of Lou-lan on the great salt-marsh of the Lop-nor. Along the road, the caravans with their hundreds of camels moved westwards carrying bright Chinese fabrics to distant Syria and Europe and bringing back pearls and glassware for the Emperor and his court. A German scholar, Baron Ferdinand von Richthofen (1833–1905), called this road 'the silk road', a name which it has retained ever since.

Albert Herrmann, the German geographer, produced evidence to show that there was not one but three silk roads. He based his contention on discoveries made by a British archaeologist, Sir Aurel Stein (1862–1943), and Sven Hedin. These roads did not follow a zigzag course, as had long been assumed, but, on emerging from an ancient gate of the Great Chinese Wall, described a wide arc in a general westerly direction. For years, even decades, they fell into neglect for political, military or geographical reasons (such as when

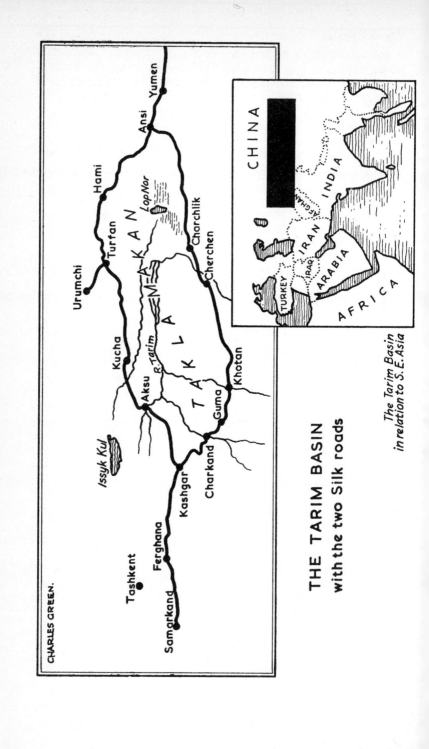

CHARLES GREEN.

THE TARIM BASIN
with the two Silk roads

*The Tarim Basin
in relation to S.E. Asia*

a river changed its course and dozens of inhabited settlements became deserted)—yet the North, South and Middle Roads formed, nevertheless, the most imposing network of trans-continental trade roads known to man.

Silk was not, of course, the initial *raison d'être* of these roads, nor was it the first commodity in which the Chinese traded. Before it came a precious stone, varying in colour from leek-green to grey-green, sometimes even to yellowish-grey, translucent and often transparent at the edges, hard, smooth and greasy. It is known to science as nephrite or hornblende, to poets and antiquarians as jade. This beautiful stone, which was admirable material for the craftsman, was used to ornament weapons and domestic utensils, also necklaces, rings and caskets, and in Chinese lyrical poetry it is treated almost as a revered household god. To acquire this mineral the Chinese were prepared to journey very long distances at a time when China and indeed silk were completely unknown in Europe. The caravans which carried jade to China travelled through the same areas which, later, played an important part in the silk trade.

The jade road passed through the Yumen Gate in the first Great Wall, the wall of the Emperor Shih-Huang-Ti (221–210 B.C.). Yu means jade, and the loads that passed through this gate were much heavier than the bales of silk that came later. The going was hard, for the jade deposits lay at the south-western end of the bare Tarim basin in the valley of the river Karakash. The mountains south of the town of Khotan contained both gold and jade. An occasional party of Indian traders may also have made their way over the Karakorum Pass, which, though 18,000 feet high, had been crossed in very early times. Traders also came over the mountains from Ferghana in eastern Turkistan, so that Khotan was the scene of almost the first, though hardly very profitable, trade contacts between East and West.

It was in this way that the first news from the so-called Western countries reached the Imperial Court. A new dynasty, the Han Emperors (202 B.C.–A.D. 220), had come to power and the country was enjoying a period of prosperity. But China still believed that the world began and ended at her frontiers.

For more than half a century the imperial chroniclers made only brief and unimportant references to the outside world, until a ruler appeared, who, oddly enough, showed much less interest in his country's internal affairs than in something that as yet did not exist: foreign trade. This emperor was called Wu-ti (140–87 B.C.) and anyone who has seen the Chinese traders in San Francisco and Singapore, Bangkok, and Java today ought not to be surprised that they have adopted as their patron saint the Emperor Wu-ti from the second century B.C.

The tyrant Shih-huang-ti (221–210 B.C.) in his short twelve-year reign had built not only the first Great Wall but also the first Chinese roads. Wu-ti saw to it that these roads were used. He established Chinese trade 'with the Western countries', a summary and somewhat contemptuous phrase which constantly recurs in Chinese chronicles and which implied very much what the Wild West meant in the nineteenth century. For after all, the Huns belonged to the West, so not a great deal could be expected from there. The Western tribes were, on the other hand, a potential market—so long as they could pay the prices asked.

It was difficult to glean much information from a few isolated merchants; it was essential to see their countries, to know what was produced in them, what their towns looked like, how the people—and their princes—lived. So the Emperor decided to equip an expedition, which would follow the foreign traders over the high mountains to the West and would bring back reliable information on the countries beyond that line—hitherto regarded as the end of the world.

Why the Emperor Wu-ti selected the eunuch Chang-tien to lead this expedition is not known. Perhaps he feared that someone else might lose his heart while he was abroad and remain with some exotic princess instead of returning to the Court to make his report. In any case it was a good choice, and what Chang-tien had to report was important not only for Wu-ti but also to modern scholars as a unique source of information about the peoples and cultures between the Caspian Sea and the mountains of Pamir. Chang-tien's journey yielded much more valuable material than the tenuous and fantastic reports that reached most writers in the ancient world indirectly by word of mouth.

Compared with Diodorus and Herodotus, the Chinese chronicles make such dry reading that they might have been written not with ink but with sand. They were, of course, all written by officials who, like their modern counterparts, do not seem to have been endowed with too much imagination. The men charged with keeping the imperial chronicles were highly respected. They had the right and duty to keep daily records which not even the Emperor was allowed to see, and no minister could afford to cross them. Although their Emperor was a despot, they enjoyed a measure of independence such as few, if any, ministers have in China today. Only when a dynasty had to abdicate, was overthrown, or was peacefully suc-

ceeded by another were the imperial records handed over to the
court historiographer of the new dynasty to be knit together into
one work of history. And in later centuries these early (and indeed
unique) chronicles were still revered almost as holy writ and were
never allowed to be altered or abbreviated.

Se-ma-Ts'ien, a Chinese historian who is frequently referred to
as the Herodotus of China, left behind on his death in 85 B.C. a work
running into many volumes, the 123rd chapter of which contains the
crucial document concerning the silk roads and the silk trade—the
report of Chang-tien, who for years had passed more or less unnoticed as the Emperor Wu-ti's palace eunuch till he embarked on
his long, dangerous and fruitful journey 'into the countries of the
West', the result of which was the first trade link between China
and the Occident.

> Chang-tien . . . together with the slave Ganfu who belonged
> to the tribe of Tang-li, was called upon to go to the tribe of the
> Massagetes [a nomadic tribe between the Caspian and Aral
> Seas]. They left the Kansu province together and reached the
> land of the Huns. The Huns seized them and handed them over
> to their Khan. The Khan said: 'The Massagetes live to the
> north of us, so how can the Chinese send an ambassador to
> them? I wish you to leave the Han Emperor. Will you become
> my subjects?'
> He kept Chang-tien with him. Chang-tien lived more than
> ten years with the Huns; and the Khan gave him a wife, who
> bore him a son [sic]. Yet the whole time Chang-tien kept the
> ambassador's staff given to him by the Han Emperor and did
> not lose it. He lived in the west of the land of the Huns and
> together with those who had been sent with him he fled. For
> some ten days they fled westwards to the Massagetes and came
> to Ferghana. There people had already heard of China's
> wealth . . . They were delighted with Chang-tien and asked him
> what were his wishes.

Ferghana is the area from which the first Turkish traders had
come to Khotan. It lies on the upper reaches of the river Syr-Darja,
which the ancient geographers called Taxartes, and was linked by
a series of passes with the great trading centre of Bactria, with
northern Kashmir, east Turkistan, and the Tarim basin. These
passes are all about 13,000 feet high and the Jyptik Pass, which leads
southwards to India, is over 18,000 feet, but they were nevertheless
accessible to caravan traffic. Although they were mere tracks rather
than the roads we know today, they enabled the first contacts to be
made between the great civilizations of West and East.

Ferghana's significance for China lay not only in its importance as a key-point on the traffic routes to the south and south-west but also in the fact that it was the gateway to the valley of the Syr-Darja, which flowed through the wide salt-marshes to the Aral Sea, traversing the area known to the Chinese as Kang-kü, to the geographers of the ancient world as Transoxania, and to the modern historian as Chorasmia. From the Aral Sea, even in earliest times, there were established traffic routes to the West and even to the Roman Empire, which always remained open in periods of peace. Heavy transport was towed on rollers over a rough-and-ready track from the Oxus (Amu Darja) to the Caspian Sea. From there it went by ship up the Volga to the isthmus of Tsaritsia, between the Volga and the Don, to be towed across to the Black Sea. The legendary Argonauts are said to have followed this route. During excavations of Greek colonies on the Crimean peninsula, silk was found. India was sending her precious wares to the Roman Empire, where luxury articles fetched good prices. Did Chang-tien know this? Had someone in Ferghana told him?

> The Massagetes sent an interpreter to conduct Chang-tien to Chorasmia. From Chorasmia he was sent to the Great Yueh-Shih. But the Prince of the Great Yueh-Shih had been killed by the Huns; his successor conquered Bactria and ruled over it. The land was fertile, there were few robbers, and the people longed for enjoyment and peace; so the Prince kept himself isolated from distant China and entirely forgot his vow to avenge himself on the Huns.

The Chinese chronicler who reports on Chang-tien's journey begins by giving the impression that it was an attempt on the part of the Han Emperor to recruit allies against the Huns, with whom the Chinese were, in fact, in an almost constant state of war. But the areas dominated by the Huns lay partly in the north, partly in the north-west, of the Chinese Empire. The Great Wall kept the northern frontier safe. Bactria, however, lay due west. Through it passed the main trade routes to the Persian Gulf and the West, to Syria, Rome and Greece. Had Chang-tien really gone there in the hope of finding allies against the Huns, or was he more concerned to establish trade relations?

The Chinese envoy, in any case, failed to contract a military alliance against the Huns. What he did bring back was a remarkably detailed account of the character and requirements of each country he had visited, even to the positions of the towns and the distances between them.

Chang-tien went to Bactria and remained there several years. When he tried to make his way back across the territory of the Tibetans, he travelled through Nan-chan, was again captured by the Huns, and remained several years with them. During this time the Khan of the Huns died, unrest broke out in the land, and Chang-tien fled together with his wife and the slave from the Tang-li tribe. After the return of Chang-tien the Emperor promoted him to high official rank and made the slave from the Tang-li tribe the envoy's servant. Chang-tien was an uncompromising, generous and trustworthy man, all barbarians loved him.

In the simple, unadorned language of the old Chinese chronicles compliments stand out as if they had been underlined. Chang-tien must have been a very remarkable man and one is tempted to quote the whole of his long report, for it makes fascinating reading. Like Christopher Columbus, that visionary genius of centuries later, Chang-tien not only showed remarkable powers of endurance and conviction in fulfilling his mission, he also had to endure the ingratitude of his royal master. Like Columbus in the monastery of La Rabida, Chang-tien waited patiently, a prisoner of the Huns. And when he had waited ten years, he still did not give up hope but fulfilled his mission as scrupulously as if he had merely paused for a brief rest. He did not even know if the emperor who had sent him on his mission was still alive. He made his way to the trade centres, to Ferghana and Bactria; he made a detailed report of the goods that were exchanged there and where they came from. What he eventually submitted to his emperor was, in fact, a detailed market report of which any commercial attaché would be proud today.

The Emperor heard that there were many precious wares to be had in such large countries as Ferghana, Bactria and Parthia, that the people there led a sedentary life and that their customs were similar to those of the Chinese; but their army was weak and they valued highly the wealth of China. He knew [through Chang-tien!] that the soldiers of the Great Yueh-chih (Wu-sun) and of Chorasmia were strong. So he resolved to send them gifts, so that the dynasty might benefit thereby. And he succeeded in subduing them without war. . . .

Now, when Chang-tien stated that it was possible to establish relations with Bactria, the Emperor ordered this to be done. Chang-tien, who held the rank of a military governor and had been installed in the newly-acquired territories, was sent to accompany the Army Commander. The Huns were dealt a severe blow. Chang-tien knew of a place where there was water and grass-fodder, so that the army did not want. There-

upon Chang-tien was given the princely title Bo-wang. This
took place in the sixth year of Yuan-choh (123 B.C.). Two
years later Chang-tien with General Li-huang attacked the
Huns in the province of Jehol. But the Huns surrounded
General Li. The army suffered heavy losses and Chang-tien
expected punishment by death. He was degraded to the rank
of simple soldier. . . .

In the same autumn Hun-ya, the Khan of the Huns,
mustered his people and subdued China. The Huns marched
unchallenged from Kan-su to Lob-nor. . . .

It must have been a disastrous period for China. The entire Tarim
basin was lost and the invading Huns swept through the settlements
along the new trade routes to the West. It seems almost certain that
Lou-lan, the capital of the tribe to which Sven Hedin's queen belonged, was also overrun by Hun-ya, Khan of the Huns.

Within a few years the power of the Huns was undermined by
internal dissension. The Chinese noticed that the riders on small,
fast ponies came less and less frequently to demand the tribute
promised to the great Hun-ya. The last of the Huns were finally
driven out, Wu-ti reorganized his army and Chang-tien was restored
to a position of honour:

> The Emperor agreed to Chang-tien's dispositions and ap-
> pointed him Commander at Court. He gave him three hundred
> men and for each one a few horses; ten thousand head of
> cattle and sheep; and sent as gifts gold and several thousand
> pieces of cloth, as well as more than ten thousand pieces of
> iron. He gave Chang-tien as travelling-companion an officer
> with the staff of an ambassador, so that they could separate
> and he could send him to another country. When they came to
> the Wu-sun tribe, Chang-tien showed them the imperial decree
> but could obtain no decision from them. . . . There he parted
> from his companion and sent him to Ferghana, Chorasmia and
> Bactria, and to the Massagetes. [A few men from the] Wu-san
> accompanied him and showed him the way. Chang-tien, how-
> ever, as token of his gratitude [for the gifts], sent an envoy
> and a dozen warriors with them and he rode back with them,
> in order that they might see China and her greatness. . . .
> Chang-tien was given the title of Great Politician. After a little
> more than a year he died.

Whether, before he died, Chang-tien saw the first great caravans
moving westwards is something we do not know. We do know, at
least, that within a few years of his death there was a steady flow
of traffic from the interior of China through the Jade Gate, which
then—depending on the military situation—spread on to the three

roads which have retained the name given to them by Ferdinand von Richthofen: the silk roads.

The southern road skirted the great Kum-tah desert (called San-lung in the old Chinese scripts), followed the Altin-tah mountains, then wound its way between small lakes to the south-west and joined up with the trade road from the kingdom of Yo-kiang. This king-dom, with which ancient geographers were already familiar and which they called Aspacara, lay, like the kingdom of Lou-lan, on the edge of a great salt-marsh which protected it against attacks from the north and enabled it to retain its independence for a con-siderable time. From Lake Gaskul the caravans had a long, slow climb over the Tashdao Pass northwards. About 17,000 feet high, it was the highest point on this road and for a long time marked the frontier of the Chinese Empire.

Some forty-five miles east of Charchlik the Southern Road joined up with the Middle Road, which passed through Lou-lan, skirting the Kum-tah desert and the great salt-marsh on the northern side. This Middle Road was the most clearly defined, for it was so hemmed in between the Lou-lan salt-marsh and the 'dragon-shaped' dunes that, unlike so many other caravan routes, it did not lose its identity in the open spaces.

Today the road runs between the Kum-tah desert and the Lou-lan marshes, so that it is much shorter than the so-called Middle Road and joins up with the old South Road at Charchlik.

So Charchlik, which in the old Chinese chronicles is called the City of Stone, was an important road junction more than 2,000 years ago and has changed its name so often in its long history that it would require the most involved research-work to list its various designations accurately.

From Charchlik the old South Road (like the present road) ran roughly south-west till it reached the once important town Tsu-mo (now Cherchen). Some thirty miles north of this town two French archaeologists, Dutreuil de Rhins (1846–94) and Grenard Ruinen, discovered the remains of an old trading centre which they believed to be Tsu-mo. Sir Aurel Stein, the British archaeologist, subse-quently proved, however, that Tsu-mo originally stood where Cherchen stands today. There are repeated references to it, though under different names, by later Chinese historians, so that it must have flourished for a long time as a trading centre and resting-place for caravans. As late as A.D. 940 a Chinese delegation stopped there on its way to Khotan. And in the second half of the thirteenth cen-tury, almost 1,500 years after the Tarim trade started, Marco Polo (1254–1324) refers to Cherchen:

Cherchen is also a province of Turkistan ... In former times
it was flourishing and productive, but has been laid waste
by the Tartars. The people are Mahometans. Its chief city is
likewise named Cherchen. Through this province run several
large streams, in which also are found chalcedonies and
jaspers, which are carried for sale to Cathay, and such is their
abundance that they form a considerable article of com-
merce.... When an army of Tartars passes through these
places, if they are enemies the inhabitants are plundered of
their goods, and if friends their cattle are killed and devoured.
For this reason, when they are aware of the approach of any
body of troops, they flee with their families and cattle into the
sandy desert to the distance of two days' journey, towards
some spot where they can find fresh water, and are by that
means enabled to subsist. From the same apprehension, when
they collect their harvest, they deposit the grain in caverns
among the sands; taking monthly from the store so much as
may be wanted for their consumption; nor can any persons
besides themselves know the places to which they resort for
this purpose, because the tracks of their feet are presently
effaced by the wind.

From this matter-of-fact description it emerges very clearly that
the fate of the silk roads and their towns depended in the last resort
on whether there was peace or war between the great Chinese
Empire and the nomads on its western and north-western borders.
Each of the Chinese trade roads to the West had to pass through a
wide nomadic belt. As far as Lou-lan, travelling on the whole was
safe, but at Cherchen—where the Tsu-mo or Cherchen river provided grazing places for the nomad horsemen—the danger zone for
raids on travellers and caravans began.

Westwards from Cherchen the road is not always easy to follow.
It appears, however, to have run almost due west as far as Romok
(formerly Tsing-tueh), which would mean that it diverges from the
present road where it turns south-east. After a further 330 Li or
three days' journey the caravans finally reached Khotan, perhaps the
oldest and certainly the most mysterious and interesting town on the
silk road. For several thousand years it had been a meeting-point
for travellers, pilgrims and missionaries, traders and warriors on
their way through the heart of Asia.

The town, which for centuries hardly saw a European—Marco
Polo, the Jesuit de Goes (1562–1607), and the Englishman Johnson
were, until a century ago, the only exceptions—has attracted a large
number of archaeologists in the present century. Their interest was
aroused not so much by the silk road as by the mixture of peoples

and cultures which resulted from this constant movement of trade. Sven Hedin and Sir Aurel Stein both made several visits to the town and its surroundings; the American geographer Ellsworth Huntington, who died in 1947, and Dutreuil de Rhins also carried out intensive research. Excavations by Aurel Stein and De Rhins revealed that the old Khotan (known to the Chinese as Yu-tien or the Western City) lay about five miles to the west of the present town. It also crops up in old Sanskrit manuscripts under the name Kusthâna.

At Khotan the desert is still quite near, but the caravan-leaders knew that the worst was behind them when they passed through the East Gate in the high mud walls and unloaded the camels. Many spent the winter there. It may be mere legend that the bales of silk spent three years on the road between eastern China and Rome, but it is certainly understandable that the caravans should prefer to winter in Khotan rather than brave the elements on the high Pamir tableland. Even today small and well-equipped expeditions can be completely immobilized by bad weather in the mountains on India's northern border. For a caravan of several hundred animals, a bout of wintry weather at an altitude of 16,000 feet meant losing all the animals and their packs—and possibly even death for their drivers.

Guma and Kargalik were smaller resting-places on the great road West; Khotan's most serious rival, however, was Charkand. Khotan, as the first major town to be reached after crossing the desert and as a transhipment centre for goods from India, occupied a special position, but Charkand lay in a fertile plain. The river Charkand rises 16,000 feet up on the north side of the Karakorum mountains, joins up with the Sarikol and other rivers which are fed by the eternal snows of the highest peaks in the world, and flows on to the edge of the east·Turkistan desert. Charkand, the first town on it, derives most advantage from the great river, for here it breaks up into innumerable channels of all sizes. The streets and alleys of the town are so narrow that a laden camel has barely room to pass through them. But some two hundred irrigation canals carry the water from the mountains to the rabbit-warren of dark, dirty mud-huts in the old town and to the fields beyond them. To the camel-drivers, exhausted from their months of travelling through the barren Tarim basin, the wheat-fields and olive-groves, the rice and the melons of Charkand must have seemed like a dream. And it cannot have been easy for them to leave this dream-like town with its abundance of water for the north-west and Kashgar.

At Kashgar the North and South Roads met, for their common destination was Ferghana, which could be reached by only one mountain pass. . . .

The North Road has not been nearly so fully explored as the South Road, but it was about 120 miles longer which meant another week's travelling for the caravans. Sir Aurel Stein made a number of important excavations which unearthed a few forts where no town exists to show where the North Road ran. It was clearly much better supplied than the southern caravan route; there was fodder and water for the animals. On the other hand, there was no security for the men, for the road skirted the mountains, of which the raiding nomads were unchallenged masters. Even today it is difficult to protect any line of communication against guerrilla fighters; two thousand years ago, when reconnaissance planes and even rapid communications were unheard of, all attempts to make the road secure ended in failure. The forts which Sir Aurel Stein roused from their centuries' old sleep were symbols not of strength but of weakness; on countless occasions the garrisons of the Chinese provincial governor were mown down or forced back into their fortresses carrying a few wounded traders with them; the raiders themselves had disappeared.

The first stretch of the North Road (if we start, as the silk caravans did, from the East) has long since been abandoned and has not been used for many centuries. It is the stretch between the Jade Gate of the Great Wall and the I-wu oasis (where the town of Hami stands today), which is almost due north. All the modern roads branch northwards farther to the east to reach Hami, in other words within the Great Wall.

While Tibet with its sparse population and high mountains offered little attraction to caravans, north of the Tien-chan range lived a number of peoples with whom trade sometimes had its dangers but was usually profitable. So whereas the South Road had only one branch—the road leading to the pastoral population of the Yo-kiang who were only too glad to trade grain against iron implements and arms—the North Road had many branches: the roads to Barkul, Urumchi and Kulja are still in use today and it seems a fair assumption that trade routes existed in very early times over the same mountain passes. The settlements of semi-nomadic tribes in the North were linked by busy roads with the Jade Gate. They are referred to only in old Chinese, not in classical, manuscripts, which suggests that they did not play a very important part in the trade with the West.

The northern silk road itself ran from Hami (also called Chami or Komul) along the southern slopes of the Tien-chan mountains to Turfan. These mountains gave the whole road its Chinese name: Silk Road would have been a much too modest description for the

Chinese, who called it 'Tien-shan-nan-lu', or 'The Road south of the Celestial Mountains'.

Turfan lies in a small, low-lying plain which is just above sea-level, while the mountains to the north of the town rise to over 16,000 feet. This oasis was already well known to the Chinese of the early Han period, although it did not come within their domains. It was in the territory of the two Yueh Shih tribes, one on either side of the mountains.

The real centre of the old silk trade through the oases of the plain was, however, not the town we know today as Turfan but Kiau-ho, capital town of the Yueh Shih 'on this side'. We know that, thanks to its favourable position, it remained the capital until 62 B.C.: two arms of the river Yar flowed round the walls of the town, thus forming a natural moat. From A.D. 91 onwards the Chinese maintained permanent garrisons here to protect the silk road as well as the northern branch-road to Jungaxei. Oddly enough the road to the north does not seem to have taken advantage of the hollow in which Urumchi, the largest town in the whole area, lies today, but crossed the mountains between Turfan and Gushen by some route no longer known. Probably the much more difficult journey through trackless mountains was preferred for security reasons: Urumchi offered raiding horsemen a natural arena, whereas they could not operate in the high mountains.

The silk road continued, taking a wide southerly bend, to Kara-shahr. It ran to Aksu, following roughly the same course as the present road by way of Chadir (Wu-li) and Kucha (Yen). From 60 B.C. onwards for some eighty years the Chadir oasis was the official residence of the Imperial 'Protector General of the Western Territories'. The caravans which 2,000 years ago passed through with their bales of silk for the Western markets followed the southern slopes of the mountains as far as Kashgar, crossing on their way the small kingdoms of Wen-su and Wei-tiu; part of the way ran alongside the river Taushkan-Darya, which must have been a great relief to the animals. The present road passes to the south of the towns, which have lost their former importance, and runs straight across a stretch of desert to the Kashgar-Darya, then along this river westwards to Kashgar.

The present road is not much shorter than the old silk road and the supply conditions are much the same; now, as then, there is a river to provide water. But the main reason for the northern bend of the old road has now disappeared: the Wu-sun. This name, which is constantly cropping up in ancient Chinese literature, was that of the most powerful nomadic tribe on the Chinese border. Estimates of size vary, but, as the Wu-sun could muster a quarter of a million armed men, they were clearly important both as friends and enemies. Chang-tien, who had spent some time with the Wu-sun, was fully aware of this.

> The barbarians love their tribal dwelling-places, moreover they covet the beautiful wares from China. One must send the people of Wu-sun precious gifts and persuade them to return eastwards to their old grazing-grounds. One must give the younger brother of the Kun-mo a Chinese Princess for his wife. In this way we bind this tribe to us and make it subject to our power. This means cutting off the right arm of the Huns. If we ally ourselves with the Wu-sun tribe, then we can safely march to Bactria and we can force the Western regions to pay tribute.

On Chang-tien's advice a Chinese princess (who cannot have been wildly enthusiastic) set out on the long journey to the barbarian prince, leader of the great tribe, and he, surprisingly, was flattered that one of the countless Chinese princesses should join him in his camp. From then on peace reigned between China and the Wu-sun, and the North Road, on that particular stretch at least, was safe from attack.

In the State of Wen-si, a principality between China and the nomad territories, the trade route branched off to the Wu-sun. Envoys and merchants came back to the cities of China with news of the new allies. What they reported makes one sympathize with the nameless princess who must have longed for the comfort of the imperial palace, for the fountains, the exotic birds and the warm climate in which she had grown up, because these were conspicuously absent in the Wu-sun country. One Chinese chronicler writes:

> In the plains it is very rainy and cold. On the mountains grow many firs and pines. The inhabitants do not till their fields but they plant trees. They move hither and thither with their flocks and their cattle in search of water and pasture; their customs are the same as those of the Hiung-nu. There are a great many horses; some prosperous people own more than four or five thousand. They are a pig-headed people, greedy as wolves and utterly unreliable.

The journey to this pig-headed people was also far from pleasant, for it meant crossing the Tien-shan mountains by no less than four passes, one of which, the Bedel Pass, was over 13,000 feet high. A Chinese chronicle from the year A.D 618 gives a fairly detailed description of this mountain road which outlived the once so-powerful tribe of the Wu-sun. Even the capital Cheh-ku, in which the unfortunate princess lived with the great Khan Kuen-mi, has virtually disappeared, its ruins covered by Lake Issyk-Kul. And the people who live there today tell countless superstitious stories of the great lake, which, in fact, is not without its mystery: forty rivers flow into it, none flows out, yet the level never rises; the water is a splendid blue, yet humans and animals alike find it undrinkable; the animal life in the jungle of rushes along its banks must be unique in the Soviet Union, among it being a considerable number of tigers. . . .

For a few years after the death of Chang-tien, who must be regarded as the father of China's Western trade, the central Lop-nor region around Lou-lan was still in the hands of the Huns. They were driven out, and the Emperor Wu-ti built a wall along the frontier to protect the area that had been conquered. Emperor Shih Huang Ti had only built the Great Wall in the West as far as Tau-ho. Wu-Ti continued this gigantic task. He wanted to give the caravans as much protection as possible and so, in the years after 110 B.C., he built an addition to the Wall, which extends far out to the West to protect the trade roads that emerge from the Jade Gate.

The first Chinese merchants who set out on camel-back for the West were true pioneers. The King of Ferghana, which was the merchants' ultimate destination, was fully alive to the hardships and dangers of the journey. He wrote:

> China lies far from here. Travellers who have come from there have frequently perished in the great, old salt-marsh. If one travels by the North Road, one is exposed to the attacks of the Hiung-nu [Huns]. On the South Road there is a shortage of water and fodder; and in many areas, where no population has settled along the road, there is great privation.

In the year 103 B.C. a Chinese general, Li-Kuang-li, made an abortive attempt to march on Ferghana with his army along the South Road. The King of Ferghana, apparently confident in the knowledge that China lay 'far from here', had seized a number of silk caravans. Li-Kuang-li's troops found that for as much as ten days at a stretch they came upon no human settlement of any size, with the result that they ran out of fodder for their animals and were unable to acquire any food supplies for themselves, as the few civilians they encountered were either frightened or stubborn and not very well disposed towards the Chinese, who gave them scant protection against marauding bands of nomads.

Countless Chinese soldiers perished between Lou-lan and Khotan and the army was reduced to little more than a collection of stragglers. Two years later the Chinese made another attempt; this time they hit on what seemed the ingenious idea of dividing up the army. One half was to take the South Road, the other half the North Road. Of the troops who marched off into the barren south nothing more was heard. Their fate is passed over in silence by the Chinese chroniclers as a particularly inglorious chapter in China's history. The troops on the North Road were well provided by the various kingdoms through which they marched. An exception was the town of Luntiu (now called Bugur, not far from Ku-Shah), which refused to provide either shelter or supplies. The town was besieged, conquered and sacked. From then on the western part of the North Road was free and secure.

The Han Emperors, however, and particularly the wise Wu-ti, were not content with isolated military victories. Long before the Cossacks were given a similar role to play on Russia's frontiers, Chinese soldiers were permanently settled in the troubled areas along the North Road. These colonies reinforced the small garrisons with an experienced militia. The annals of the Han dynasty record with satisfaction: 'Now there were in Luntiu several hundred people, who were both peasants and soldiers. An Imperial Commissar was appointed to keep watch on these fields and collect the grain in order to meet the needs of the envoys who were sent out to foreign lands.'

So the Chinese peasant-soldier colonies not only protected the road, they also supplied travellers with food and provided them with guides! In subsequent years more of these settlements arose; the Ödmäng oasis, for example, which was a short distance away from the main road, may have been settled in this way by the Chinese. The I-sün oasis near Lou-lan also became a Chinese military colony and acquired so much importance that in a Chinese chronicle of A.D. 500 it is described as the new capital of the Shan-shan State.

Only when conditions on the South Road had also been made secure could trade really prosper. Cheng-ki, who from 60 B.C. was Protector-General of the Western Regions and therefore responsible for the great trade roads, appears to have been a man of great drive. He extended the chain of military colonies to Yarkand and set up his headquarters in Chadir, far over to the north-west. As a result traffic between China and the West increased considerably.

In the early years of the Christian era the situation in China deteriorated, mainly due to a usurper, Mang, who seized the throne in A.D 9 but was dethroned a few years later, in A.D. 23. During this period of unrest the power of the Huns increased and China lost the South Road. On the North Road a few military colonies held out, so that at least the stretch between Turfan and Ku-chah remained open, but eventually that too was overrun by the Huns.

For almost a whole half-century, between A.D. 23 and 73, trade on the silk roads came to a standstill. 'The rest-houses were deserted, the water-points became silted up, and the small stone markers which showed the travellers the way crumbled and disappeared.'

In the year 73 a Chinese general, Pan Ch'ao, decided to try to restore the Empire to its former position of power and began by advancing northwards. He conquered Hami and defeated the Huns at Lake Pu-lei (Barkul), then he sent his Governor on towards Turfan, where the nomads were defeated in the year 76, while he himself marched westwards along the South Road, subduing one small kingdom after another. Pan Ch'ao advanced far beyond the Hun territories in the north, then swung west and crossed the Jaxartes (Syr Darya). He not only reached Samarkand in the heart of Chorasmia, but even crossed the Oxus (Amu Darya), which to the geographers of the ancient world was a sort of dividing-line between civilization and the unknown world in the Far East. Somewhere in the Karakum desert, north of the mountains on the Persian border (an area that was even better supplied with water then than it is today), he turned about and when he returned after an absence of twenty years to his headquarters on the North Road, he immediately dispatched his adjutant Kan-ying with orders to march as far as Syria. He did, in fact, reach the Euphrates.

The important Middle Road and the Western sector of the North Road, however, were still barred by the King of Kusha. The General appealed to the Emperor, Chang-ti, but he was not greatly interested in wars and it was not until three years after Chang-ti's death, in the year 91, that the energetic Pan Ch'ao received the troops he needed to free the network of roads that was so vital to China's trade.

In the meantime, trade with Ferghana and its vast hinterland had been resumed on the South Road. After Pan Ch'ao's victories over Kusha and Karashahr, the Middle and North Roads were also open again, and Pan Ch'ao himself, as Protector-General of the Western Regions, took up his residencé in Kusha bearing the melodious title Tu-hu. Traffic on the silk roads must have been considerable. Everyone was anxious to take advantage of the improved conditions, for no one could know how long the improvement would last. Caravan after caravan moved westwards. The exports of merchandise grew steadily and travelling conditions became steadily better. 'Peasant colonies were established in the fertile districts,' reports a contemporary source, the *Hou-hanchu.* 'Along the main roads at certain intervals pavilions for changing the horses were set up as well as post-offices. The carriers of urgent dispatches and the interpreters travelling to and fro were busy at all times of the year. Both country-men and strangers, who were engaged in trade, knocked daily at the turnpikes for admittance.'

For two decades trade flourished. News from the West reached China, news from China penetrated to Syria. Then, in the year 102, the great General Pan Ch'ao died. China gave up her conquests in the West and trade declined; the merchants in Syria waited in vain for fresh deliveries from the Orient. But Pan Ch'ao's son, Pan-yung, felt it his duty to continue the great work done by his father; he reconquered so many of the lost territories that the North Road could again be used by caravans. In the year 123 he moved his head-quarters to Linchung (Lukchun); and at that time the North Road had become even more important than the South Road through Lou-lan. It may be, however, that Pan-yung was also looking for a new route to the West which would not run through Ferghana, for, as a result of internal unrest and struggles for power, the extension of the road to Samarkand and Merw was blocked, and in the year 127 traffic came to a complete standstill. The tremendous achieve-ments of General Pan Ch'ao and his son, which must rank as the most remarkable campaigns since those of Alexander, proved in the end to be fruitless.

The attraction of the West for the East was at least as strong as the age-old longing of the Europeans to penetrate as far as possible into the mysterious Orient. But while the Huns, driven from their homes north of Turfan by Pan Ch'ao, plundered their way west-wards without need of roads, the Occident was sending to the East small groups of peaceable men whose long robes trailed in the dust of what had once been the silk road: the Nestorians.

In 440 the Patriarch of Constantinople died. He had spread the doctrine that the divine and the human in Jesus Christ were distinct and separate and that Mary had therefore given birth not to a divine child but merely to a Chosen One. In 431 the Council of Ephesus had condemned this doctrine and the Patriarch's followers moved steadily eastwards for safety. In 505 there were already Nestorian Metropolitan sees in Samarkand and Sina (as China was then called). In 635, after a long journey down the silk road, Nestorian mission-aries reached the Chinese capital, Hsi-ngan-fu. In 638 an imperial edict gave them the right to work as missionaries throughout the whole of China, and in 781 they erected at Hsi-ngan-fu the Nestorian Stone, which was found in 1625, and its inscriptions have become the chief source of information about the activities of the Nestorians in China. Meanwhile the Emperor Tai-tsung of the Tan dynasty had conducted a victorious campaign against the nomad peoples in 634, thus reopening the trade route to the West, and for more than 150 years the Nestorians wandered eastwards along the old silk roads, while Chinese merchants travelled West.

There can be no doubt as to the important part played by the silk road in the development of human culture. In the midst of an enormous desert, through the heart of a vast continent which comprises great wastes of sand, inaccessible mountains, salt-marshes and phantom rivers, runs a double chain of oases: Kashgar, Kucha, Karashahr and Turfan in the north, Yarkand, Khotan, Charchlik and Lou-lan in the south. René Grousset (1885–1952), the French orientalist, compared the role of these oases in the history of civilization to that of the Aegean Islands in early Mediterranean history. Grousset, in fact, went further: he referred to the Gobi Desert as 'a sea of sand through which the caravans ploughed their way as through the Mediterranean of the Asiatic Continent, and thanks to these caravans all the shores of this sea were interlinked. . . . Just as Hellenism in the Alexandrine world brought about a fusion of the Egyptian, Sino-Chaldean and Greek cultures, so Indian Buddhism (from the second century A.D. onwards) spread throughout central Asia and so produced the most fruitful mixture of spiritual and artistic influences from the Greek, Indian and Iranian countries.' (*Les Civilisations de l'Orient*, Paris, 1930, III/143.)

The great trade roads of Central Asia gave rise to a unique, mixed culture with which a fairly wide public has become familiar during the last twenty-five years. In the most westerly part of Turkistan, where the silk roads had to cross the high Pamir passes, and in the area round Bactria, the reigns of Demetrius of Bactria (386–283 B.C.), of Menandros and of the great Kanichka (first century A.D.) produced the Gandhara style with its magnificent sculptures.

Many of the carvings and murals which were discovered by various expeditions in the nineteenth and early twentieth centuries show merchants as they travelled over the centuries along the silk roads. Some are wearing turbans, others mushroom-shaped caps, and others again are depicted with their riding and pack animals, with camels, horses and donkeys. From the various racial types one realizes what a mixture of peoples used the roads through Central Asia. One painting, for example, which now hangs in the Berlin Folklore Museum, shows two merchants offering a Buddha small bags—possibly of gold dust—on golden salvers. The one with the red beard, red hair and green eyes is probably a Tochar from the land of the Wu-sun. Another picture, however, shows men who are clearly western Asiatics, while the King of Kucha and his consort are just as clearly eastern Asiatics.

Along the great roads not merely caravanserais but also monasteries had sprung up, which were inhabited in turn by Buddhists, Nestorians and Mohammedans. In some cases Manichaean manuscripts were even found containing beautiful miniatures: sacred scripts of the ascetic order whose founder, Manes, was crucified about 250 years after Christ and who believed that man's redemption came in many successive stages. The discoveries which were made by Albert von Le Coq, the German archaeologist, and others in Turfan showed that for some two centuries Manichaism was almost a world religion whose influence ranged from Spain to China.

This coexistence and succession of different religions at the same key-points on the great roads had not only a stimulating but also a negative effect. Whereas the Nestorians and Manichaeans, when they moved into an abandoned monastery, painted over the Buddhist murals, the Mohammedans scraped off everything they found, thus depriving posterity of many artistic treasures. The superstitious Mohammedans were particularly careful to erase the eyes and hands of old religious images in order to render the 'evil spirits' powerless. Le Coq described with understandable despair how a peasant from Karakhoja admitted that he had taken a whole cartload of 'rolls with small writing'—many of them illustrated with red and gold pictures—and, being terrified of evil spirits, had thrown them in the river. These specimens of Manichaean scripts were priceless, because, till they were found at Turfan, almost the entire source-material available was *about* the Manichaeans, they themselves having left little or nothing that was authentic.

Here in the no-man's-land between the great Chinese Empire and the outposts of Rome a Manichaean centre had been established, where the sect could worship in safety and create works of art which in their realism are reminiscent of the finest works by the catacomb Christians.

For centuries the only records of the silk roads were more or less terse accounts by chroniclers. Then monks and pilgrims and zealous missionaries ventured to explore the vast solitude of the desert and wrote down their experiences. For the most part they were Buddhist monks from China who set out along the silk roads for India—the birthplace of their faith, the land of Buddha. Fa-hien made the pilgrimage in A.D. 399, Fayung twenty years later, Sung Yün about 510, and U-Kung took three years from 781 to 784. (The last was a contemporary of the great poet Li-tai-po.) Finally, Hüan-tsang, who

spent no less than sixteen years on the old silk roads, had, one sus-
pects, become so engrossed in the adventures of such a journey that
he lost sight of its original pious purpose. . . .

Reports on journeys from the Western side began somewhat later.
The famous Nestorian tablet tells us that a priest named Olopun
came in the year 635 'out of the land Ta-tsin [Syria] guided by blue
clouds and thanks to the heavenly signs passed unharmed through
dangerous countries', but that is somewhat vague to qualify as a
travel report. It merely reminds us that the extension of the silk
road westwards by way of Ferghana and Samarkand to Syria was
exposed to considerable hazards. A more detailed account was given
about the same period by an Egyptian Greek, Theophylaktos Simo-
kattos, who actually succeeded in travelling along the half-
abandoned silk roads as far as the Chinese capital, Hsi-ngan-fu. He
speaks of civil wars and reports that the Emperor of China called
himself 'Son of Heaven'.

At some point in the first thousand years of the Christian era Jews
also mingled with the pilgrims of other confessions. According to
traditional Jewish hearsay, Persian Jews emigrated to China by way
of Samarkand as early as the Han dynasty. A Hebrew inscription
at Kaifong, which Richard Hennig (1874–1951) quotes in the first
volume of his work *Terrae Incognitae*, announces the erection of a
synagogue at Kaifong in 1164. In 1488 a Chinese emperor is said
to have welcomed seventy immigrant Jewish families with admirable tolerance: 'You have come to China. Preserve the customs of
your forefathers and settle in Pienlang. . . .'

Around 1850 a fairly large group of people decided to settle in
the Tarim basin, despite its barrenness, in order to be able to pursue
their faith undisturbed: the Starowerts, an old Russian sect which
put up an obstinate resistance to the liturgical reforms in Russia.
They do not seem to have realized, however, what they had let
themselves in for: from 1858 to 1861 they searched for a legendary
'White Water Land'. A Russian Asian explorer, Petr Koslow, on
one of his expeditions in 1899 met a member of the sect called
Rachmanow, who was still searching for the White Water Land and
wanted to move 'to a quiet area because of religious persecution'.
He had travelled steadily eastwards along the South Road till he
finally reached the salt-marsh at Lop-nor. Most of his companions
—Russian peasants—were, quite understandably, not happy to remain there and wandered on southwards over the Altyn-tag, where
they began to plough and hunt. But almost all of them became so
homesick that they made their way back to Russia. Rachmanow,
however, had to leave his beautiful daughter Pelageja behind: she

had been abducted by a local ruler in the Turfan area and remained as his favourite concubine, bearing him three children. . . .

That more or less completes the list of world religions and sects which found their way to the Tarim basin. In the course of time the pilgrims' tracks and the traces left by the pious or peace-seeking travellers formed a great invisible network across the vast desert.

Even today it is the immense solitude that makes travelling in Central Asia a unique experience. And just as there are certain stretches and places on modern roads where, for some unknown reason, fatal accidents seem to be particularly prevalent, so there are points on the great North Road, the road 'along the Celestial Mountains', which seem to be haunted by the spirits of past travellers. To judge by the experiences of various expeditions, one of these mystical gates between two worlds is the country on the Edsin-gol river, the area in which the North Road emerges from the Great Wall and winds from the interior of China in a great arc towards the wild North. Sven Hedin writes:

> From time to time death paid a visit to the members of our previous expedition (1927–33). In the course of time seven men were snatched away. Strange that six of these deaths should occur on the Edsin-gol. Stranger still that two members of the staff took their own lives and in parts of the forest that are quite close to one another. In a fit of melancholy and acute depression the young Chinese student Ma killed his Chinese servant and then inflicted fatal wounds on himself with an axe. The other case was the Balt called Beick, near whose grave we have now passed.
>
> One Chinese servant died of a sickness, while another missed the spot on the bank of the Edsin-gol where the camels were taken to drink. He was drowned in the shallows. The last was Josef Söderbom, a brother of George, who had only been active on one transport from Su-chou to the river-camp. He had been ill for some time but had managed to stay on his feet. On the way down-river his condition grew worse. One evening he felt death approaching. He called his servants and said to them: 'I shall die tonight. Do not worry about my body. Do not take me home or bury me but simply throw me in the river.' Shortly afterwards he died and his servants gave him temporary burial.
>
> It happens, of course—not infrequently—that travellers die on their journeys, but how can one explain that two civilized and cultured men took their own lives and in the same district? In the eyes of the superstitious Mongols and Chinese it was certainly no accident that a young woman from Torgoth dropped dead a year after Ma's tragic end. She was passing

the very spot where he had pitched his tent and where he had taken his servant's life and his own. We, who look upon such tragic occurrences rather more coolly and soberly, felt strangely moved by these mysterious deaths. Our imaginations, however, did not take refuge in a similar train of thought to that of the natives. For as long as they could remember people had died on the Edsin-gol. The fatal spots were haunted by demons and ghosts. Restless spirits wandered abroad there, working their spells in the dusk and in the darkness. They could drive living mortals to desperate and accursed deeds.

There were many such mysteries in that immensity of space. The fact that crossing the Tarim basin is still a hazardous undertaking gives us some idea of the daring of the Chinese silk-caravans, which travelled round the desert, either to the north or the south, or made their way from Lou-lan along the Kuruk-Darja to Kurla, the old Wei-li, and on from there to Kashgar. On the North Road the caravans were at least nine weeks under way (assuming that they were not held up by some unforeseen accident or incident), on the South Road eight weeks, even on the Middle Road by way of Lou-lan and Wei-li it was seven weeks. And that only covered the stretch from the Jade Gate of the Great Wall to the town of Kashgar! Caravans coming from the interior of China could use the fairly well-kept imperial road as far as the Jade Gate, but from Kashgar onwards there were fresh difficulties to contend with: passes had to be crossed to reach Ferghana, where the merchandise had to be disposed of or transported farther with new drivers to Samarkand, the fabled city from *The Arabian Nights' Entertainments*, to Merw, to Palmyra or to Bactria. . . .

Hundreds of camels, tied in an endless file with long halters, moved along the tracks, and their footprints together with the wheel-tracks of innumerable carts turned the roads into defiles six or seven feet deep. The road was not built up, either in the South, the Middle or the North. On the long journey the merchants who accompanied their caravans or did their own trading were forced to lead a nomadic life. One of the liveliest descriptions of life on a caravan road is by a merchant named Afanassi Nikitiu around 1470. It was found and quoted by a Soviet writer, Konstantin Kunin, in his book *Hinter drei Meeren* (Berlin, 1952):

> Slowly the caravan climbed up the mountain-side. It took three days to reach the summit of the pass. During the night a halt was made in small camps.
> Gradually the trees thinned out. More and more frequently the caravan passed through clearings, in which wild mint and

fennel grew. At last the final rise had been surmounted and the pass crossed. Before them stretched bare, treeless mountains; in the distance shimmered the snow-covered peaks of Demawend.

For sixty years wave after wave of conquerors had swept across Persia. But, far from being concerned about the wretched lot of the sorely afflicted peasants, the Persian Shah and his toadies tried to lay their hands on the little that had been overlooked by the invaders. In the villages from which contributions had been extorted it was difficult to get food. All too frequently, the travellers, who after their long day's march looked forward to a hot, satisfying meal, had to be content with dry bread and a mouthful of cold water distributed by the provident Hadji-Jakub.

The farther south the caravan travelled, the hotter it became. Hadji-Jakub proposed therefore that they should travel by night and spend the day resting in the villages. In the early summer the nights were still cool, the animals moved faster and the caravan made more rapid progress.

From time to time they met another caravan. As with them, the caravan-Baschi rode in front on a small donkey. Behind him, in splendid, richly-decorated harness and hung with countless small bells, came the finest mule in the caravan, the leading-animal. As a rule it carried the most precious load. Then came the other mules, the camels, laden with carpets from Kirman, and donkeys, which were almost completely hidden under the heavy, grain-filled pack-saddles.

Once they met the caravan of a princely family. In front rode the bodyguard, then came the pack-camels, and behind them, fastened to the saddles of two white mules, swayed a woven, tent-like basket, the Tacht-i-revan, in which the richly-jewelled and veiled concubines of the Prince were seated. This was followed by a white horse, on which a splendidly dressed boy gave a display of horsemanship. . . .

Then the caravan entered the region of the Kewir salt-desert. The bluish salty soil, which was sparsely overgrown with dark green and grey-brown grass, gave way here and there to rows of sandhills and stony depressions. . . . For two days they travelled through the salt-desert, without finding any drinking water. On the third day when the caravan finally came upon a well there was great rejoicing. One of the servants lowered a leather bucket on a rope into the dark pit. Deeper and deeper it sank but the splash all were waiting so anxiously to hear did not come. At last from the depths echoed a dull thud. . . . The servant drew the bucket up again; its rim was smeared with damp clay, inside were only a few centipedes and a small sand snake. The horses had to move on without water, and each man received only a few drops from the reserve container over which Hadji-Jakub kept a close watch.

The next stage of the journey without water was agony for all. Heat and thirst became almost unbearable. A strong wind blew sand and red dust into the travellers' faces. And thus the caravan plodded wearily on. . . .

At last night began to fall. The sun stood low in the sky, touching the western mountains. In the south, behind desolate sandhills, dark blue domes appeared, shimmering in the sun's rays, and the sharp-pointed minarets of Kum.

Chapter 4

KHANS AND CARAVANS

As we have seen, the long roads through the least known and inner-most part of Asia were particularly dangerous; when the Mongols under Genghis Khan were the masters in Asia, the silk roads had already been in existence for 1,300 years, but during this whole time they had only been open to traffic for at most 300 years. The period of Mongol rule bears out the thesis put forward at various points in this book that good roads are the product of strong government and that weak rulers seldom go together with any major achievements in the development of transport.

Apart from the fabulous communications network which a court official by the name of Yü is said to have built up in China in the year 2300 B.C. (!),[1] the Mongol postal and road laws of Genghis Khan and his successors represent the first comprehensive solution of Asia's traffic problems.

Genghis Khan (1155–1227) decreed that on all roads in his empire post stations were to be set up a day's journey apart. At each of them as many as twenty horses had to be kept in readiness for the imperial couriers.

Occoday, who was Great Khan from 1229 until 1241, extended this postal system still further. Solely for his own use he set up an express postal service on the North Road between Iran, northern China and Karakorum, while the normal postal service was made

[1] A. Birk, p. 19.

available to all State and military officials (but not to merchants!).
After Occoday's death, however, the merchants found ways and
means of using the service and even derived considerable profit from
it. Even at that time reliable information was worth its weight in
gold. The Great Khan Mangu (1251–59) had to threaten those who
abused the State postal service with dire penalties. The couriers were
instructed only to call at places where the State had sent them; all
too often they had found it well worth their while to make detours
with the result that important State papers were delivered late.

With the decline of the Mongol Empire this magnificent system
also broke down, which meant that the maintenance of the roads
themselves and at least a measure of protection from robbers were
no longer guaranteed. At many staging-points the Great Khan's
couriers found only two horses waiting instead of ten or twenty. The
profession of State courier, which entitled him to the best lodgings
and attention, wherever he went, had become so profitable and so
coveted that 'even the Mongol notables vied with each other to have
their children given this appointment with one of the Princes'.[1]

At Kashgar, where the North and South Roads join, two hundred
mounted couriers are said to have been assembled once. As these
couriers had found it to their advantage not to use the prescribed
main roads but to make detours through wealthy villages in which a
courier's pass was a useful extortion weapon, even large stretches of
the main roads were neglected and abandoned.

This situation was remedied by Gazan (1295–1304), who issued
strict orders that all couriers were to confine themselves to the postal
roads. As many of the villages lay some distance from the old trade
roads, which frequently passed through the ruins of former settlements, special accommodation was built for the couriers. They were
no longer allowed to requisition lodgings and had to pay for horses
and food. Although the State was charged very high prices, expenditure on the courier service was nevertheless reduced by ninety per
cent. This gives one some idea how much had found its way into
the couriers' pockets.

They were issued with new papers which were stamped at all post
stations; there was even a special stamp for late-comers. Anyone
who violated the new regulations was immediately punished by the
Great Khan with death. Even travelling princes could not claim
more than four horses, however urgent their assignment.

Gazan hoped, when he introduced these new regulations, that a
courier would be able to travel from the most remote corner of his
great empire to the imperial residence in four days, but this hope

[1] Spuler, p. 424.

turned out to be premature. But at least Gazan did not live to experience a still greater disappointment: the sensational news of his death took no less than twelve days to travel from Rajj (south of the Caspian Sea) to Khorasan, which, as the crow flies, is barely 600 miles. One can imagine how long it took for less important news to travel! That conditions had not greatly changed in modern times is clear from Sven Hedin's complaint in 1934 that a letter took twenty-six days to reach Shanghai from Anhsi, while a post-rider needed nine days to travel from Urumchi along the eastern part of the silk road to Hami and on to Suchow and Liangchow (about the same distance as from Rajj to Khorasan).

Conditions for the ordinary traveller in the Mongol empire were similar to those for the postal traffic. Guides were mainly concerned with lining their pockets and had precious little regard for punctuality. For example, when Wilhelm von Rubruck, envoy of the Pope and of King Louis IX (St. Louis) of France, travelled to Karakorum in 1254, a few days before reaching the imperial residence the guide urged him to make a detour in order to see the beauty and vastness of the Mongol Empire (in the Gobi Desert!).

In this respect, too, the centuries have brought remarkably few changes. Not only have conditions and traffic on the silk road remained almost the same but the population have retained to this day, in spite of all the admixtures that have taken place, the same not always pleasant characteristics.

Nikolai Michaelowitsch Prjevalsky (1839–88), who unlike Sven Hedin was plagued by misfortune and illness on his expeditions and yet made some of the most important discoveries in Central Asia, tells how one of his guides compelled him once to make a laborious detour merely to visit his sister, and on another occasion he writes angrily about some natives whom he was forced to accept as fellow-travellers.

> The whole trouble stems from the fact that Saman-Beg is travelling with us. While we are on the road the entire band rides ahead, hunting hares with falcons and singing songs. At the overnight stops twenty people always join the visitors. Five times a day they recite their prayers at the top of their voices. That it is impossible, in such circumstances, not merely to kill but even to catch a glimpse of an animal is clear. If it were not that the geographical exploration of Lob-nor is so important, I would long since have turned back. . . .
>
> Moreover, experience has now convinced me that an expedition in the deserts should not be as large as ours. Not only is this unnecessary, it is even a serious handicap. . . . A large

caravan moves so slowly, because at every ford or any other difficult point a great deal more time is needed than with a small caravan—the camels often break loose, not to mention other unpleasant incidents of this kind. After Tibet I will take no more than four men with me. . . .

Ibn Batuta, the great Arab explorer and traveller (1304–77), took part as a young man in a journey during the Mongol period with the rich Abu Seid and wrote a description of it. The Khan, surrounded by all his retinue, was followed by flag-bearers, drummers and trumpeters, and, bringing up the rear, the slaves. A band of some two hundred players had to make continuous music at each stop. A company of this size could only be held together by strict discipline and this was always enforced by severe punishment. Anyone who arrived late at a meeting-point received twenty-five strokes of the lash and had to walk barefoot across the sand next day, his sand-filled shoes hung round his neck by a cord. . . .

A start was always made early in the morning, a rest was taken in the midday heat, and the march was resumed towards evening. The technique adopted was, therefore, substantially different from that employed by the silk caravans, which turned the camels loose in daylight to search for food.

When a Mongol ruler died, the roads were deserted, for during the period of national mourning no one except the express couriers was allowed to travel. This ban sounds more pious than it in fact was; it served the very practical purpose of preventing the ruler's death from becoming too widely known. The danger of unrest in the remote parts of the vast empire was considerably reduced.

The biggest source of trouble to the Mongol Khans, however, was highway robbers. They may have been chiefly the same nomadic tribes which the Han emperors had so often been obliged to fight in order to keep the silk roads reasonably safe. But peasants whose homesteads had been looted—and runaway slaves also—formed waylaying bands, which raided not merely travellers but also caravan stations and supply posts. Even in the Mongol time one could consider oneself lucky if one completed the long journey between Iran and China with a whole skin.

The most energetic in dealing with this scourge was Gazan, who gave the Mongolian postal service a new lease of life. He not only condemned to death all robbers he could lay his hands on but also anyone who sheltered a robber. Furthermore one of his Emirs was given a special security force of 10,000 men, its sole function being to keep the empire's roads clear. At points which were known to

be particularly dangerous, strong military detachments were stationed. They knew that they would lose their pay if they did not
catch robbers—this threat being the only way of preventing the
police from making common cause with the robbers.

To encourage the soldiers still more, Gazan allowed them to levy
a road-tax on the caravans, which varied according to the number
of riding and pack animals. Although we have little or no reliable
information about the value of coins in circulation at that time, one
can assume that this tax, compared with its modern counterpart,
was very low. (Sven Hedin in his book on the silk road mentions a
large caravan in 1934 which had to pay not less than 1,300 silver
dollars inland duty.) Gazan's 'Tables of Justice' fixed the taxes,
made them public and, for anyone who could read, gave the name
of the postmaster (lest some unauthorized person should collect
the tax). In order to control the villages which came so readily to
terms with the robbers (because they regarded this as a sort of
national guerrilla war against the Mongols), Gazan decided upon a
masterly move, which showed how well he knew his people: in any
district which was not completely free of robbers the villages had to
shelter and feed the caravans. The villagers had, therefore, every
interest in keeping the robbers out.

The precautions taken in Gazan's decrees give one a fairly clear
idea of the degree of corruption among his officials, the unreliability
of his soldiers, and the rebellious mood of the villages. He had to
work out all kinds of subterfuges to match the cunning of these
mixed peoples of Central Asia. And yet he never lost sight of his
goal, to give his great empire a reasonably efficient road-system
and a good postal service—safe communications for both travel and
trade.

The Mongol rulers had, of course, the power, even before these
reforms were introduced, to secure for some individual caravans a
safe and even pleasant journey. An impressive example in the reign
of Genghis Khan was the journey by the Chinese scholar, Chang-
chun, perhaps the wisest man who ever travelled on the silk road. . . .

Not one of the thousands of merchants who rode westwards
before Chang-chun through the desolate Tarim basin or through the
northern chain of oases has left any record of his journey. It is
doubtful whether even Marco Polo, the great Venetian, would have
written his famous *Travels*, had he not spent four years in a Genoese
prison. It is quite another matter with Chang-chun. True, he did not
write himself, for he was an old man whose seventy-eight years made
him chary of too much exertion, but his pupil and disciple, Li-chih-
chang, kept a faithful record of his revered master's observations.

Chang-chun, who by virtue of his age and his profound faith was almost closer to the hereafter than to life on earth, dictated a report on his journey which is almost scientific in its detachment. He explored the courses of rivers and described the mountains, the position of the stars—in short, all his impressions from the simplest botanical detail to the cosmic experience of a solar eclipse.

Why Genghis Khan should summon the old man across the breadth of China remains a mystery. It may be that he simply wanted to consult the wisest man of his time, but it is equally possible that he hoped the old man, who was reputed to be 200 years old, might give him a potion against death. At all events Chang-chun was conducted in state along the northern silk road. ('Never in history has a scholar been treated with such honour as was the Tao monk Chang-chun by the barbarian chief Jenghiz Khan,' writes Michael Prawdin in his biography of the great warrior.) The solemn cortège passed to the north of the Ferghana basin, finally reaching Samarkand, where Genghis Khan had his official residence when he was not absent on some campaign. Chang-chun reported that he had reached 'the great post road' and that shortly afterwards he met a Chinese envoy returning from a mission. We can deduce from this that the oasis road, at least between Hami and Aksu, was still busy under the Mongols, although Chang-chun frequently mentions ruins of former settlements.

A few years after Chang-chun's journey, Giovanni Pian del Carpini, who travelled on a papal mission in 1245 'to the Tartars and other nations of the Orient', also took a northern route round the high mountains on the edge of the Tarim basin to Karakorum. He did not touch the silk road: he started his journey across Silesia to Cracow and travelled eastwards across southern Russia. So he took the old caravan trail to Olbia.

The Mongol city of Karakorum lay some five hundred miles northeast of Hami. When the silk trade was at its height, Karakorum was barely in existence. It was founded in the eighth century by a Khan of the Hoei-hu peoples; in the thirteenth century the ruined city again became a prince's residence. Chang-chun's journey from Peking to Samarkand took about fifteen months, Carpini left Lyons in April, 1245 and reached Sira Orda, the summer residence of the Great Khans near Karakorum, on the 22nd July 1246. His entire journey lasted two and a half years, that of Chang-chun three years. But Carpini was also impressed by the splendid facilities provided by the Mongols, which made traffic and travel on the roads a great deal easier. Albert von Le Coq, who made a special first-hand study of Turkistan and the areas through which the northern roads pass, declared that these facilities brought the Peking of the Mongol Khans closer to Europe than it ever had been before, or than it was to be until the opening of the Trans-Siberian Railway.

About the middle of the thirteenth century Andrea de Longjumeau and the Franciscan Wilhelm von Rubruck travelled from Europe to the Mongols, both as envoys of Louis IX of France. Both travelled by way of Talas, a place already mentioned by Chang-chun, and travelled on north of the Tien-shan mountains. So the road 'south of the celestial mountains', as the northern silk road had been called, was not at that time in use, at least for diplomatic journeys to Karakorum. Even the Armenian King Haithum II, who had visited Mangu-Khan and returned home in 1254, did not travel to his southern kingdom along the silk road and through Ferghana, but by way of Dsungarei and Talas. Not until after 1259, when Mangu-Khan took up residence in Kaipingfu, and later under the great Kublai-Khan (1259–94), whose residence was in Peking, did China as a country become once more of such widespread interest to Europeans that the southern route through the Tarim basin was used not only for goods traffic but also for diplomatic journeys.

The most instructive reports on the state of the silk road and on conditions at its transit-points came not from a diplomat but from a merchant—the justly famous Marco Polo (1254–1324), whose colourful descriptions earned him the nickname of Messer Millione from his contemporaries.

Had Marco Polo been as meticulous as Chang-chun, his account of his travels might well have been the greatest work of its kind. But Marco Polo was not over-meticulous and, quite understandably, when he began to dictate from memory in October, 1298, many of the details had slipped his mind. As a result the obscure passages in this comprehensive record have been subjected throughout the centuries to a variety of new interpretations, each designed to trace the precise route followed by Marco Polo on his two journeys through China. One thing is certain: at least on his second journey in the spring of 1275, Marco Polo crossed the Pamir, passed through the old gateway used by the silk caravans on the way to Kashgar, and then travelled on by way of Yarkand and Khotan to Lake Lop-nor.

Marco Polo knew that Kashgar had been at one time an independent kingdom and he noted that its inhabitants spoke a different language from that of their neighbours. His impressions of both town and country were much more favourable than those of the Chinese pilgrim Hüan-tsang, who, however, travelled in the seventh century when conditions on the silk roads were nothing like so good as under the Mongol Khans. Yarkand did not make a particularly good impression on Marco Polo: 'The people are expert artisans. They are in general afflicted with swellings in the legs and tumours in the throat, occasioned by the quality of the water they drink. In this country there is not anything further that is worthy of observation.'

The Venetian devoted a whole chapter to the city of Khotan, which had also made a profound impression on the pilgrims Fa-hien and Hüan-tsang and must, therefore, both in the year 402 and in 644 have been a flourishing commercial centre with a very active spiritual life in the many Buddhist monasteries. In the eighth century the Arabs, led by the bloodthirsty Kutaiba Ibn Muslim—who also spread fire and slaughter in Chorasmia—fought for a quarter of a century against the Buddhists of Khotan, before they succeeded in forcing the new religion on the country. In 1220 Genghis Khan conquered the city, and half a century later Marco Polo wrote: 'Everything necessary for human life is here in the greatest plenty. It yields likewise cotton, flax, hemp, grain, wine and other articles. The inhabitants cultivate farms and vineyards, and have numerous gardens. They support themselves also by trade and manufactures, but they are not good soldiers.' Constantly subjected as they were to foreign domination in one form or another, they may well have lost courage. . . .

From Khotan Marco Polo travelled farther east along the southern silk road. In that particular area it is not always possible to reconcile his journey with the course followed by the road. There are certain inconsistencies which were only clarified when Sven Hedin noticed that the desert between Khotan and Cherchen moves. Whole towns are buried under the dunes, which are constantly changing the contour of the desert. Clearly it did not cover such a large area in the thirteenth century as it does today. That mysterious region round Lake Lop-nor, Sven Hedin's wandering lake, intrigued Marco Polo just as much as it did other travellers before and since. From the accounts given by Fa-hien, Hüan-tsang, and Sven Hedin we can gather why the southern silk road was abandoned for whole centuries and why the North Road took precedence over it. The ancient city of Lou-lan, which was engulfed at the beginning of the fourth century by a fearful sandstorm, or by the waters of the wandering lake, remained buried and forgotten till Sven Hedin rediscovered it 1,600 years later. But both Fa-hien and Hüan-tsang provide some very interesting information of the country and the old caravan road. The pilgrim Fa-hien wrote:

In this desert there are numerous evil spirits; hot winds frequently blow, which kill any traveller who encounters them.
There is a complete absence of birds and no wild animals are
to be found; but as far as the eye can see the road is easy to
identify by the bones of men who perished in the attempt to
cross the desert.

Two hundred years later Hüan-tsang gave a description which
was almost as bleak (and yet since the end of the sixth century the
caravan traffic had been resumed, though somewhat sporadically!):

If one . . . travels eastwards, one reaches a great desert,
where the sand covers a vast area and is in constant movement.
The dunes pile up and scatter according to the whim of the
wind. Travellers find no trace of human life and it often happens that they lose their way. The desert stretches on all sides
as far as the eye can see, so that one cannot know which way
to turn. For this reason travellers have made heaps of animals'
bones to point the way. One finds neither water nor grass and
at times raging hurricanes blow up. When these winds rise,
men and animals fall sick and as if drugged to the ground.
Sometimes one hears singing and whistling sounds and cries
of pain; but when one looks about and listens, one is completely confused and without any sense of direction. Hence it
is that travellers frequently lose their lives in the desert. These
disastrous happenings are the work of demons.[1]

Sven Hedin also reported similar phenomena from the South
Road, to which the accounts by Fa-hien and Hüan-tsang refer.
When he stayed in Yarkand in 1895, he heard of a man who, a short
time before, had wandered out into the desert in search of gold. He
had not returned, and anyone who cared to venture into that same
region where the gold-prospector had disappeared would occasionally hear voices calling the traveller by his own name. If he followed
them, he would lose his way and die of thirst. In fact the desert
storms in the Tarim basin appear to have a particularly high sound-
volume, for Sven Hedin remarked that neither shouts nor rifle-shots
could be heard above the storm. All one could see was the camel
immediately in front, otherwise nothing; and the countless grains of
sand, as they whirled past, gave out a strange whistling sound. The
Russian explorer Prjevalsky also experienced several such storms,
one of which, in spring, 1877, he described in his diary:

[1] The passages from Hüan-tsang and Fa-hien are taken from the Marco
Polo Edition of Dr Hans Lemke, Hamburg, 1908, whose versions of place-
names have, however, been corrected in various instances.

26 March. Yesterday towards seven o'clock in the evening a violent hurricane suddenly burst upon us from the north-east. At that particular moment we were with Saman-Beg, whose Jurte was five hundred paces from our tent. The storm approached from the distance with black and brown clouds of dust, and it moved so quickly that, after we had noticed this phenomenon, we had no time to return to our tent.... The sky became pitch black, so that we were compelled to spend the night with Saman-Beg... In the morning the wind dropped and finally abated altogether, but a thick cloud of dust remained all day in the air; we were forced to remain stationary for a day (N. M. Prjevalsky).

Apart from these sand- and dust-storms, the salt-storms in the Lop-nor area, to which many travellers have testified, are particularly dangerous, because they cause chronic eye diseases. So it is not surprising that Marco Polo had all kinds of things to report on the caravan traffic in this area, which show the silk road, or at least its southern branch, in a fairly gloomy light:

For the purpose of crossing the desert travellers load a number of strong donkeys and camels with foodstuffs and with their wares. If the first of these are consumed before the end of the journey, then they kill and eat the pack animals; as a rule, however, camels are preferred as pack animals, because they carry heavier loads and need little feeding. As far as food is concerned, at least a month's supplies must be carried, for that is the shortest time needed to cross the desert. ...

During these thirty days the journey continues unceasingly over flat sandy wastes and bare mountains; but at the end of each day's march a halt is made at a point where water is to be found, though not enough for a large number yet sufficient for fifty to a hundred persons together with their pack animals. At three or four of these stopping-places the water is salty and bitter, but at other points, of which there are probably twenty-eight, it is sweet and good. On this road one finds no four-footed animals and no birds, because there is no food for them.

Then Marco Polo gives a detailed and impressive account of the illusions in the desert—the strange noises, the sounds of voices and even the imaginary thunder of hooves, as if bands of horsemen were attacking, causing one to lose all sense of direction. He writes in conclusion:

For this reason travellers consider it necessary to exercise foresight before retiring to bed and set up a sign well ahead to point the way they are to follow next day. Moreover, a bell is

hung on each of the pack animals to prevent them from stray-
ing too far [a practice which has continued to the present day].

Within the Great Wall, on the river Tan-ho, lay the town of
Sachow, which Marco Polo described on his journey eastwards. In
Sachow, he reported, the great desert came to an end; the Jade Gate,
which for so long was the gateway to the wealthy interior for all
caravans moving eastwards, is not even mentioned. In Sachow, as
elsewhere on the silk roads, the Venetian found a mixture of Turks,
Mohammedans and Nestorians, all of whom had a lively recollection
of various Buddhist monasteries. The majority of the population
lived by the roads and indeed it was probably only because of them
that they had settled in the barren country, which, as the centuries
passed, became drier and more barren.

Hami—the first caravan-station on the road that wound northwards from the Jade Gate to link up with the northern silk road—
was not, in the opinion of the experts, visited by Marco Polo. But
it was only natural that, while in Sachow, he should hear all kinds
of stories about the great caravan city in the north, and the fact that
he combines the strange reports he has heard with his own description of Sachow seems to prove that in the thirteenth century all three
silk roads, the South, Middle and North Roads, no longer passed
through the Jade Gate. It seems that the trade caravans coming
from the interior of China branched off to the north-west, like the
modern caravan routes, at Ansichow (about sixty miles east of
Sachow) or at Sachow (about seventy miles east of the Jade Gate).

Hami or Komul, as the town was called in Marco Polo's time and
as it is still called today, seems to have owed its prosperity to the
large number of caravans and to have developed a life of its own.
Marco Polo reports (if not at first-hand at least reliably):

> The men are addicted to pleasure and occupy themselves
> only with music, singing, dancing, reading and writing, in short
> they are very fond of pleasure. When strangers come and ask
> for lodging and comfort, this causes them the greatest plea-
> sure (!). They give their wives, daughters, sisters and other
> female relatives the strictest orders to fulfil all their guests'
> wishes, while they themselves leave their homes and retire to
> their country houses in the midst of the orchards where they
> see to everything that the family and the stranger need. For
> this, however, they expect payment, as should be made
> clear ...
> The women are, in fact, very pretty, very sensual, and in
> consequence obedient to the commands of their husbands in
> every respect. It so happened, when Mangu-Khan held court

in this country, that he heard of the aforementioned offensive custom; he issued an edict according to which the people of Komul were strictly enjoined to abandon such a humiliating habit and forbade the people to shelter strangers who should seek accommodation in the public caravanserais. Filled with anger and sorrow, the inhabitants obeyed their master's orders for about three years; but as they found with time that the earth was no longer producing the accustomed fruit (!) and that many unhappy occurrences were befalling their families, they resolved to send a delegation to the Great Khan craving his permission to resume a custom which had been inherited through their fathers from their forefathers since time immemorial; for since they had neglected their duties of hospitality to strangers, the wellbeing of their families had suffered and misfortune had fallen upon them.

After the Great Khan had heard this complaint, he replied: 'As you are anxious to persist in your own life of shame and degradation, so be it. Go, continue in your unworthy habits and customs, and earn in future through your wives the reward of your dishonour.'

Armed with this reply, the delegation returned home to the great joy of the whole people, who to this day have maintained their ancient custom.

At this point we turn our backs on the silk road. It was an impressive illustration of the fact that roads can create life even in the desert. The almost invisible trail which thousands of camel-hooves had beaten out between the shifting sand-dunes attracted countless human souls. Who began this great trek we do not know. Was Chang-tien the first, or had the seventy Jewish families sought out and found the way across the desert? Pilgrims and traders followed close on one another's heels, and finally the Occident and the neighbouring Russian Empire sent explorers who rescued the silk roads from oblivion. The great Trans-Asiatic Highway, of which Sven Hedin dreams in his book on the silk road and which he even includes in his maps, is not likely to be built now. For some time past freight-traffic has been going round India; since the Suez Canal shortened the sea route, the silk road has slipped even more into the background, and in a world of aeroplanes[1] that fly high over the dragon-shaped dunes, the few caravans which still follow the old trail are dying reminders of the fabulous and adventurous glamour that the silk road enjoyed in its heyday.

[1] The region is now served by air—two flights a week Moscow–Peking and other local services.

Chapter 5

GOLD AND SLAVES ON EGYPT'S ROADS

Because the women of Rome loved silk, caravans from the west of China spent months on the road carrying the precious bales to Syria; because the women of Greece liked wearing amber brooches and bracelets, traders bravely traversed the marshy steppes of north-eastern Europe; because a woman of Egypt dreamed of planting myrtle trees on the terrace of a temple and of breathing in their heady scent, she equipped five triremes and sent them to a far country, the precise location of which is still not known. This country was called Punt and the Egyptian woman was the Pharaonic Queen Hatshepset, who ruled from 1501 to 1480 B.C.

A thousand years earlier the Egyptians had brought incense from Punt: on the tomb of the helmsman Khnemhotep from Elefantine it is recorded that around 2350 B.C. he sailed no less than eleven times to Punt with a captain named Hwj. So Hatshepset was merely renewing a link which had been broken under the Hyksos, the Asiatic conquerors of Egypt (around 1720 to 1580 B.C.).

One cannot travel in a trireme by road (although Cleopatra tried it in 31 B.C., only to lose almost her entire Mediterranean fleet), so Hatshepset's expedition would have no place in this story if her ships had not brought so many goods that a new road had to be built from the Red Sea to the Nile. It was the first trade road to be built by the Egyptians themselves, who until then had only made artificial processional roads and had relied entirely on the Nile for commercial traffic. Ancient Egypt was a gift from the Nile: 800

miles long but often only a few miles wide, it stretched alongside the great river which was and still is its vital artery—and its main highway.

At Koser or Kosseir, in other words about the 26th latitude, the distance as the crow flies between the Nile and the Red Sea is only some ninety miles. Presumably these two shipping lanes were connected by a road of some kind from very early times. Throughout the ancient world we see how the first roads were linked with the inland waterways or coastal shipping. We must therefore assume not only that the Nile was used for transport before the desert but also that the connections between the Nile and the sea are older than the oldest desert roads. Where, after all, would these desert roads have led? To the West for thousands of years lay endless and unexplored desert, whereas to the East there was at least a known destination in the shores of the Red Sea. Southwards the Nile became shrouded in mystery, a land of sagas and fables, for its sources were only discovered in the time of our grandfathers.

For a long time the camel was unknown in Egypt; it came presumably from Arabia. It made its appearance in Egypt in the fourteenth century B.C., but another thousand years passed before it really became a native of North Africa. So until then an extremely important prerequisite of desert travel was lacking, and, to begin with, even the hundred-odd miles between the Nile at Kene and Coptos and the seaport of Kosseir represented quite a problem to the Egyptians. Following the tortuous wadis, the traders with their donkeys or ox-carts had first to reach the top of the watershed. The hills there rise to over 6,000 feet—even at the lowest crossing-point they are 2,500 feet above sea-level. On the other hand, the rocks at least provide water and occasionally there is grazing for the animals.

Since the reign of Sesostris III (1878–1841 B.C.)[1] this route appears to have offered a further attraction—a variety of green slate which was particularly suited to Egyptian craftsmanship. When properly treated, this beautiful, hard stone became wonderfully smooth. Gold and semi-precious stones, dark granite and diorite were discovered at an early stage in these mountains, as can be seen from the Egyptian mosaics. These minerals, together with the porphyry which was later discovered in the Jebel Duchan, gave rise to a large number of side tracks from the main route into the wadis.

Road-making in this area does not seem to have been particularly difficult. Hatshepset's road was quickly built because it followed the old towpath; when the Romans came and Mons Porphyrites was forced to surrender its treasures, several roads had already been

---

[1] All dates are taken from Alexander Scharff.

built across the eastern desert to link the ports of Myos Hormos (on
the Gulf of Suez), Safaga, Kosseir and Berenike (now Siketab-el-
Kebir) with the Nile. Under the Ptolemies (305–51 B.C.) the town of
Berenike in particular had acquired considerable importance; it was
therefore linked with the Nile port of Coptos farther to the north
by a direct road. This road ran some 230 miles across the desert and
its ten staging-points enabled travellers to use it without risk. It was
included in a Roman travel-guide and even today it is still used
occasionally, mainly because it passes by a series of ancient ruins
such as the old emerald mines south of the Jebel Sebara and the
ruins of Aristones, Dios, Compasis and Didymos.

South of this road there were only the ancient gold roads, tracks
leading to the gold-mines and of no importance for through traffic;
they branched east and south-east of the rock temple of Canais,
which Sethos I built about 1300 B.C., and led partly to the Jebel
Sebara, the so-called Emerald Mountain, partly to the gold-mines
at Barramiya, Sucari and Samut. The traffic on these roads cannot
have been very heavy, for, although gold is still found near Samut
today, the mines have never been very rich. For the most part the
gold had to be sifted laboriously out of the quartz. Hundreds of
miserable stone huts, flanked by houses for the guards, have been
found in this area—evidence of the bitter fate of military and
civilian prisoners who toiled and sweated here thousands of years
ago, long before Rome sent her *damnati in metallum.*

At some of the staging-points on the Coptos–Kosseir route, within
reach of these southern gold roads, rock-carvings of prehistoric
hunters were found. It may well have been the treasures of the
eastern desert that made the area east of Coptos a centre of the
Nekade culture in the fourth millenium B.C. Long before the first
Pharaohs, therefore, at a time so early as to be dateless by European
standards, this area was already traversed by traffic routes which
were later taken over to a large extent by the caravan trade.

The course followed by the second of the ancient Egyptian roads
was also dictated by nature: the so-called Horus Way, the Pharaohs'
military road along which Thutmosis III (1502–1448 B.C.), Haremhab (1345–1318 B.C.), Ramses II (1301–1234 B.C.) and later Marcus
Antonius and Octavius marched their troops.

The Horus Way ran between the lagoons and the Bitter Lakes
which today flank the Suez Canal. Its terminus, Egypt's gateway to
the Orient and Asia, was the town of Sile (about 1½ miles east of
the modern town of El Kantara, which means a 'bridge'). Sile itself
was a bridge-town, and so many crocodiles had been imported into
its canals as a safeguard against invasion that it was impossible to

swim across them (Gardiner). But if it was virtually impossible to get into Egypt unobserved, it was equally difficult to get out. A doctor named Sinuhe, in the story of his life—one of the main sources of information on conditions in ancient Egypt—gives this account of his experiences on the Horus Way:

> Now I directed my steps northwards and came to the Princes' Wall, which was built as a defence against the Bedouin and to strike down the nomads who traverse the sands of the desert. I ducked behind a bush lest the sentry on duty on the wall should see me. During the night I moved on and, when the earth grew light, I reached the Peten desert and made my way down to the Great Bitter Lake. I was overcome by thirst and forced myself to continue. I struggled to remain conscious, my throat was burning, and I said: 'This is the foretaste of death.' Once more I roused my flagging spirits and summoned the last of my remaining strength—then I heard the lowing voices of cattle. I caught sight of Bedouin and the chief there recognized me, because he had been in Egypt. He gave me water and boiled some milk for me. I went with him to his tribe and they received me well.[1]

Even on the return journey, although one solitary individual could hardly represent much of a threat, Sinuhe was held by the frontier guards on the Horus Way till he was taken under escort to the residence of the Pharaoh Sesostris I (1971–1930 B.C.). Not only the hinterland but also the frontier area was controlled, and, as a rule, particularly capable men were selected to carry this responsibility—before he ascended the throne as Paramessu, Ramses I had been commandant of this military area and his son Sethos (1317–1301 B.C.) held the same post after him. From many of the inscriptions and carvings in the temples we know that most of the Egyptian campaigns against Asian countries were launched from here. If the Pharaohs returned home victorious, they were given a ceremonial reception on the Horus Way by priests and officials.

But armies invading Egypt—if they did not enter by way of the Mediterranean—almost always chose this route. The Hyksos from Asia, who not only conquered Egypt but even established themselves as rulers, set up their official residence on this land-bridge from which they could control both Egypt and Palestine. Not until later was Sile superseded by Pelusium, the fortress which lay farther

---

[1] About 2000 B.C. The reason for Sinuhe's flight is not clear. Günther Roeder, whose text (*Ancient Egyptian Tales and Fables*, Jena, 1927) I have followed here, assumes that Sinuhe had become an accessory to one of the frequent harem conspiracies.

north on the coast and in which, under Alexander the Great and in Cleopatra's time, Egypt's destiny was decided.

Traders with the Sinai area used either the difficult desert route by way of Lake Timsah in the middle of the isthmus and through the sparsely-populated Wadi Tumilat, or, preferably, the better maintained caravan and pilgrim road through Suez. Today, of course, this cross-traffic leads mainly to the holy places of Islam in the Arabian cities of Mecca and Medina. In ancient times the chief attraction was the turquoise mines in the mountainous Sinai peninsula, where other less valuable brightly-coloured minerals, including perhaps even copper, were also found. These roads, too, appear to have been in use from a very early date, for turquoise—as a German Egyptologist, Hermann Kees, discovered—figures in the ancient Egyptian Badari culture (about 4000 B.C.).

In the so-called Thinite period in the early third millenium B.C. —the time of the royal tombs of Abydos and the foundation of Memphis—the use of precious and semi-precious stones was so common that there must have been a considerable volume of traffic between the centres of ancient Pharaonic culture and the sources of the mineral supplies. A whole network of trade routes and caravan roads must have existed from early times, covering the various sources of precious metals, many of which were widely separated. Garnet, onyx, rock crystal, amethyst, agate, jasper and cornelian are not found side by side, and as lapis lazuli, which was also very popular, is not natural to Egypt, there were presumably trade connections with Transoxania and its ancient commercial centre Bactria. Amethyst, on the other hand, could be obtained fairly near by, in Arabia.

West of the Nile, in other words, inland from its left bank, there were—and still are—relatively few roads across the desert. Yet even in ancient times they were important; they spread the influence of the country far beyond its narrow riparian limits. This explains why the highest official in the empire of the Pharaohs, the Wazir, was responsible for these roads in his capacity as 'Governor of the Western Desert'.

As we look back from a distance on these desert tracks that led to the western oases, they seem to acquire a romantic appeal. The western part of Egypt which they penetrated was also the dark, mysterious, unknown Egypt; the official Egypt remained—as it still does—close to the Nile, a wide, unhurried conveyor-belt that carried Egypt's main flow of trade in the broad light of day and under the watchful eyes of the Pharaoh's officials. The chain of oases, on the other hand, created a second link, which was both dangerous and difficult to control, between black Africa and the unruly Libyans in the north-west, who only accepted the domination of the Pharaonic Empire a few centuries before the Christian era began.

The oases, which formed natural links for the caravan roads, lie more or less parallel with the Nile and in this sequence form such a regular pattern that geologists and hydrographers believed until recently that they were all that remained of a second, prehistoric Nile river-bed. But while the oldest rock-carvings by prehistoric tribes of hunters indicate that the climate in those areas was more humid, there is no suggestion of a large river.

Taken from south to north, the oases are called Dungul (which links up through the Kurkur oasis with the Nile at the First Cataract at Aswan), Kharga, El Dakhla (west-north-west of El Kharga), and finally Bahriya (on roughly the same latitude as El Behnesa and El Keis). El Kharga (The Inner) is about 100 miles from the Nile, El Dakhla (The Outer) about 150. El Kharga was populated as early as the first half of the third pre-Christian millenium, in other words about 5,000 years ago. The early Egyptian kings had vineyards there, and for many centuries there was regular caravan traffic between these vineyards and the Nile valley. The old vineyards appear to have been acquired later by the temples, which owned a great deal of property in Egypt, or, as the Egyptians themselves believed, they became the property of the god concerned. For this reason we do not know exactly which god became responsible for protecting the caravan routes: Amun, the owner of the vineyards, or Seth, or the lesser known god Asch, who in ancient Egyptian inscriptions is sometimes called Lord of Libya, which means, in fact, God of the Desert.

El Kharga is of particular interest as the most important point on the so-called Road of the Forty Days (Darb el arbain); forty days which, however, must have seemed like 400—if not their last days on earth—to the hordes of black slaves trudging along in their chains.

The Road of the Forty Days connected the Nile at Assiut with Darfur, which until the nineteenth century was an independent kingdom in western Sudan, the main transhipment centre between north and central Africa. The road linked up a series of large and small oases, some of which, as for example the Selima oasis, are not permanently inhabited but only occupied by Bedouin at certain times of the year. From Selima the road bends south-west to Saghawa (Bir el Malha) and from there runs more or less due south to the Jebel Medob and El Fasher, the capital of Darfur, which lies about 2,500 feet up on Lake Tendelti.

El Fasher is still a busy centre for many caravan routes, which link up not only the Lake Chad area with Abyssinia and the Red Sea, but also the Tibbu country—to which the Tripolitanian routes lead—with Fashoda. But this market had its heyday with the slave trade. It had a very long tradition behind it. The Pharaohs had imported many of their slaves from black Africa, to which the Road of the Forty Days led more directly than any other. The superiority of the Arabs with their commercial acumen over the simple blacks produced appalling results; even today many a dark-skinned child finds his way, bound and gagged, by camel-back to Arabia and Persia.

Georg Schweinfurth, a Baltic German, travelled through the whole of this region in the last century, often with slave-traders or their caravans. He described the terror aroused by these traders who had divided up the country between them and who searched village after village; he gave a graphic account of the decline of village life, which was governed by panic and the need for armed defence. As a result, the richest of these traders, Zobeir Pasha, was summoned to Cairo and arrested. The power wielded by these uncrowned tyrants is clear from the events that followed the arrest: Zobeir Pasha's son started a revolt; Zobeir's foster-brother and army commander Rabah waged a determined struggle against the Egyptians and the French—after a desperate flight westwards he was finally shot by the French in the Lake Chad area. By then, however, through his senseless resistance, he had kept the whole region in a state of war for twenty-two years.

For the very early Egyptians Darfur was practically inaccessible, as neither oxen nor donkeys could hold out for forty days in the desert. Not until camel-breeding on a large scale began did trade join the melancholy slave-traffic on the Road of the Forty Days.

The ancient Egyptian records tell of a slave-raid by Prince Harchuf (about 2300 B.C.) 'on the oasis trail', which was specially equipped with water-supply-dumps for these ventures. One of these supply-dumps was discovered in 1917 in the middle of the desert far from any of the modern caravan routes; it consisted of hundreds of clay jars which could hold quite a sizeable supply of water. At a later period, the Nubians, who for thousands of years provided Egypt with slaves, appear to have taken their revenge on the Kingdom of the Nile, for there are known to have been repeated raids on the oases road in the fifth century A.D.

In the peaceful times of its four thousand years' history, almost everything that comes from the Dark Continent passed along this caravan route: ivory, ostrich feathers, followed later by rubber, natron, and alum among other goods. The caravans which assembled in Darfur to take the oases road to Egypt consisted of as many as 15,000 camels; yet they stayed only a matter of hours—at the most a few days—in the oases, which never made any lasting contact with the rich life of the Nile valley. Only fugitives from justice or from enemies sought refuge there. From more than one Egyptian source we know that all kinds of shady characters were at large on the oases road, and that while criminals had to be rounded up by special police patrols in Egypt's 'Wild West', many went to ground and were never tracked down. Under the XXI Dynasty about 1000 B.C. the El Kharga oasis with its 65,000 date palms was used as a place of banishment particularly for religious offenders and political opponents. And in the early Christian era, in the fourth and fifth centuries, when Bishops Athanasius (died 373) and Nestorius (died 440)[1] fell into disfavour, they were sent along the Road of the Forty Days into banishment. The indomitable Athanasius, who suffered this fate several times only to be reinstated, must have walked the oases road many times.

The monks, who found in this solitude the life ordained by their faith, left behind on the Road of the Forty Days no works of art to compare with those of the Nestorians and Buddhists in the Tarim basin. Yet the Christian ruins in the El Kharga oasis are still impressive, if only because they stand in the midst of the desert and at the heart of a great Islamic territory; they will bear comparison with the buildings from ancient Egypt (the Temple of Hibe) and the Roman citadels.

Although the oases road showed itself hospitable to the monks, it revealed all the horrors of sand and drought when the desert was invaded by armed men. In the year 524 B.C. a Persian king, Cambyses, not only conquered Egypt but also planned to subdue Nubia. He divided his army in two, sending one part by the Nile, which describes a wide eastward curve in Upper Egypt, and the second by the overland route which cuts across this curve like the string of a bow, passing through the Kurkur, Dungul and Selima oases. The famous 'Stele of Dongola', which was discovered by Count von Schlieffen in 1853, contains a report of the defeat which the Nubian King Nastesnes inflicted on the first Persian force which advanced on the Nile. He was not called upon to fight Cambyses's land army, for 'before the army had covered the fifth part of the way, its supplies ran out, and the pack animals had to be slaughtered, but they too were soon consumed. Had Cambyses, when he saw this, exercised self-discipline and, as the affair had gone awry, turned back with his army, then he would have acted sensibly. But he would not listen

[1] Compare section on Nestorians in Chapter 3 on Silk Roads.

to reason and continued on his way. As long as the soldiers could find anything in the ground, they ate grass and herbs and managed to keep alive. But when they came to the sandy desert, many adopted the most horrible method of keeping death at bay. Lots were drawn and each tenth man was eaten. When Cambyses heard this, he was afraid they might all eat one another. He therefore abandoned the campaign against the Ethiopians and ordered the retreat; after losing a large part of his army, he arrived back at Thebes. From Thebes he continued on to Memphis. . . .'

Although there can hardly have been 50,000 men involved, as Herodotus reports—even a Persian tyrant in his right mind could not have sent so many men into the desert—a great many soldiers undoubtedly died a horrible death.

The roads from the Nile Valley ran in three directions: the east road led to the Red Sea, the west roads linked up the oases with the river, but the roads running south, which formed a communications network on both sides of the Nile where it was barely navigable, owed their existence to the most powerful of all incentives— gold.

On a stele from the period of Ramses II (thirteenth century B.C.) we read:

> On one of these days it happened that the Exalted One sat on a great throne of electrum [alloy of silver and gold], wearing his crown with the double plumage, and counted the countries from which gold is brought. He then turned his mind to plans for boring wells on a waterless road, as a report had reached him that there was much gold in the region of Akita, but that the road thither was entirely without water. If a few caravans of gold-washers were to set out, only half of them would arrive, for they die of thirst as do the donkeys which they drive before them. The drinking-water which they need for the outward and return journeys is not to be found in the gourds [i.e. cannot be carried]. So, because of shortage of water, no gold is brought from this country.

Ramses, one of the greatest rulers of the ancient world, consulted his princes and highest officials about the report of the stele. The viceroy of the area around Akita, which, being desert, is always referred to in Egyptian records as 'miserable Kush', referred to the vain attempts made by former rulers to bore for water, but he added cautiously: 'If, however, thou thyself sayest to thy father Hopi [the Nile God]: "Let water come to the mountains", then he will approve all that thou hast told us, as well as all thy plans which thou hast put before us.'

What happened shortly after looks not unlike a miracle, and it certainly seems to have come to Ramses's contemporaries as confirmation of the understanding that existed between their Pharaoh and his father, the Nile God. Whereas Sethos I only a few decades before had drilled more than 200 feet deep without finding water, Ramses II's well-borers struck water at only twenty-five feet which immediately rose ten feet in the shaft. This well is believed to have been situated in the Wadi Alaki near a rocky hill called Hukal el Haskar, and made gold-mining possible in this area. Ancient Egypt needed every grain of gold she could find for exchange and ornaments and fully realized its value. The gold-bearing veins of quartz were traced and hewn out of the rock with such astonishing thoroughness that attempts in more recent times to reactivate the gold-mines with modern machinery have been abandoned as uneconomic.

Water was a vital element in gold-mining, because gold was washed out according to an ancient method, and it was no less vital to the transport of gold, because waterless roads could not be used either by donkeys or by oxen and the camel was still almost unknown at that early period. At some of the old gold-mines the hoof-paths can still be recognized—paths which were trampled out by endless columns of donkeys as they carried water. Despite these difficulties the Egyptians were sufficiently attracted by Nubian gold at an early stage to make expeditions to the south, and the fortifications and control-points on the uneasy southern border were better than the patrol-posts on the Horus Way. Military victories over the half-savage Nubian tribes were relatively easy and had the same kind of appeal for princes and young rulers as the chase, except that here the quarry was much more varied; slaves, cattle, gold, ivory, hides, precious stones, and so on. On one occasion a dwarf was even captured, 'a temple-dancer from the land of the horizon-dwellers', over whom the young Pharaoh Phiops II rejoiced so much that he 'issued a special decree to protect this rare prize and suspended all privileges in the country while he was being transported to the royal residence'. (Kees.)

Ancient Egyptian records of the military expeditions which paved the way for trade caravans give few geographical details. In the west they speak only of an oases route, in the south of the 'Way of the Ivory Traders'. Peaceful caravans and punitive expeditions were never far apart. It presumably took centuries before the areas south of the Second Cataract acquired the habit of exchanging rather than simply stealing the goods imported from Egypt (slaves, honey, textiles, jewellery). Egyptian traders were particularly interested in the leopard-skins, which were the ritual dress of the priests and could always be sold at good prices.

A considerable number of Egyptian caravans must have penetrated deep into darkest Africa in search of gold and leopard-skins. But the gold-mines in the hinterland of Sofala (in the Rhodesian area of the so-called Zimbabwe culture), if the Egyptians ever knew of them, can only have been discovered from the sea. A German geologist, Heinrich Quiring (b. 1885), in a letter to Richard Hennig, the historian and geographer, maintains, on the other hand, that in the gold country on the Zambesi and Sabi around 1180 B.C. and until almost 750 B.C. a method of mining gold was being employed which Ramses III (1197–1165 B.C.) had introduced. The dimensions of the shafts and galleries suggested that the mineworkers were Bushmen. This theory has not remained unchallenged but is worth mentioning if only to emphasize at what an early stage—whether with or without Egyptian help—mining, industry, trade and communications started even in Africa, covering the continent gradually and imperceptibly with a complex network of trade and transport routes.[1]

One of the oldest and most important caravan routes was in the most southerly part of the Nile bend, in the ancient country of Dongola, which was closely linked with the junction at El Fasher in Darfur. The people living today between Dongola and Darfur are the direct descendants of the slave-traders. The Pharaohs went to this part of the country not only for the best slaves but also for the best policemen. The administrative and cultural centre was the town of Napata; the ruins of its temples—crude by-products of Egyptian culture—can still be seen on the southern corner of the Jebel Barkel. Hermann Kees supposes that the first to penetrate this far was Thutmosis III around 1450 B.C.

About 750 B.C. King Kasta founded an independent Ethiopian kingdom with its capital in Napata. This introduced entirely new conditions into the Sudan trade and the traffic on the caravan routes. There were a good half-dozen well-tried caravan routes between the strange loops and bends of the Nile, which made the new kingdom independent of the Nile delta. In addition, Napata became a junction of all the caravan routes that led northwards from the interior of the Sudan. Later on in Egyptian history, however, they lost all but purely local importance, as through traffic virtually ceased. Napata, it was found, lay too far north, and about 300 B.C. Meroe (120 miles

[1] The interesting question of Zambesi gold and the early African gold trade has been the subject of lively discussion for some decades.

north of Khartoum) became the capital. Napata was given its death-blow by Roman legions under a general named Gaius Petronius, who in 23 B.C. carried out reprisals for Nubian raids and razed the old capital to the ground.

The Romans subsequently advanced well south, particularly under Nero—A.D. 37 to 68—but they did not build any roads in these remote areas. The main trade centre in Roman times was Coptos, which lay on the Nile and was a mere hundred miles or so from the Red Sea. So many merchants passed through here that, as the contemporary writer Xenophon reported from Ephesus, all the Syrian robbers congregated on the road from Coptos to Kosseir, where Indian and Arab goods passed in great quantity. The itineraries from the time of Ptolemy and Diocletian (A.D. 284–305) only describe the roads in Egypt as far as Hiera Sycanimus, the frontier-town on the Nile not far from Korosko, where the river turns south-west and the caravan road branches off to Abu Hammad. Here lay the southernmost of the Roman military stations. The oases road in the west, on the other hand, ran much farther and military fortifications went out as far as El Kharga, which had seven forts.

These were by no means the only roads to be improved by the Romans. Augustus (63 B.C.–A.D. 14) had already started a programme of repairs, and in the subsequent decades and centuries local commanders were apparently quite active. A Greek geographer, Strabo (63 B.C.–A.D. 20), reports, for example, that in his time the important caravan route from Coptos to Kosseir (the Romans called it Myoshormus) was a journey of six to seven days. This was only possible thanks to the new water-points and camping-sites. The road from Coptos to Berenike by the route south-east of the Nile and across the desert took twelve days.

Three hundred years after Gaius Petronius's victory over the Ethiopians or Nubians, the roads between the Nile and the Red Sea ran into difficult times. Not only did the Syrian desert bandits know that there was plenty of rich loot to be had there, but the Nubians had not forgotten their defeat. Savage tribes kept pushing northwards, making traffic on the roads and even on the Nile unsafe. They only became reasonably peaceable when Diocletian started paying them tribute (which was naturally given another name, 'Yearly contribution to frontier-control').

It is reasonable to assume that the roads of the Sudan, just because they were no more than caravan roads, outlived the various kingdoms. The historian Speck, in his *Commercial History of the Ancient World*, points out that on the Ptolemaic maps the whole territory between Lake Chad and the Sudanese Nile is shown with remarkable accuracy; he concludes from this that Nubian exports of gold, ivory and hides must have continued even from the remote Niger area, which was linked with the Nile through Darfur and even with central Egypt through the Road of the Forty Days. The *Periplus maris Erythraci* (a description of the Indian Ocean), which may have been written by a merchant some time between A.D. 56 and 71, speaks of an extensive network of communications in Africa 'on the far side', in other words west of the Nile, by which ivory was brought to the Red Sea coast. The very lively trade with India from the port of Kosseir (around A.D. 25, 120 ships were leaving Kosseir for India each year) is another factor that points to supply routes from the Sudan, which supplemented the flow of goods from Egypt herself.

So we see Egypt, a narrow strip of a country on the banks of the Nile, becoming the gateway to a continent which is still called 'dark'. We know that the Emperor Nero, who had a great diversity of interests, sent two companies deep into the Nile marshes (where no one was again to penetrate till European explorers went there in the nineteenth century), but nevertheless Africa remained, on the whole, much more of a closed book to science than to industry and trade, which will always find a way if there is profit to be made. It was not explorers but traders, not expeditions but slave-caravans and ivory-hunters who blazed the first trails from the cities of ancient Egypt into the jungles of Africa, defying deserts and crossing mighty streams.

At some points the roads were little more than footpaths, at others wider than any military road; they wound their way through humid jungle forests and swept majestically across the Bisharin plain and the deserts east and west of the Nile; their hallmark was the dust clouds that rose from caravans of hundreds, often thousands of camels.

Egypt's traders walked, like many a modern peasant, behind their teams, but for the most part their goods were carried by pack animals: donkeys and camels, which had no difficulty in negotiating the narrow bridges over the canals, for, particularly since the reign of Ramses II, the whole of the lower Nile Valley was irrigated by canals.

Solitary travellers were obvious prey for highway robbers. At many stages in Egypt's history reports have come down to us of strong measures being taken by the Pharaohs against robbers, but under weak rulers the peasants who lived in the oases and had to travel through deserted country were constantly being robbed. There is an account of a trial which reveals that even vagrant soldiers were convicted of attacking a peasant and his daughter and leaving them both naked at the roadside. From ancient Egypt, a typical story (which undoubtedly has more than a grain of truth to it) tells of the shrewd peasant Chun-Anup, who with a dogged sense of justice made no less than nine pleas for satisfaction. The trick employed by a corrupt official to seize his fully laden donkeys is so cunning that it could hardly have been invented: Thotnacht (the official) spread a damp cloth on the road (apparently to dry) and told Chun-Anup, who had to pass that way, not to tread on it. When the good-natured peasant led his donkeys to one side and thereby took them on to the field, trampling a few oats, Thotnacht felt entitled to confiscate the pack animals and their loads.

Within the immediate Nile area conditions were better. The canals were policed and with them the roads which ran along their built-up banks. Progress, admittedly, was fairly slow, for the canal banks were also used for grazing and as towing-paths; very often they proved too narrow for the various duties they had to perform.

Crossing these canals was usually a simple matter, for, although bridges were few and far between, the water was shallow and crocodiles were only found near the frontier. To build a bridge over the Nile itself would, of course, never have occurred to even the boldest of the Pharaohs, who, in any case, would not have had the necessary technical resources. But the Nile was the god who brought fertility to the land; to place a man-made structure over his body would have been regarded as an outrage by any Egyptian. So ferries were the only alternative. In the towns ferrying was a recognized profession; in the country it was rather frowned upon, but it was taken as a sign of a charitable disposition when a boatman pulled in to the bank where people were waiting and took them across.

The introduction of horse-drawn vehicles into Egypt was a very painful process; the peoples of Asia Minor had a new weapon, the war-chariot, which proved so effective in battle that the Egyptian army was finally compelled to adopt it. But it was not until a much later period that the horse and chariot really became a common feature of the Egyptian scene. Driving a chariot in the cities of ancient Egypt was a costly business, for it was impossible to make any progress through the crowded streets of a city like Thebes unless the chariot was preceded by Nubian slaves who ran ahead and forced a path through the crowd with bamboo staves. Even litters, which required four or more bearers, were reserved for the Pharaoh, wealthy citizens and high officials, and warlike characters such as the Pharaoh Haremhab (a former general) seem to have preferred the chariot. Neither by chariot nor by litter, however, could an Egyptian get very far, for sooner or later he had to take to the river, which was broad and powerful enough even to carry a ceremonial barge.

Travelling in the desert, on the other hand, continued to be quite an adventure. However many caravan routes might cross the desert, it still remained for the Egyptians a mysterious region in which supernatural or diabolical powers held freer sway than in the Land of the Nile itself. Wild animals and snakes were not only a constant threat to the desert traveller, they were also regarded as manifestations of the desert gods and a powerful spell was needed to protect oneself against them. On the caravan route from Heliopolis to the Red Sea there was a statue of Ramses III with a goddess, which was reputed to have this power: anyone who touched it or, still better, offered a sacrifice could be sure that he would not lose his way or fall foul of robbers. A prospector by the name of Antef, who lived about 1500 B.C. in Thebes, left a document, since published and annotated by Garies-Davis, in which he complained eloquently of one employer who sent him out to find a Bekhen stone, one of those extremely hard and beautiful jewels which are found in the mountainous country of the eastern desert.

> For eight days I wandered through the desert searching for this particular pocket, which was not known even to the hunters. Then I flung myself in the dust before Min and Mut, before the Great Sorceress and all desert gods and burned cones of the terebinth [turpentine] as sacrifice. And behold when dawn broke I found myself on a mountain which was the one I had been seeking and it was called Rohanu.

Similar votive tablets give the names of those courageous men who searched for wives on behalf of the viceroys and Pharaohs, staked out roads and drew many maps, which can be regarded as the first land-maps ever to be made. One is preserved in Turin, a roll of papyrus on which the gold-mining areas east of Coptos are marked in red; there is also a road, which is designated as a main highway, and a few houses.[1] As in the pioneering days in America, ancient Egypt probably also produced a special breed of tracker and desert-trapper; Egyptian sources of the pre-Ramses period report of a man named Sankh who frequently led military expeditions to explore and protect desert roads, and even at the age of sixty refused to give up this dangerous life.

[1] Leo Bagrow: *The History of Cartography*, Berlin, 1951.

Chapter 6

LAND OF INCENSE AND PILGRIMS

Of all the roads that led to Egypt, one wielded immense power for several centuries, conjuring kingdoms from the desert sand and making a long and inhospitable strip of coastal land so rich that the writers of the ancient world named it 'Arabia Felix' (Happy Arabia). The road in question was the incense road—also known as the spice road—on which the most precious cargoes in the history of trading travelled by camel from Oman and the Hadramauth to Egypt and the Mediterranean ports of Syria. Aloes, balsam, myrrh, incense trees and other rare plants gave southern Arabia a unique place in the Old World. We have read of Queen Hatshepset's longing for incense; we know that some 1,500 years later Cleopatra haggled obstinately with King Herod over a few balsam plantations and finally gave the splendid city of Jericho in exchange; but the Phoenicians also regarded incense as a rarity, while Darius, the great Persian king, exacted an annual tribute of the aromatic gum from Arabia to the value of 1,000 talents, roughly twenty-five tons; China consumed large quantities, which came by ship across the Indian Ocean, or overland by the silk road; and when Nero's wife, the beautiful Poppeia, died in A.D. 65, he burned whole chariot-loads of incense.

'In the south ... Arabia is the furthest inhabited country,' wrote Herodotus in his famous History (III, 107), 'and it is the only one in which incense, myrrh, cassia, cinnamon and labdanum grow. But the Arabs gather all these, with the exception of myrrh, only with

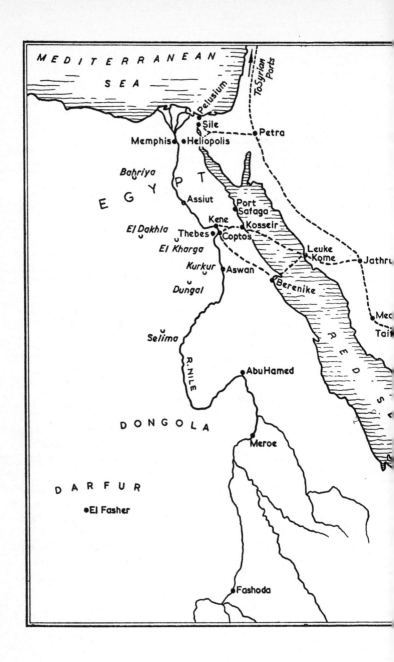

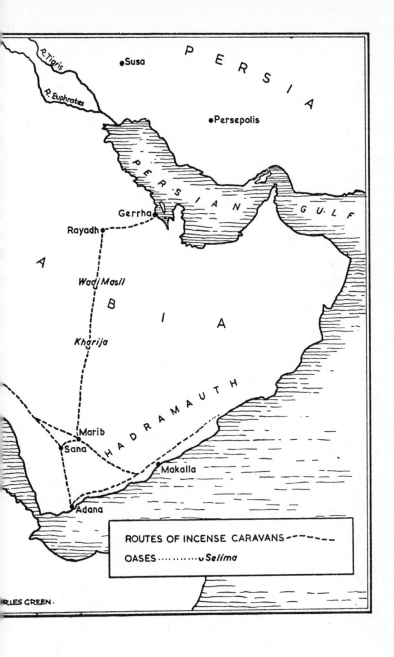

PERSIA

●Susa

R. Tigris

R. Euphrates

●Persepolis

PERSIAN   GULF

Gerrha●

Rayadh●

A

Wadi Masil

B   I   A

Kharija

HADRAMAUTH

●Marib

●Sana

●Makalla

●Adana

ROUTES OF INCENSE CARAVANS --- --- ---

OASES .... ꞌSelima

RLES GREEN.

difficulty. To gather incense they burn styrax gum, which the Phoenicians import into Greece; for when they burn it, they are able to reach the incense: the trees on which it grows are all guarded by countless small, gaily-coloured, winged snakes. . . .'

As a rule Herodotus was careful to avoid anything that seemed to verge on the fantastic, so his account can be taken to indicate the sort of romantic conceptions that were current in the ancient world about the land of incense; but it also confirms that Arabia enjoyed a monopoly in aromatic gums and spices. That they were so much in demand was due, according to a young American archaeologist, Wendell-Phillips, to the simple fact that the ancient peoples of Arabia were so malodorous. As recently as 1951/52, when he travelled through southern Arabia, camel's urine was being used as a kind of hair shampoo and for washing wounds. (W. Phillips.)

There may, however, have been equally strong religious reasons, for the gums exhale that unmistakable fragrance which induces and stimulates a sense of piety—every bit as welcome to the priests of ancient Egypt, Asia Minor and Greece as it is to Christians of our own day.

The spice cassia, which Herodotus mentioned, is probably 'qat', a plant whose leaves the Arabs still chew, and which has a very stimulating effect; the eventual results, however, are even more detrimental than they are from the South American Indians' addiction to kola leaves. After a few years this dangerous drug causes increasing amnesia and dullness.

Like most of the caravan roads the incense road cannot be traced precisely. All one can say with certainty is that some towns and points in the landscape (wadis and passes) were linked by a trade road; and from this one can gather roughly what direction it took.

Starting in the Hadramauth, the road ran westwards more or less parallel with the southern coast of Arabia, and then to the north of ancient Adana (Aden) it turned north-west, following the coast of the Red Sea at varying distances, but seldom more than 120 miles from it. The most important branches were:

1. Those tracks that sought to cut the bend at Aden by crossing the tongue of land which juts forward to the Bab-el-Mandeb straits. This secondary road, which at certain periods was more popular than the original highway, passed through Marib, the capital of the old kingdom of Saba.

2. The caravan route that turns north and then north-east at Marib. It passed through the great desert in the centre of Arabia to the port of Gerrha on the Persian Gulf, at which Indian, Persian and

Elamite traders called in their ships. From here the large trading centres in Persia—Seleucia, Ekbatana, Susa, Persepolis and others—were supplied with the precious gum, and fresh caravans carried the cargoes on to Trebizond, Hekatompylos, Samarkand and Baktra.

3. The west road from Jathrib (Medina) to the Red Sea at Leuke Kome, which cut out the long, unsafe road across the Sinai Peninsula. There was a short journey by sailing-boat to the east Egyptian ports of Kosseir and Berenike, which were connected by good caravan routes with the Nile Valley. The incense that was not destined for Upper Egypt could easily be taken down the Nile to the Delta.

The incense road itself ran from Jathrub through the desert country of the Nabbateans to Petra, the capital of a small Bedouin State, which became very prosperous through the incense trade, but figured only once in the affairs of the region—when the young Queen Cleopatra fled from her brother into this impregnable rock-bound fortress and found there a dark-eyed Bedouin prince, who led his desert warriors into battle on her behalf and laid down his own life for the beautiful Egyptian before the fort of Pelusium.

At Petra the incense road forked, one branch leading to the Nile Delta, the other to the great ports of Palestine and Syria, where Phoenician and Greek ships were waiting to carry the merchandise from the south across the Mediterranean. Some towns, by virtue of their natural resources, became important road-junctions. The town of Shabwa (today Saba), for instance—between Bir Asakir and Beihan in southern Arabia—had large salt-mines. Here, two caravan routes met, the incense road and the northbound trade road from the port of Cana.

Shabwa was for a time capital of a small kingdom which was so barren that it lived entirely on trade and disappeared with the incense traffic. At the fork of the incense road near Aden, where one branch led to the ports and through them to Ethiopia while the main road swung to the north-west, lay a town whose name is still unknown. The hill under which it is buried is called Hadjar bin Humeid. William F. Albright, the famous American archaeologist, examined a dozen different layers of remains, which showed that town after town was built on the same spot, so that the tenth century B.C. lies about seventy feet down. A small bronze plaque from the first pre-Christian millenium, which was found here in 1949, shows a camel, the animal which first made traffic possible in those parts and was at least as important to all the towns on the incense road as the modern motorway to the towns that are serviced by it. This discovery suggests that somewhere under one of the countless sand-dunes is also lying that great silver camel of which St. John Philby, for many years adviser to King Ibn Saud and probably the most prominent Arabist of our time, was told.

While Pliny the Elder (A.D. 23–79) mentions the town Shabwa under the name Sabota and reports (from hearsay) that it has sixty temples, the town on the Hadjar bin Humeid hill has not so far been traced in ancient writings. Albright was able to establish, however, that, thanks to its favourable position in the middle of the Wadi Beihan, it was still populated in the Middle Ages (between 1000 and 1400). Only two to three miles from this particular spot, the Wendell-Phillips expedition of 1951 discovered graffiti, rock-carvings and inscriptions from the eleventh century B.C.; it can therefore be assumed that Hadjar bin Humeid and the incense road were busy and prosperous for a period of some 2,000 years.

Between the two deep incisions made by the Wadi Beihan and the Wadi Harib the Mablaka Pass formed a link which still remains one of the most impressive sections of the old incense road. The final stretch before the top of the pass was so steep that further bends were impossible; so the builders of this pass-road simply cut steps into the mountain, which, considering the primitive tools available, must have been hard work and have required an enormous number of workers. Only a few miles farther north, where the climb is much easier, all this trouble could have been avoided, but this would have meant that the incense road no longer passed through the ancient kingdom of Kataba and other tribes would have cashed in on the caravan traffic, on the taxes and duties it paid and on the general trade it brought with it.

A second flagstone pass on the old incense road today lies in the Yemen—an area which is so torn by tribal feuds as to be practically inaccessible. It is called Nejd Mergat and shows, according to Phillips's report, the 'remains of a flagstone pavement between two still extant walls'. Not far from this pass a nameless town lies buried under a sandhill, which is known only from coins that have been found—gold coins which King Warawil Ghaylan had minted about 50 B.C. . . .

The inscriptions that cover stones, rock walls, the pedestals of pillars and statues tell a much fuller story than the coins. On expeditions in 1951 and 1952 the Belgian orientalist Albert Jomme, working in tropical heat, made thousands of copies, all the texts of which have not yet been interpreted. But he was not the first. A strange lone wolf, Eduard Glaser, an Austrian, had visited southern Arabia in 1883, 1888 and 1892, gone as far as Marib and collected as many as 1,800 inscriptions. As the means at his disposal were extremely limited, he taught Arabs to copy the inscriptions. He also made a cartographic survey of the area from Hadramauth to Mecca and collected a number of ancient Arabic manuscripts. Then in 1924 an Austrian scholar of Greek origin, Rhodokanakis, proved that the ancient city of Timna, capital of the kingdom of Kataba, lay on the incense road and is buried under a hill in the Wadi Beihan.

According to the inscriptions found by the Wendell-Phillips expedition, in early times Kataba and Saba had a common ruler; Kataba appears to have been ruled at that time by Sabbaeans and it can be assumed that the same Queen of Saba who around the middle of the tenth century B.C. conducted trade negotiations with the biblical King Solomon ruled not only over Kataba but also over Saba.

As indirect evidence of the importance of the incense road even in those early times, there are the ancient Egyptian temple-accounts showing the consumption of aromatic gums and the statement in the Bible (2 Kings x. 2) that the Queen of Sheba 'came to Jerusalem with a very great train, with camels that bore spices, and very much gold, and precious stones ...' Later in this chapter there is the significant phrase: 'There came no more such abundance of spices as these which the Queen of Sheba gave to King Solomon.' Whether the Queen was in fact called Bilkis (as tradition has it) or not, it is certainly true that in the Jewish sacred scripts southern Arabia was already known as the rich Arabia in contrast to the Arabia Deserta, which was nearer to Palestine. But the prosperity of the southern Arabian kingdoms derived from the trade in spices and incense. The gifts of gold and precious stones mentioned in the passage from the Bible may have come from the Hadramauth, but, as resources in that area were limited, the Queen of Saba is more likely to have acquired her treasures by trading with Egypt and East Africa. The kingdom of Saba enjoyed a monopoly in the spice trade and could therefore demand in exchange ancient Egypt's most treasured commodities, gold and precious stones, for it is written in the Old Testament (2 Chronicles ix. 9) 'neither was there any such spice as the Queen of Sheba gave King Solomon'.

A further proof of prosperity is the towered south gate of Timna, which a priest-ruler, presumably Yadiab Dhubyan, built four to five hundred years later. It was through this gate that the caravans from the Hadramauth entered the town; here the tolls and duties were paid which made Kataba and its capital so wealthy. The hewn stones of the gate-towers were between thirty and sixty cubic feet in size so that each one weighed several tons. Their outer walls were steep and of a dazzling white that must have shone in the Arabian sun and been visible to travellers from a considerable distance. Be-

tween some of the stone blocks the remains of charred beams were
found which, together with other deposits of wood-ash, indicate that
the town was destroyed by fire. It was sacked, however, not by the
Romans, who in 25 B.C. invaded southern Arabia, but by a neighbouring people who, apparently as trade rivals or from sheer rapa-
city, reduced the wealthy city on the incense road to ashes, and
about the beginning of the Christian era conquered parts of Kataba.

During this period of unrest, however, trade itself does not seem
to have suffered any permanent damage, otherwise the kingdoms on
the incense road would not have attracted the Romans, whose expeditions were never organized at random. Compared with the fairly
brief and not particularly detailed information given in the Bible,
in Herodotus, and on the coins that have been found, contemporary
reports of the campaign of Aelius Gallus, one of Augustus's generals,
are positively verbose and show the incense road and Arabia Felix
for the first time in a historical light.

In Rome itself the prices of aromatic gums, unguents, cosmetic
products and spices were very high, for Rome was the final stage in
the trade chain which linked her with the Hadramauth through
Petra, Syria and the Mediterranean. So in Augustine Rome the
riches of Arabia were no less proverbial than in the kingdom of
Solomon, and the news of a military expedition to Arabia Felix
appears to have caused a veritable gold fever among the debt-ridden
young bloods of the Eternal City.

'Iccius, dost thou look now with envious eye at the rich treasures
of the Arabians, and prepare dire warfare on Sabaean kings . . . ?'
wrote Horace in his 29th Ode (First Book), and Victor von Gard-
thausen, one of the most reputable historians of the time of
Augustus, writes: 'He may have hoped by conquering Arabia with
its immense wealth to acquire the funds which he needed to run his
army and his administration . . . What the merchant had taken there,
the soldier was to regain.' For centuries merchants and caravans had
taken much of the produce of Egypt, Greece and Rome to those
parts of southern Arabia from which the precious camel-loads came.
What could be more obvious than to recover all this with simple
and compound interest by means of force? The Greek geographer
Strabo leaves us in no doubt: 'The Arabs were also known from
earliest times to be rich, as they traded their spices and precious
stones against gold and silver and gave nothing back to strangers of
what they received. For this reason he hoped either to exploit them
as rich friends or to conquer them as rich enemies. . . .' (Strabo XVI,
776.)

Arabia, in fact, was not a very accommodating trade partner, for it bought little or nothing from its clients, insisting on payment in hard cash. As we see, this was unpopular—and dangerous—even in the ancient world. Every road runs in two directions, even the incense road, thought the Romans angrily, and got ready to mete out to Arabia Felix the same punishment they had imposed on Carthage. Had they kept to the incense road, they would probably have succeeded, particularly as in Egypt they had an excellent base, from which to launch their campaign, and well-stocked supply depots in Syria. But either they were badly advised or they took the whole operation too lightly. They certainly appear to have had a completely false picture of the Arabian terrain. That 'merchants on camels with many people and animals can make their way safely and unimpeded amongst the hills and rocks, so that they have no need to fear even an army' (Strabo), this was something the Romans became aware of too late, when their fleet had already crossed the Red Sea and suffered heavy losses on the rocky coast. Moreover, they landed much too far north, so that they were compelled to undertake an endless march through the desert. For safety's sake they stuck close to the coast, instead of following the inland caravan trail that ran parallel with it. For no less than half a year the Romans wandered through sand and desert wastes, losing a great many men from sickness and exhaustion, till they were finally obliged to turn back within two days' march of the land of spices. With the help of native guides, Aelius Gallus on his retreat covered the same stretch which had taken him six months in sixty days, which was roughly the time taken by the Queen of Sheba. 'It was not through enemy action but through starvation and bad marching conditions that he had lost his soldiers: in actual combat only seven men had fallen.'

It is, however, difficult to believe that Aelius Gallus, once he had marched as far as Marib, decided to retreat on other than purely military grounds. Marib was a large and wealthy city, capital of the kingdom of Sheba. 'At our first inspection it seemed to us that ten Timnas might easily fit into the area of Marib,' writes Wendell-Phillips. 'The present Arab village occupied only a small portion of the ancient city area. Columns, walls, and pillars extended everywhere as far as our eyes could see . . .'

Two thousand years ago the sight that met Aelius Gallus's eyes must have been even more impressive. He may have felt that with a mere handful of soldiers—all that was left of his army—he could not hope to conquer such a large city. It is also possible that the Sheban army engaged the Romans in a bloody desert battle and defeated them. The huge Marib dam alone—which had been standing for close on a thousand years, storing up the water of the Wadi Denne for irrigation, and which ranked as one of the wonders of the ancient world—must have made the Romans realize how rich this country was and how well worth conquering.

Arabia Felix remained unconquered, protected by its deserts against the armies that invaded it from the north and north-west, yet through these same deserts passed an endless chain of camels, taking out incense and spices and returning with gold and silver. A full five hundred years after Aelius Gallus, the Ethiopians invaded Arabia—the Red Sea was more easily subdued than the desert; fifty years later came the Persians who had only to cross the Gulf, and then the new religion united the whole peninsula with strong spiritual bonds.

At this stage, however, the incense road had already lost much of its importance. The main traffic had moved north; anyone wishing to travel south by way of Mecca boarded a ship in one of the Egyptian Red Sea ports. Navigation had improved, the underwater reefs were well charted, and maritime trade provided a cheaper form of mass transport than caravans. In Egypt the old religion had long since lost its hold; the temples had been stripped of their riches. Arabia's export of incense no longer passed across the Sinai peninsula, but in the opposite direction, eastwards to India. The Hadramauth lost interest in the old incense road; Timna and Marib lapsed into decay; and the harbour towns prospered from the trade that now passed across the Indian Ocean. The Greek seafarer who first discovered the monsoon with its steady, regular rhythm had created a much more serious threat to the incense road and the wealth it conveyed than the sabre-rattling Roman Aelius Gallus. Marib and Timna were superseded by the wealthy metropolis of Zufar, whose prince controlled the incense trade right up to the seventh century, but today this city also lies buried under a high hill on the coast.

Whether the incense road will ever come back into use is doubtful. In 1914 Cadi Ragheb Bey introduced the first motor-car into the Yemen, but the population, who depend on the caravan trade and camel-breeding for their livelihood, are not at all well disposed towards the combustion engine and their antagonism will take a long time to overcome. King Saud's enormous limousines equipped with refrigerators, television, bullet-proof glass and fittings in precious metals owe their existence not to incense but to the less fragrant petroleum which has proved much more potent than the trees for which the Pharaoh Hatshepset longed.

In the early part of the seventh century, trade on the incense road came to a complete standstill. One man from the city of Jathrib, later called Medina, had conceived a grudge against the city of Mecca and with a small, ragged band of men carried out enough raids and forays to disrupt Mecca's trade. This man, who was called Mohammed Abdul Qasim ibn Abdullah, was already in his fifties and might have continued to live quietly in Jathrib, if he had not become convinced that he was destined to found a new religion and to conquer for this new faith the ancient and sacred black stone of Mecca, which for several centuries had been attracting pilgrims.

In the year 624 one of these raids on the incense road to Mecca developed into a fierce battle at a place called Bedr. The people of Mecca outnumbered the men from Jathrib, but the small band of marauders fought with desperate ferocity, killed Mohammed's arch-enemy, Abn Djahl, and emerged victorious. In a second engagement in the spring of 625 the men of Jathrib were again victorious, but at the crucial moment their looting instincts got the better of them. Finally, in 628, Mohammed himself went on a pilgrimage to Mecca at the head of a great concourse of the faithful, and, when he died on June 8th, 632, the incense road had become the holy road of a new religion, the Pilgrims' Way of Islam.

Until Mohammed's lifetime, only the Arab tribes from the hinterland had made the pilgrimage to Mecca—together with isolated groups who came more out of curiosity than piety from the remoter parts of Arabia. The temple which housed the Kaaba is said to have been built by Abraham, a legend in which even many Jewish tribes believed, and, in consequence, they also made the pilgrimage to Mecca (till Mohammed had seven hundred of them slain). It is certainly true that the stone was considered to be sacred before the birth of Christ, and that the Koreishite tribe and particularly one member of it named Kossai organized the pilgrim traffic in the fifth century B.C., building shelters for the caravan travellers and thereby laying the foundations of the city which, in spite of frequent raids and fires, must be regarded today as one of the richest cities in the world. The dark basalt block, of which barely two square feet are visible and which has a mysterious crystalline glitter, attracts hundreds of thousands of pilgrims every year, who have created an immense network of pilgrim roads over the length and breadth of the Islamic world, from West Africa to India, and from the Somali coast to the Bulgarian frontier. Up to a thousand people die every year on this holy journey, as many as six or seven hundred alone from sunstroke in the Arabian desert, and while the human victims can at least console themselves with the thought that death brings them closer to heaven, tens of thousands of donkeys and camels perish without any such consolation.

It is only in this century that modern means of transport, though only available to the more prosperous pilgrims, have brought these casualties down—as far as the animals are concerned. In 1951 the sun exacted the same toll as for centuries past: in September of that year 700 pilgrims died of heat-stroke within three days.

In earlier times, the pilgrims from Anatolia and western Persia assembled near Damascus—often several months before the pilgrim caravans set out. They were up to 50,000 strong and carried with them all kinds of supplies and commodities, for these trading peoples, for all their piety, would not undertake such a long and expensive journey without doing some business on the side.

The pilgrims from West Africa spent as much as a year on the journey. They used the old trade routes straight across the continent, or blazed new trails if a particular area was impassable for political, economic or health reasons; plagues were one of the most appalling hazards on these journeys. About the middle of the last century the British and the Dutch introduced a system of plague-control, which was mainly directed against cholera, but it functioned—somewhat arbitrarily—in only two areas, El Tor (to the north of the Red Sea) and the island of Camaran.

In the African caravans, princes travelled together with poor peasants, game-hunters with wealthy merchants, and plundering (or at best gold-hunting) Bedouin swarmed about this gigantic convoy like sharks, their principle being: We neither sow nor reap, the soil we cultivate is the pilgrims. The way was long. The Moroccans had to travel through the oases of Tafilet eastwards by way of Tripoli to the assembly points around Cairo, where they were joined by the Egyptians who came from the Lower Nile Valley and the Sudan. From Cairo to Mecca took about another forty days. When Islam spread to the negroes of West Africa, pilgrims also came from Ssonghay (around Timbuctoo) and other areas, which until then had only known the crudest of communications by way of Lake Chad and the Darfur area. These particular pilgrims took not only riding and pack animals but also enough livestock to keep them in food during the journey. Not surprisingly, for many of these primitive dark-skinned pilgrims such a journey had all the perils and adventure of an Odyssey.

Countless stories have been told of the pilgrimage, but none more intriguing than that of Yussuffu Hamadu, the peasant who in 1911 at the age of thirty-five set off for Mecca from French Equatorial Africa with his herd of cattle. He drove them more than 500 miles to the Gold Coast, where he sold them; then he travelled by train to Accra; proceeded from there on foot across the Ivory Coast,

Liberia, Sierra Leone, Guinea and Gambia till he reached Saint-Louis in Senegal. Throughout this long journey he made one business deal after the other with the capital from the sale of his cattle, buying and selling kola nuts, amulets and anything else he could profitably lay his hands on, with the result that he was able to take a boat from Saint-Louis to the Canary Islands. He travelled on by way of Barcelona, Marseilles and Alexandria, walked across Egypt, and took a sailing-boat from Suez to Jeddah. He arrived eventually at Mecca, saw and kissed the Kaaba, and returned home contented via Medina, Jerusalem, Haifa, Marseilles, Bordeaux, the Canary Islands and Dakar with about £20 in his pocket. But he also brought home with him enough goods and souvenirs to sell at a handsome profit.

If one compares Yussuffu's experiences with those of many other pilgrims, one is tempted to conclude that his shrewdest move was to avoid the normal pilgrim routes in the interior of Africa, on which so many lost everything they possessed, and not a few their lives. Sultan Zakura of Mali in western Sudan, for example, was murdered and robbed on his way back from Mecca in the year 1300. When his successor decided to make the pilgrimage thirty years later, he took an escort with him of no less than 15,000 men. Askia Muhammed, who made the pilgrimage to Mecca a hundred years after the Sultans of Mali, managed with a bodyguard of 'only' 800, but on the outward and return journey he spent, according to Romain Roussel, the considerable sum of 100,000 louis d'or. Even in the nineteenth century—to judge by a report from a German explorer, Richard Kund—the son of a Sultan of Timbuctoo lost, in three months, one-third of his personnel, almost all his mules and some 500 head of cattle. It seems almost as if the poor pilgrim, travelling alone, came out better in the end. A mendicant pilgrim from West Africa set out on November 9th, 1794, from Walata, 250 miles west of Timbuctoo, and after walking for $7\frac{1}{2}$ months reached Mecca unscathed on June 25th, 1795.

That these pilgrimages are almost as hazardous as ever and that even modern means of transport are no match for the desert is clear from the fate of 200 Pakistani pilgrims, who in 1952, after a short sea voyage down the Persian Gulf, tried to cross Arabia on their way to Mecca. In March the first group, forty strong, set off to walk across the Nejd desert, but only one reached the holy city of Islam. The Arab pilgrim roads on all routes, via Damascus, the Sinai Peninsula and from the Persian Gulf continued to be a severe test, thanks partly to the Wahabis, a puritanical and cruel sect of nomads, who between 1783 and 1795 kept the pilgrim road in a constant state of

uncertainty, and in 1803 even descended on Mecca, conquered
Medina, and blocked the four roads to Egypt, Damascus, Persia and
the Yemen.

This insecurity affected not one but two major religions, for by a
strange dispensation of providence both Islam and Christianity have
their holy places in the same area. Mohammedan pilgrims on their
way to Mecca and Christian pilgrims on their way to Jerusalem
frequently travelled on the same ships. At a time when Spain was
only half-Christian, not merely was the normal way to Jerusalem
blocked by the Saracens, but the conquests of the crusaders compelled countless pious Mohammedans to take roundabout routes to
the Mosque of Omar in Jerusalem, which after Mecca and Medina
is the third holy place of Islam.

In sharp contrast to the four clearly recognizable pilgrim roads
to Mecca is the maze of routes by which the crusaders, the 'pilgrims
with sword in hand', made their way to Palestine. And there were
others, innumerable men, women and children, who made the gruelling journey across a continent, which about A.D. 1000 was much
more difficult to cross than in the heyday of the Roman roads.

So many shiploads of pilgrims from Spain and France and from
Italy and Greece passed through the Mediterranean, with which seafarers had become familiar since the very earliest times, that the old
Roman roads through the Balkans—or what was left of them—
could never have competed but for two developments which forced
many pilgrims to travel overland. One was the increase in the number of Islamic corsairs, whose ships preyed on the main routes from
Barcelona, Marseilles, Genoa, Brindisi and Venice; the other was the
victory of Christianity in Hungary. The change was already apparent in the year 999, when the monk Gerbert (perhaps the greatest
scholar of his time) became Pope Sylvester II and called upon
Christendom to recover the holy places from the heathen; and the
transformation was completed two years later when Stephen, son
of the wild tyrant Geisa, was crowned King of Hungary and subdued the last of the heathen tribal chiefs. Once Hungary was won
over to Christianity, the pilgrims could travel through Christian
countries right to the very gates of the Orient.

This marked the beginning of a mass movement, which until
then had been a mere trickle. True, the Emperor Hadrian as early as
the second century A.D. had erected a statue of Venus on the Hill
of Calvary and a statue of Jupiter on the scene of Christ's resurrec-
tion in order to prevent the establishment of a Christian mythology;
about A.D. 212 Alexander, Bishop of Cappadocia, made a pilgrimage to Jerusalem; and in 325 Constantine's mother, the saintly

Helena, followed in his footsteps. But even half a century later, in 382, when Porphyrius, Bishop of Gaza, made the journey to Jerusalem with his servant Marcus, organized pilgrimages and pilgrim roads were still unknown. These two pious travellers worked their passage to the Holy City as cobblers and scribes.

In 1064, however, 7,000 people followed the Bishop of Mainz, to be attacked and robbed by Bedouin in Syria. Then came the high tide of pilgrims in the late Middle Ages as a result of fiery sermons by Sylvester II (999–1003). But soon the tide began to recede. In 1589 a French pilgrim, Villamont, encountered barely half a dozen compatriots in Jerusalem; in 1656 a French traveller and writer, Melchisedec Thévenot, counted altogether twenty-two visitors to the Holy Sepulchre; and another Frenchman, the poet René de Chateaubriand (1768–1848), in his *Itinéraire de Paris à Jérusalem* reckoned the number of pilgrims for the whole of the eighteenth century at a yearly average of two hundred, 'which includes the missionaries from the Levant and pilgrim priests'. It was only with the marked improvement in transport in the nineteenth and twentieth centuries that the number of pilgrims increased again. But as recently as 1958 they were still well below the figures for the Middle Ages.

As I have pointed out, the medieval pilgrims travelled to a large extent on the old Roman roads. But for considerable stretches they were in a state of dangerous disrepair; new wooden bridges were built at many points, but more often than not they were too flimsy to carry the heavy traffic of pilgrims and crusaders. Where no Roman roads existed, the travellers used the rough tracks across country, which for a large part of the year were in a shocking state.

In the first Crusade, in 1099, Raimund de Toulouse travelled along the Via Egnatia, the old Roman military road which linked Aquileia, Salonae, Dyrrhachium and northern Greece with Byzantium, while Godfrey de Bouillon, who died in Jerusalem in 1100, made his way through Mainz, Regensburg, Vienna and Belgrade (the ancient Sirmium), and from there through Thrace to Byzantium.

The majority of pilgrims on these roads, however, were not protected by a crusaders' army, so they banded together in large groups, for the roads were so unsafe that the smaller the group the greater the risk involved.

A German, Bishop Willibald, on the other hand, was the victim of an incident which could have happened even on an asphalt road. With his seven companions he was suspected of espionage and thrown into prison. Some time elapsed before they were set free. Then, though already a small group, they divided up into four in order to attract less attention. But in general the poor state of the roads and mountain passes was the major hazard with which all medieval pilgrims had to contend; as a result, journeys took so long that the Council of Rouen in 1072 had to threaten with excommunication all married women who prematurely announced the death of their husbands on pilgrimage in order to marry another.

Because of the overall duration of these journeys and the short distances covered each day, innumerable hostels sprang up along the great pilgrim roads. The monasteries offered simple but safe accommodation; from less spiritual motives the villages also welcomed the pilgrims and erected proper caravanserais for them where their animals could also be accommodated. As these pious travellers spent months on their journey, they lived on the roads, which acquired a special character of their own from these hordes of pilgrims, who were not allowed to engage in trade like other road-users, were strictly rationed in their food, and wore distinctive clothing. At the larger staging-points the tired travellers were offered all kinds of entertainment, though only if—like the immortal hero of Eça de Queiroz's satire—they carried well-lined purses. While the Mohammedans knew that if they had intercourse with a woman they must abandon the pilgrimage to Mecca, and therefore waited patiently for the moment of absolution after the ritual cutting of hair, the Christian pilgrims could always look forward to eventual indulgences and forgiveness for the sins committed in Alexandria or Venice, Athens or Budapest. They lived, loved and died on the road to salvation—exhausted, robbed, but never losing faith and grateful to Heaven for allowing them to die on pilgrimage.

In unpopulated areas or at particularly dangerous points were specially built hostels which, even in later centuries when the tide of pilgrims had long since receded, still continued to function. The first of these asylums was almost certainly the great hospice of Edessa in Greece, which was founded in the fourth century by the prominent theologian and preacher Ephraim and, to begin with, supplied food and lodging for three hundred, later for anything up to a thousand or more sick pilgrims. In Europe Charlemagne had revived the tradition of Roman hospices but under the aegis of the Christian Church, and in the year 789 he issued instructions that his hospitalia should cater primarily for pilgrims. These rest-houses had not only eating and sleeping quarters but also latrines (which were something of a rarity in those days), a bakery, a drinking saloon and a small room for cooling beer. Charlemagne levied a hospice-penny on church revenues, which proved such a profitable source of income that before long hospitalia appeared on all the main roads—at Liège and Grenoble, at Nîmes, Sens, Nevers, Toul, Le Mans and other places. An equally important factor was the interest taken by the monks in maintaining and improving the roads. Bridge-building fraternities were even formed, which emulated the achievements of their heathen predecessors, the priests of Delphi and other Greek sanctuaries. In both cases the basic principle was the same: pilgrims could only be encouraged to visit the holy places if the way was prepared.

Among the impressive structures that still exist to remind us of that wave of public spirit are the hospice on Mont Cenis in the western Alps which St. Louis equipped so handsomely, the castle of Bourrines on the way to Santiago, the bridge of Saint-Benezet, at Avignon, and the Pont-Saint-Esprit in the village of the same name in southern France.

Sometimes the pilgrims benefited by a chance accident, a misfortune that befell some powerful figure and opened his eyes to the hardships which the common people suffered on the roads. When Adalard, Count of Flanders, was attacked and surrounded by a band of robbers on his way home from the famous shrine at Santiago de Compostela, he vowed that on that same desolate Rouergue plateau he would build a hospice. The result was a fortress rather than a house of charity, but at that particular spot and in that period (1120) the Flemish count had undoubtedly done the right thing. From then on the pilgrims could cross the Via Mala of that high plateau without fear; armed knights escorted them, while their wives cared for the poor and the sick. The Order of Chevaliers d'Aubrac, which was created from this foundation, contributed a great deal in subsequent decades towards the security of travel in that area and, in consequence, towards the general economic development. No less famous was the Order of Knights of Santiago, which protected pilgrims to Santiago de Compostela.

In view of the difficulties and dangers involved it is hardly surprising that quite a few people did not themselves make the pilgrimage to the Holy Land, but delegated others to make it for them. The choice invariably fell on someone who had nothing better to do, who preferred the open road to some dingy cellar and who was quite happy to trudge the dusty, dirty roads of Europe and Anatolia so long as he was paid for it. So, in addition to the many trades and professions that lived by the road, a new group made their appearance: professional, per procura pilgrims, whose employers were sometimes no longer alive, but wished to protect themselves against the fires of purgatory by a proxy pilgrimage to the Holy Land.

One can easily imagine what a motley and not always pious collection of people made their way along the pilgrim roads of the

Middle Ages. Very few were in a hurry to get back home to the familiar treadmill—so long as they remained on the long road they were serving God and their own cause as well. Others found on the road ample opportunity to commit petty and not so petty offences, for here every man was a stranger, and in the crowded hospices and monasteries it was much easier to pass unnoticed than in the walled towns with their narrow streets, where the officers of the watch were always on the look-out for strange faces. Offences of various kinds became common on the roads at quite an early stage; in the fourth century a distinguished Father of the Church, Gregor of Nyssa, called upon the faithful to honour and praise Christ at home, and the holy Bonifacius wrote to Cuthbert, Archbishop of Canterbury, a letter—which has since become famous—about the many women who made the pilgrimage to Rome and lost their virginity on the way, with the result that 'in Gallia and in Lombardy there is literally not a single town left in which English women are not living as whores.' This was, of course, an ideal subject for satire, and a whole literature emerged—from Chaucer (1360–1400) to Erasmus of Rotterdam (1465–1536), from the anonymous *Pélérinage de Renart* to the *Reliquie* of the Portuguese Eça de Quieroz (1887)—which with a wealth of imagery shows the seamy side of the holy roads.

Chapter 7

THE SACRED TRAIL

Between Sicily and Tripoli, in the middle of the Mediterranean, lies the little island of Malta, no bigger in area than a modern metropolis.

The island's bare limestone plateau, which drops steeply on the southern side from about 700 feet to the coast below, was the scene until recently of one of the most intriguing riddles of ancient history. With an air of mystery, every visitor to Malta was shown the strange ruts which are a feature not only of the main island but also of the tiny island of Gozo. Those ruts do not run between villages—which might have suggested some kind of prehistoric railway without steam —but wind their way in pairs up the hill-sides to the tableland. At some points ten or twelve of these double tracks run side by side, almost giving the appearance of a Stone Age marshalling yard. To judge by the dimensions of these ruts, quite heavy loads must have passed along them; they are as much as a foot deep in the rock, about four inches wide at the bottom and become markedly uneven on the bends. The gauge is surprisingly uniform at 137 centimetres (nearly 4½ feet).

These ruts cannot have been produced naturally; they can only have been made by men who spent countless hours chiselling them in the rock. It is one of those gigantic communal achievements which we find at various stages in the early history of the human race, the best-known examples being the Pyramids of Egypt and the Great Wall of China; lesser-known examples are the ancient artesian canals in Armenia and the tunnel of Nimrud in Mesopotamia. In all these cases an explanation was eventually found for such tremendous human effort. Rarely, except in periods of decline and under half-crazy Caesars, was work of this magnitude undertaken merely to gratify the whim of a dictator.

We know from the evidence of tombs and graves that Malta formed part of the main stream of Megalithic culture (Late Stone Age), which left behind massive stone buildings on the Gulf of Riga, on the south coast of the Baltic and North Seas, in Great Britain, in the Channel Islands, on the eastern shores of the Atlantic and on the southern shores of the Mediterranean, as well as in Palestine, Persia and India. They formed a ring that almost encircled the world, but was never far from the sea-coast—a ring to which, some archaeologists claim, the ancient monuments of South America such as the ruins of Tiahaunaco on Lake Titicaca also belonged. The men who built with these gigantic blocks of stone—and were, therefore, believed for a long time to have been giants—were ruled by priests or priest-kings, and were so devoutly religious that some scholars have interpreted the long journeys and endless wanderings made by the Megalithic peoples as a form of missionary activity. (W. J. Perry.)

Unfortunately, we know very little more than that about the people who lived more than 3,000 years ago in Malta; that is why the origins and purpose of these groove-roads remained un-explained until a few years ago. It was safe to assume that the Phoenicians, who later conquered the island, were not responsible, for they clearly did not know what the object of them was: right across these laboriously-hollowed grooves many Phoenician tombs and graves were found which belonged to the eighth and ninth centuries B.C. and which blocked the tracks.

A Maltese historian, Themistokles Zammit, who has a unique knowledge of the natural history of his native island, found an explanation in the climate and the structure of the soil. Malta is hot and dry—except in December, January and February, when the rainfall is so heavy that the soil is washed down from the tableland into the valleys below—and before the Maltese peasants could culti-vate their fields, they had to carry up the soil and then the water in truckloads.

At Birzebuggia in St. George's Bay one can still see three dozen bell-shaped containers from prehistoric times, which were hewn out of the rock and were used to catch and store rain-water. Today they lie under the sea, but drinking-water in Malta is still collected in large cisterns.

The groove-tracks run down the hill-side to the bay, where the high, single-axle trolleys—double-axle trolleys would not have negotiated the bends—were loaded. On the hub of the wooden wheels a second wheel was fixed in such a way that the trolley could not stick on the worn parts of the track. As no hoof-marks were found, one must assume that men and women of this unknown Stone Age race themselves hauled and pushed the earth and water up the mountain-side; this was probably the only way they could be sure of their crops.

We shall probably never know definitely whether these groove-roads, the ancient roads of Crete and the short flagstone paths in Egypt—which were presumably used only for processions—can be regarded as the oldest man-made roads in the world, or whether in distant China thousands of soldiers built the first road across a chain of mountains. None of the known road-systems was influenced by the others. The road was simply built where it was needed, and the form it took was dictated by nature. Between the natural track beaten out by animals or men and the surfaced road a new type has appeared: the groove-road. It was built not with any ideal in view but to meet an emergency, so it is, if not a common, at least a fairly frequent occurrence in pre-Roman and even Roman times.

The German sociologist and historian, Heinrich Bulle, who died in 1945, discovered one of the most striking examples of this type of road on the Federauner Sattel in Carthenia. Commonly referred to as a Roman road, it belongs, in fact, to a much earlier period, when salt, amber and other commodities were transported for long distances across pre-Roman Europe. A prehistoric settlement on a hill-top near Oberfederaun, which goes back to 1800 B.C., indicates that the road through the Federaun mountains was one of the oldest north-to-south communications in the whole of the eastern Alps.

Heinrich Bulle carried out the most thorough research into this three-thousand-year-old road.

> The outstanding feature of the soil in this stretch is ... that at several points the limestone rock appears, sometimes quite smooth and flat but more often in the form of ridges or mounds of rock which ... protrude more or less steeply and represented, in each case, a serious obstacle for passing vehicles. Here the old road-builders set to work as stone-masons and cut these ridges down to a certain depth to produce a tolerably even surface over which vehicles could pass.
>
> Where the rock was cut as well as where it is flat ... we find the groove-formations which must be regarded as belong-

ing to what, as we shall see, was a simple, economical yet quite deliberate method of road-building.

Modern agricultural vehicles gave 'the walls of many of the grooves, where they ran deep, a permanent smooth polish'; at some time earlier an attempt had been made to render the track skid-proof. The Romans were able to carry on where the Celts had left off, for they had hewn tracks through all the ridges of rock, and farther up the mountain-side Bulle found traces of an even older groove-track built by the Illyrians, who had clearly set the example which the Celts and Romans subsequently followed.

'But,' writes Bulle, 'there was undoubtedly a prehistoric track there in the first instance, for in mountainous country of this kind such tracks are virtually products of nature.'

These grooved tracks have stood the test of time as well as any rock-carvings or ancient runes. They give us an unexpected glimpse of the history of a road which, as Bulle says, is 'dictated by nature' and therefore made its appearance at a time when the first settlers wanted to make contact with their neighbours on the other side of the mountain. And it remained a road: it became part of the network of Etruscan trade routes to the North, and then of the important Noric main road which ran through Pontebba–Saifnitzer Saddle–Tarvis–Maglern, across the small river Gail to the village of Unter-federaun, to Oberfederaun over the saddle, and on northwards through Völkendorf to Villach and across the Drava.

It was an old trade road even under the Romans. Not only iron and gold but also hides, skins, timber, resin, cheese and honey passed along it. (Derringer.) Later, between A.D 167 and 174, when Marcus Aurelius subdued the Marcomanns after bitter fighting, Roman soldiers marched along this road with their baggage.

The grooved type of road reached its highest point of development in Illyria, the Karst area of Dalmatia, Bosnia and the former territory of Herzegovina. Long stretches of it are still extant—one of them about six miles long between the northern Dalmatian towns of Ervenik and Krupa.

As Illyria had neither trees nor enough clay for building, there was nothing else for it but to level out the jagged and creviced rock and make one or possibly even two tracks. To build a wide road in such rock would have been a tremendous and, indeed, superfluous task, for all the vehicles needed were grooves for the wheels. The bases of these grooves were filled with loose rubble, which provided a certain amount of give and acted, so to speak, as springs. These tracks undoubtedly remained in use for several centuries, otherwise one track, which in many of the curves was subjected to greater friction and pressure, would hardly have been as much as two feet deeper than the other. Some of the Illyrian roads, most of which were single-track and only about five feet across, were later widened by the Romans to as much as twenty feet and provided with several tracks. At many points stones and the remains of embankments can still be seen, which the Romans had erected to protect the track; in northern Dalmatia the Romans even built walls to buttress the road.

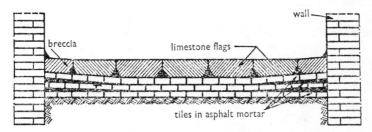

Processional road 'Aibur Shabu' at Babylon (about 600 B.C.)

The discovery of the Illyrian road-system was of particular interest to archaeologists, because this coast-dwelling people had for some two thousand years been dismissed as pirates—the Illyrian War (229 B.C.) of the Consuls Gnaius Fulvius Centumalus and L. Posthumius Albionus was known simply as the Pirate War. The roads prove, however, that these pirates were able to produce sufficient from their barren country to develop an appreciable barter-trade with the Greeks and Romans. The Illyrians extracted gold, silver, copper and iron from their mountains, quarried marble at Tragurium, and transported cheese and honey wine down into the valleys. There are even traces of a modest industry in bronze weapons and jewellery. Unfortunately, any such traces are few and far between; even the knowledgeable Herodotus does not credit the Illyrians with being industrious—he does, however, describe their rare marriage custom whereby the most beautiful girls, who fetched the highest prices at the marriage-market, helped their uglier sisters to find a husband by contributing to their dowries.

In Malta the grooved roads served almost as goods lifts, but in Illyria they were essentially trade routes; in Asia Minor they fulfilled a third function as splendid, wide processional routes along which the festive cars rolled, bearing images of the gods. Hittites, Assyrians and Babylonians all carried their gods in such processions

on feast days. One of the greatest rulers of Asia Minor, Nebuchadnezzar II (605–562 B.C.), built a particularly splendid processional
road which ran from the Gate of Ishtar to the High Temple of
Babylon at Etemenanki and which was fringed by two rows of
lions in relief. This road, which was about twenty yards wide, has
a particularly flat lane in the middle, and when some of the blocks
were removed the following inscription was found in cuneiform
characters: 'I had the Road of Babel laid with Shadu stone flags for
the procession of the great Lord Marduk.' In another inscription
Nebuchadnezzar expresses himself even more clearly: 'Nabu and
Marduk, when you wander happily along these roads, may benefac-
tion for me rest upon your lips, a life of distant days, bodily wellbeing. I shall wander along them before you. Grant that I may
become old for ever.'[1]

The King was anxious, it seems, to serve not merely the gods but
also, and above all, himself: all eyes were upon him when he rode
along the processional road before the images of the gods, and the
slightest accident was regarded as an ill omen. 'If a horse stumbles
on the god's chariot, then the whole land will lose its reason,' according to an ancient Babylonian book of omens. The meaning is very
clear. The monarch, who was protected by the gods and received
their homage, was untouchable and beyond blame, but once the
gods had made known their displeasure, the land lost its 'reason'
and was in that case likely to defect from its ruler. And, like most
of his predecessors and successors, Nebuchadnezzar feared nothing
so much as the defection of any one of his territories, unrest in any
corner of his vast kingdom, which took several weeks to cross from
one side to the other.

Nebuchadnezzar had precedents for taking out some insurance
against accident. Before his time the Assyrian king Sargon II (721–
705) and Sanherib (704–681) had built similar stone roads for the
safe transit of the divine images. There are known to be three
Assyrian temples with deep-grooved roads leading up to them; one
of these, in the Sin and Shamash Temple of Assur, even has grooves
more than two feet deep, in contrast to the much shallower grooves
of the Assur temple. Before the cars with the divine images began
their journey the rails were filled with a special material to prevent
the wheels, obviously for some superstitious reason or other, from
touching the stone. Stone and earth were taboo to the gods. What
kind of material this was has not so far been discovered. The

---

[1] Taken from Robert Koldewey (1875–1925) whose life's work it was to
excavate Babylon. After digging at Sendjirli, Baalbek and other places, he
devoted eighteen years almost continuously to this great task.

archaeologist Walter Andrae, in his work on 'Ancient ceremonial roads in the Near East', suggests wood or metal, but Heinrich Bulle believes it was 'a pavement-like material possibly of solidified plaster or something similar ... which has not stood the test of time.'

It is hard to imagine why it should occur to anyone to look for prehistoric roads in an island the size of Malta, which covers only a few miles from one end to the other. And yet this is one of the few places where irrefutable evidence was found to show that roads

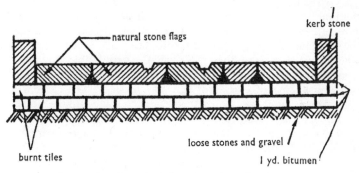

Processional road to the Ishtar Temple of Assur

existed in the Stone Age. No less surprising are the discoveries which were made on another Mediterranean island—Crete. In area, Crete is about the size of Wales, but it is so shaped that at its widest it is only 35 miles across, and it is five times as long as it is broad. The mountains in the interior of the island rise at several points to over 7,000 feet and are so wild and inaccessible that from 1866 to 1878 Cretan irregulars were able to keep the Turks and their Egyptian troops permanently on the hop.

A narrow island washed by the warm waters of the Mediterranean and with so much of the interior virtually inaccessible—all this would seem to point to the sea as the obvious means of communication. Yet when the archaeologists made their sensational discoveries of Minoan culture (2600–1150 B.C.), they also found an ancient network of roads in Crete, which showed a standard of workmanship that was only equalled by the Romans and only surpassed in our own time.

Until the discovery of the royal palace of Cnossos virtually nothing was known about Crete's early history apart from the semi-legendary King Minos and Queen Pasiphae, who hid herself in a specially-made bronze cow in order to acquire the archaic wildness of a sacred bull and then conceived the Minotaur.

The impressive royal palace with its labyrinthine passages, its flights of steps, terraces and columns, does suggest that architecture had already reached a very advanced stage about 2000 B.C., but of particular interest to us is the idea that the architects of that early period knew how to build not only splendid palaces but also excellent roads. About the time when grooves were being hewn in the rock in Malta for the use of trolley-cars, the science of road-building in that particular period had reached its peak in Crete.

To make this clear we must go into a certain amount of technical detail and examine the cross-section plan of a typical Cretan road more closely. It shows that the Cretans began by carefully levelling and stamping down the subsoil to produce a flat, even ditch about eight inches deep and five yards wide. Then rubble and broken stones were packed into the bottom of the ditch and made watertight with a kind of mortar of clay and plaster. Then came a soft layer of clay about two inches thick, on which the surface stones of lime or even basalt were laid. The road was thus sprung or cushioned with the result that the paving-stones proved much more permanent than in Greek and Roman roads centuries later, and the Cretan roads of the Minoan period have remained in an extraordinary state of preservation for over 4,000 years. The road surface was cambered to let the rain-water run off into stone drains on both sides of the road. These drains alone must have required considerable manpower; they were made of long blocks of stone which were specially hollowed out for the purpose. Limestone walls up to fifteen feet high bordered the road. Their purpose is not quite clear, but they must at least have provided the traveller with some shade.

When one considers the Cretan climate, this is not quite such an exaggeration as it might seem to be. One must also remember that most of the roads ran from north to south and crossed mountains that were devoid of trees. Only by taking a fairly straight course could these roads offer any advantage over coastal shipping. On their way across the mountains both men and animals had to negotiate some steep climbs.

One of the roads started at the south coast near Gortyna and Komo, climbed through the Messara valley, and crossed the mountains at a height of 5,000 feet. Its destination was the royal residence at Cnossos and the near-by port. This was probably the main road, and was almost certainly in use long before it was technically completed in the second millenium B.C. Other roads branched from it to other parts of the north coast, or to the few points in the mountains where a crossing was possible. Owing to the barrenness and wildness of the interior, the rulers of Crete had been compelled from earliest times to protect travellers and merchants by means of military outposts, and to provide them with rest-houses.

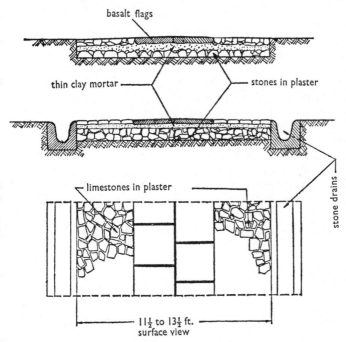

Cross-section and surface of an ancient Cretan stone road

Where the Cretans acquired their highly specialized knowledge it is impossible to say with any certainty. It is true that the older Egyptian culture exercised a strong influence on the Minoan culture of the early and middle periods, and the Egyptians knew something (though not a great deal) of the art of road-making: ramps were used as supports in the building of the Pyramids, short roads were specially laid down for processions, and there were roads in the towns. But it looks as if road-making was developed in Crete itself. The fact that the roads are so remarkably straight, only deviating where the lay of the land makes it absolutely essential, suggests a determined, ruthless guiding force behind these very early masterpieces of road-building. If in Malta it was sheer neccessity, a vital need, that made those ancient priest-kings demand of their people such gruelling work on the stone grooved roads, under the early Cretan kings the driving force was the power of the State. Crete was rich: Homer speaks of ninety towns and cities on the small island and reports that they mustered a flotilla of eighty ships to fight against Troy. Excavations have produced ample evidence of this wealth, and road-building clearly kept pace with it.

In the small town of Devizes in Wiltshire there is a wooden button which has been so carefully preserved that one might imagine it to be the only one of its kind in the world. But there is another exactly like it; both are painted in gold and decorated with precisely the same motif. The second button was found at the other end of Europe under the mounds of earth that cover the city of Troy. It dates back 2,000 years B.C. At that time Greek goods from the eastern Mediterranean were reaching southern England by way of Spain and the Bay of Biscay. This trade, of course, was not confined to wooden buttons, which even England could have done without; also in southern England a piece of tin was found shaped like a swallow's tail—the shape in which Cretan merchants used to export this particular metal. . . .

One could quote many other such examples to show that there was considerable long-distance maritime trading in those early times and that land communications were, by comparison, primitive. The fact that the Cretans had such good roads was an indirect result of the maritime traffic which had made the island so rich. The Cretan roads were not absolutely essential; they were built quite simply to make travelling comfortable and because the island could afford expensive roads.

The situation in Greece was quite different. No point in this mountainous peninsula with its rugged, heavily indented coast is very far from the sea, but to sail or row along the coast was a laborious business that called for endless patience.

Theseus was not a patient man; he was a hero. When his mother told him to sail to Athens to see his father, he preferred the land route across the Isthmus of Corinth, which in those times was full of danger: bandits made the roads unsafe, attacking and robbing travellers.

The beginning of the Theseus saga is of particular interest because it gives a precise description of the route Theseus took and names the robbers whom he worsted by his strength and fearlessness: Periphetes with the club, who terrorized the Epidauros country; Sinis, the bender of firs, who killed travellers by bending fir trees, tying his victims to the tree-tops and releasing the trunks; and finally Phäa, the Crommyonian wild boar, which was also a constant threat to travellers. After overcoming these various hazards, Theseus, accompanied by Perigune, the beautiful daughter of a bandit, reached Megara, the country opposite the island of Salamis. Now that he was so near Athens, Theseus must have thought the worst was behind him, but suddenly he found the road to Attica blocked by Sciron, who required all travellers to wash his feet. If they obeyed, as soon as they bent down he pushed them over a steep cliff. Thanks to his lightness of foot Theseus was able to turn the tables on Sciron, who plunged to his own death. Theseus also disposed of Kerkyon at Eleusis before he finally encountered Damastes, better known as Procrustes. According to the legend there were two beds of Procrustes—a short one for tall men and a long one for short men. The giant Damastes suffered the fate of many of his victims when Theseus forced him to lie on the short bed and cut him down to size with his sword.

Theseus' first agreeable experience on his dangerous and adventurous journey was with the Phylatides, who inhabited the banks of the river Cephisos and lived on the fig trees which the goddess Demeter had given them.

It seems clear that the hero's mother and grandfather had advised him to go by sea because the journey overland was so dangerous. It is also worth noting that Theseus had to contend not only with fabulous monsters but also, and above all, with simple highway robbers, who had presumably been making the main road of ancient Greece virtually impassable. And Theseus was, in fact, remembered as the man who freed Greece's roads; at many crossroads and city gates small monuments were erected in his memory. The river Cephisos, however, where Theseus is said to have committed his first deeds of heroism, may well be the site of the first Greek bridges. Ernst Curtius (1814–1896), the great German historian, in his famous lecture on the history of Greek road-building speaks of ancient dam structures in the Boeotian valley and bridges over the river Cephisos. As the country is marshy, the ground had to be drained and levelled in the region of Lake Kopais, and this work is said to have been done by the semi-mythical tribe of Minyans, who seem, therefore, to have produced not merely adventurous sailors like the Argonauts but also good builders of dams, bridges and roads. In Lake Kopais, stones and the remains of arches were actually found. The first bridges, however, had no arches and were built with corbel stones, which gradually converged from the sides till they met in the middle. Arches were frequently superimposed at some later period on the pillars of these bridges, as, for example, on the rivers Pamisos and Pylos. Instead of corbel stones long beams were often used.

Even in the prosaic field of technical history we find this strange mixture of reality and legend. Theseus, the first of his epic exploits behind him, encounters the men who had drained the great marshes in northern Boeotia and whose daughters became the mothers of the Argonauts. Lake Kopais and the river Cephisos, with all that human labour had built on and around them, were a natural goal for the man who freed the roads, the first place where he felt at ease.

Looking back over thousands of years, one realizes that in those ancient times the road was something sacred. To the Greeks, the power to blaze a new trail was an attribute of the gods. They believed that the gods themselves had once walked on their roads. If they did not come by sea like Aphrodite, then they strode along the highways like Dionysus, who, according to legend, linked the most remote countries of the Orient with the West and bridged dividing streams. And Apollo is said to have wandered, playing his lute, along an ancient ceremonial road from Delphi to Krissa, a sacred road. Delphi, the centre of the worship of Apollo, was not regarded as the original home of the god, but as his final destination after he had completed his travels. At the Feast of Apollo of the Daphnephoria, a beautiful boy, representing the god, walked before the procession along the road from Parnassus to Olympus, bearing an olive-staff garlanded with wreaths of laurel and flowers: he symbolized the arrival of the god from the valley of Tempe. Nikias, the Athenian statesman and soldier, who was also the richest Athenian of his time (about 420 B.C.), built a bridge in honour of Apollo over the wide bay between Delos and Rhenaia.

The very first treaties concluded between the confederate states of ancient Greece emphasized the importance of internal security. Access to the holy places was guaranteed, and pilgrims of all races were assured that they could travel overland without danger. This meant that the public highways, like the temples themselves, gave the traveller a right of asylum. For centuries wayfarers were virtually inviolable, till looting by mercenary armies reached a point where even religious scruples were ignored and the roads again became unsafe. But up to that point the main highways leading to the temples were safe in time of war. This was true, for example, of the Eleusine ceremonial road throughout the Thirty Years' War between Sparta and Athens. When that great soldier Alcibiades returned home in 404 B.C., the first thing he did was to clean up the roads and solemnly escort the Mystic choir to Eleusis. And it is said that King

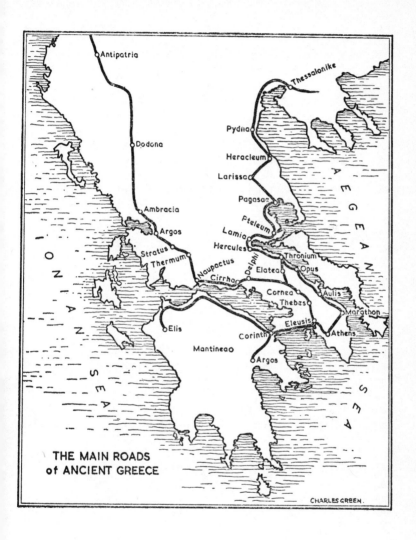

THE MAIN ROADS
of ANCIENT GREECE

CHARLES GREEN.

Agis I, the Spartan, though at war with Athens, did not dare molest the pilgrims on their way to Eleusis. In other words the roads were sacred, protected by the gods.

Although the various Greek tribes were almost constantly at war with one another, the roads continued to be maintained and even extended. In fact, war was in itself a pretext for building roads. In most cases the victor made no attempt to interfere with the worship of his defeated enemy, but as a symbol of his victory he would build a temple to his own particular god, which had to be linked by road with the mother-temple. Hence the roads between the young kingdom of Sparta and the ancient shrine at Amyclae, and between Olympia and Elis. Megalopolis, a small market town in Arcadia, was linked by a series of roads with the sacred shrines of the neighbouring Pelasger tribes. So highways originally built for religious purposes also came in time to serve political and economic ends.

On the roads themselves religion was predominant, sometimes in a way that made travelling most agreeable. For example, fruit growing at the roadside could be picked quite freely, and hungry travellers were even allowed to eat the sacrificial food-offerings which were left in the wayside shrines of Hermes and Apollo. The traveller, as a privileged guest of the country, enjoyed a degree of protection which it is hard to visualize today. Even to misdirect him was tantamount to sacrilege, while to protect him was regarded as a sacred duty.

Not merely the road but also the roadside was sacred and the property of the gods; near the road from Athens to Eleusis, for example, were two salt lakes in which only priests were allowed to fish. Furthermore, as the Greeks were naturally anxious to be buried in holy ground, the roads were fringed by burial-places—a practice which was later continued by the Romans. Sites near the towns, where various roads converged, were particularly sought after. The same was true of road-junctions where traffic was heavy and, above all, of city gates.

Herodotus records that Queen Nitokris was buried over the main gate of Babel. Antiope, the wife of Theseus, who fought by his side against the Amazons when they invaded Attica and is said to have met her death then, was buried, according to legend, near the Phalerian Gate in Athens. The town of Sikyon near the Gulf of Corinth honoured its fallen with a heroes' tomb outside the town on the great military road to Corinth.

It must have required patience and endurance to travel through the wild mountain country of ancient Greece with its extremes of climate, its burning sun and sudden gusts of wind, for most of the travelling was done on foot. Curtius suggests that there was a politico-psychological reason for this: to the ancient Hellenes, especially when republicanism was at its height, the use of a vehicle was regarded as incompatible with the simple, manly life—which meant that vehicles of any kind were reserved almost exclusively for women (but priestesses were strictly forbidden to use them!). Anyone who travelled by chariot within the precincts of the city was regarded as proud and overbearing, but even on the open road a man who used a vehicle was looked upon as either effeminate or ostentatious. When a group of Athenian envoys returned from a mission by chariot, they were publicly taken to task for putting the poor footsore pilgrims to shame. On the other hand, Homer records that Telemachus, son of Odysseus and Penelope, and anything but an effeminate youth, crossed the entire Peloponnesian peninsula in two days by chariot. But even State officials were no exception to the general rule: express messages were carried by foot. In 479 b.c., when the Greeks defeated the Persians at Platea and celebrated their victory by rekindling the flames in their shrines, a man named Euchidas ran in one day from the battlefield to Delphi and back to bring a sacred torch from Delphi: that was a distance of about a hundred miles, an athletic feat which cost the messenger his life.

Apart from this network of sacred roads, a second gradually emerged. Under the legendary King Pompos of Arcadia, the first traders penetrated into the wild mountain country, and between Pontium and the Adriatic there were undoubtedly ancient trade routes through Greece, along which wine and other goods passed by caravan. The religious significance of road-travel in ancient Greece was such that even the trade routes had a status which was only enjoyed elsewhere by ceremonial and temple roads.

As steep gradients were rare on the sacred roads, they frequently took considerable detours, and short-cuts and flights of steps were provided for pedestrians and traders. Hundreds of these short-cuts can still be seen, where once 'the bad stairs' led from Delphi to the summit of Parnassus. A similar road existed in pre-Roman times from Eleusis to Corinth, till it was replaced under the Emperor Hadrian by a proper highway. The Greeks were proud, and rightly so, of their particular skill in road-making, which interfered as little as possible with the natural surroundings. Only sacred roads were thought to justify any major alterations in the landscape, which the Greeks regarded otherwise as barbaric.

In order to make the roads as safe as possible and to give vehicles a firm hold even in the mountains the Greeks cut grooved tracks in the road similar to those found in Malta among other places. Near the ancient citadel of Orchomenos—the area in which, there is reason to suppose, the earliest Greek causeways and bridges were built—remains of these man-made wheel-tracks can still be seen, with jagged spurs of rock and deep holes between them; other tracks of this kind were found on the ancient road across the Taygetos mountains in southern Greece, which runs from Sparta to Messenia. Similar discoveries were made between Athens and Thebes, between Cirrha and Delphi, and in the Tretos mountains. All the evidence suggests that the whole of Greece was covered at one time by a network of these grooved roads and that they were not merely used by priestesses but also by the general public—they were the key trade and transport routes.

Travelling on these roads was, of course, not always pleasant: the grooved tracks were fairly deep in places, sometimes as much as a foot. When two vehicles approached from opposite directions, one or other of them had to give way. No one liked doing it, for it was no simple task to remove a vehicle, especially if it was loaded, from the track and replace it in the grooves. We know that Oedipus was one of those who refused: he struck down his father Laios (of whose real identity he was, admittedly, unaware) on the way to Thebes after quarrelling with his driver. Quarrels of this kind must have happened frequently, for, especially in the mountains, there were very few points at which vehicles could pass.

The gauge of these tracks seems to have presented much less of a problem. Ernst Curtius believes that a gauge of about five feet was in general use at quite an early stage; in the Taygetos mountains in the southern Peloponnesus, however, a track only three feet wide was found, its grooves about three inches deep and six inches wide at the base. It is possible that this is all that remains of an old double track, but it seems more likely that the vehicles used to cross these mountains were specially designed with a narrow gauge for difficult country. In any case the surface between the tracks had not been made up; the Ancient Greeks had also realized that the artificial wheel-track was a more rational form of transport than wide, made-up roads.

This assumption is borne out by the Greek language: the Greeks speak of 'cutting' a road (as in Latin: *secare viam*) and all the words in Greek for a road or way are feminine gender, which suggests that the road itself was synonymous with the furrow or depression in which the wheel was lodged.

The shape of the country compelled later road-builders to follow, at least for long stretches, the same pattern as their predecessors in the fifth, fourth and third centuries B.C. The Roman roads in Greece, like the main roads of ancient Greece, ran in two great arteries from north-west to north-east, converging on Athens; and many cities like Naupactos and Corinth retained their key-positions. Naupactos owes its importance in history to its geographical position, for it was here that the old road from Dodona and Argos touched the narrowest part of the Gulf of Corinth before it swung eastwards to Athens. As early as the fifth century B.C. and right up to the Middle Ages it was an important trading centre, possession of which was, from time to time, hotly contested. In the year 1477 it was besieged—unsuccessfully—for four months by 30,000 Turks, and in 1499 Bajesid II needed no fewer than 150,000 men to conquer it. On the 7th October 1571, near Naupactos the naval battle of Lepanto was fought, at which Don Juan of Austria defeated the Turks and—a fact that aroused no interest at the time—the poet Miguel de Cervantes lost his right arm. Today this once flourishing city has a mere 3,000 inhabitants and is surrounded by crumbling Venetian walls.

Corinth has not stood the test of time very much better, in spite of its unique position at the gateway to Peloponnesus and on an isthmus, on which since time immemorial there has been a slipway for ships. According to legend, the city was founded about 1350 B.C.; it is certainly clear that at such a key junction of overland and sea traffic a city of some kind was bound to arise. It had a very chequered career. It was conquered and reconquered by the Romans, Goths, Slavs, Turks and others, and sacked and rebuilt till an earthquake finally razed it to the ground in 1858 and a new town had to be built three miles away. Even the opening of a canal across the isthmus in 1893, a project which Nero, among others, had planned, failed to give the town a new lease of life. Greece has long since ceased to be the centre of the world, and the Isthmus of Corinth is merely the umbilical cord that links northern Greece with Peloponnesus. Along the old roads, instead of grooved wheel-tracks, run the rails of modern Greece's few railway lines; between Megara and Athens one can follow by car in the footsteps of Theseus and gaze at the fearsome cliffs between Megara and Corinth, where Sciron lay in wait for passing travellers. Today one drives up the mountain-side at Gerania where two and a half thousand years ago the Greeks had to use steps cut in the rock. But driving through Greece one is constantly reminded of the times when the altar of the twelve gods on the Agora at Athens afforded protection to a far-flung network of roads, along which travellers could walk without fear. . . .

Chapter 8

ALL ROADS LEAD TO ROME

After the defeat of Napoleon and the withdrawal of the French army of occupation from Dalmatia, the Emperor Francis of Austria toured the country and inspected, among other things, the magnificent coastal road which the French had built but left uncompleted. He stared thoughtfully at the impressive ribbon of road that ended abruptly in rubble and mounds of earth, and then said to his entourage: 'A pity they didn't stay a bit longer. . . .'

In fact, what Napoleon contributed in the space of nine years to Europe's network of roads is much more impressive than all the Roman roads which have come to be described as among the wonders of the world. The Roman roads acquired their almost legendary reputation during the Dark Ages—the thousand years in which Europe remained in every respect far behind the ancient world and therefore looked upon all the authorities and achievements of Greece and Rome with a reverence that was as near to worship as the Christian religion would permit.

Whether they deserve to rank as wonders of the world or not, the Roman roads were certainly built on the principle that anything worth doing is worth doing well and that Rome herself was not built in a day. By the time the whole of Europe from Scotland to the Sahara and from western Spain to the Euphrates was finally covered by a network of Roman roads, Rome had spent on this monumental achievement more than five hundred years, in fact more than six hundred if one goes back to Appius Claudius Caecus, who in 312

B.C. gave orders for a military road to be built from Rome via Aricia, Fundi and Sinuessa to Capua. (The fact that it is still possible to drive along stretches of this road, though rather slowly and circumspectly, shows how well it has stood up to the ravages of time.)

A hundred years ago a Dane wrote a three-volume work on the Via Appia alone, and a German devoted one hefty volume to the short stretch of the old road between Rome and Albano, which was excavated last century at the instigation of Pope Pius IX. If one considers that the first-class Roman roads alone cover a distance equivalent to twice the circumference of the earth, and that all the roads built by the Romans would stretch ten times round the equator, one has some conception of the vastness of the subject I am endeavouring to cover in one chapter.

They were undoubtedly a miracle of execution; and in road-building execution counts for more than planning, for between the roads of ancient Crete and the modern U.S. Highway No. 40 no more than half a dozen technical discoveries have been made that are of any significance. So it is not only of secondary importance but virtually impossible to ascertain from whom the Romans learned road-building: Rome did not lie at the end of the world like the kingdom of East Asia, which called itself the Middle Kingdom yet was nowhere near the middle. Rome, in fact, was situated at the centre of a world which was itself 'Mediterranean', and it even lay in the heart of a country, Italy, where Etruscans and Greeks had been building roads since very early times. Anything the Romans may not have learned from their contact with these peoples they learned from the Carthaginians, Phoenicians and Egyptians. As, however, all these peoples built roads without creating any road-system, the achievement of the Romans remains without parallel.

The Romans were the first to recognize that a road is worth just as much as the individual places it connects. A road between two towns is only of importance to these towns. For the empire as a whole, what was clearly needed was a closely-woven network of roads—a continuous and, in fact, endless band in which one section would lead to the next. We shall probably never know who built the first road, but the first man-made road-system was produced by the Romans, by their censors, their consuls, their emperors, their generals and their ordinary soldiers.

During the last few decades so much has been discovered about Rome's relations with the Etruscans that one is not surprised to learn how much the Romans owed to the Etruscans in the making of roads. The pre-Roman barter trade between Italy and the Alpine peoples was almost entirely in the hands of the Etruscans, who, unlike the Romans, showed a natural talent for trade and handicrafts. In the Alps themselves no trace has been found of early made-up roads (apart from a few exceptions which we discussed in connection with the Illyrian roads); when Hannibal (246–182 B.C.) crossed the Alps, he complained bitterly of the absence of roads. In Etruria, the modern Tuscany, the Etruscans made several roads, some of which were later built over by the Romans.

At Remedello Sotto a paved road about fifteen yards wide runs between two pre-Roman burial grounds, and near Canatello paved roads of varying widths from two to four yards were made. But it was not until the eighth century B.C. that a specifically Etruscan type of road emerged: it is a hollow road, which cuts a miniature gorge through hills and hillocks, has a built-up wall on either side as much as eighty feet high, and yet is only about ten feet wide. This type of road cut out quite a number of bends, but required a special drainage system, which is astonishingly reminiscent of the ancient Chinese loess road. When one considers that on both sides of these roads burial chambers were built deep into the rock, one realizes how uncomfortable travelling must have been in Etruscan times. The Greeks and Romans also buried their dead at the roadside, but these were roads that ran across open country and gave a clear view of the tombstones. The Etruscan defile-roads ran through the graveyards like tunnels. ... Although the stone in Etruria is often soft and easy to work with, the road-surface was not, as a rule, uniformly smooth: special wheel-tracks were cut for vehicles, there were frequent points where they could pass, and there were even kerbstones, some with Etruscan inscriptions.

The Romans probably gained their most lasting impressions of Etruscan road-building in the fourth and third centuries B.C. when they occupied the Etrurian cities. During excavations in the small Etruscan town of Marzabotto (near Bologna), for example, four paved roads each about fifteen yards wide were found, which also had sidewalks for pedestrians and drainage channels. In rain or bad weather the pedestrians were able to cross the road on stepping-stones without wetting their feet. The stepping-stones at Pompeii are a clear indication that the Romans adopted this same procedure and were still using it five hundred years later.

On the whole, however, pre-Roman Italy had no overland roads because the main prerequisites were absent: political unity and a strong central government. It was only after a long struggle and many reverses that the Romans finally succeeded in subduing the Italian tribes in the north and south. Up to the beginning of the second century B.C. the only roads in Italy were the old trade routes, which were no more than beaten tracks on which gravel was strewn to provide a reasonably firm surface.

The most important of these early roads seem to have arisen as a result of agreements between the individual tribes, which for economic reasons had to sink their differences. The Sabines, for example, who lived on the upper western slopes of the Apennines, south of Umbria, needed the salt from the mouth of the Tiber. It reached them by the Via Salaria. For considerable stretches the Via Appia also followed an old gravel road about ten feet wide.

It would be wrong to deduce from these examples, however, that people at that time were really aware of roads and road traffic as a factor in their lives. When the foundations of the Roman Empire were laid about 450 B.C. with the famous Law of the Twelve Tables, roads were mentioned, but it was also plain that the central government was still not seriously interested in roads as such. According to the old law, roads were the responsibility of those who tilled the land on either side of them. If they did not want people wandering across their fields, then they must keep the roads in good condition. It is not hard to imagine what the country roads were like in those days.

Ernst Speck in his book on trade in the ancient world holds Roman law responsible for another defect of the early Roman roads:

> The slow development of the Roman road-system was a direct result of the stipulation that the State roads must be the property of the Roman people. . . . The Via Appia, which was 132 Roman miles (122 English miles) long, was entirely within Roman territory. But almost a century passed before in 220 B.C. the Via Flaminia (190 miles long) was built, partly through land which had to be surrendered by Umbrian communities.

While law was the dominant factor in Roman thinking, war was their chief form of action. In their military campaigns the Romans discovered talents in themselves which were otherwise conspicuously lacking. If one compares the Etruscan and the Roman arch and considers how long the Greeks had been using mortar—in southern Italy—then one is forced to the conclusion that from a technical point of view the Romans were not particularly inventive. But they had the best sappers and very clear ideas about what is today called the theory of employment. Isidorus Hispalensis, who became Bishop of Hispalis (Seville) in A.D. 594, said of the Romans in his *Etymologies* that they had built roads 'throughout almost the entire world to enable them to travel in direct lines and to prevent unemployment

amongst the population.' Much more dangerous, however, than unemployed people were unemployed soldiers, for they were potential
rebels who not only possessed arms but knew how to use them.
Moreover, as military law from time to time superseded Roman
law, censors and consuls kept soldiers busy with road-building—
usually immediately after a battle but sometimes even during the
fighting.

In this way, although there was a great deal of grumbling, the
road from Bonia to Arretium (Arezzo) was built in 187 B.C., also,
among others, the roads from Salonae to Andetrium in Dalmatia—
the work of the 7th Legion—from Carthage to Theveste, and the
Via Septimiana from Lambaesis in North Africa. The legions stationed in the colonies, who for months and even years at a stretch
led a pretty quiet life, particularly distinguished themselves at work
of this kind. The veterans of the Legio XXX Ulpia Victrix took
less than a year to build a town on the land which the Emperor
Trajan gave them to settle on (Thamugadi, twenty-five miles east of
Lambaesis)—a walled town with public buildings, streets and
squares, with a market-place, a library and thermal baths.

When the Roman State was still in its infancy, there was a special
branch of the army which moved on ahead of the troops and repaired the roads. This 'Centuria accessorum velatorum' remained in
existence for several centuries and did excellent work on Italy's
roads. Yet it was not the first Pioneer Corps: Alexander the Great
had a special road-building unit, which advanced ahead of his army
and was expected, in an emergency, to work at very high speed; the
Persians, too, in their campaigns against the Greeks, not only recon-
noitred but also improved the local roads.

Native labour in the occupied territories was much less productive than these specialized and highly-disciplined units, but it was
cheap and these long, straight roads enabled the Romans to keep a
constant watch on the subject peoples. So victors and vanquished
worked side by side on the great military roads of the Roman
Empire; slaves and prisoners of war laboured for six to seven
hundred years on these roads throughout almost the entire known
world.

It was not, on the other hand, 'dirty' work. Although the Roman
roads were not sacred as the Greek roads were, although they were
not designed primarily for priestesses and pilgrims but for the
cohorts, arms and supplies of the greatest military power in the
world, yet for that very reason Rome was as proud of them as she
was of her army and her great empire. It was impossible to maintain
such a vast network of roads, much less extend it with each fresh

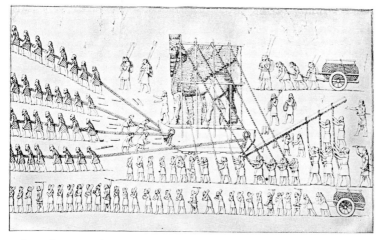

Assyrians moving a piece of statuary. The enormous weight required a smooth 'slipway', sometimes provided with grooved tracks in order to prevent the statues of the gods from shaking, which was regarded as an evil omen.

Grooved road. Malta.

A stone grooved track from the Hallstatt period on the Federauner Sattel in Carinthia.

The Roman arched
bridge in stone over
the river Marecchia
at Rimini
(Ariminum); the
town stood at the
end of the Via
Flaminia, which
linked it with
Rome.

The Via Appia
at Rome.

Part of Hadrian's Wall in Northumberland. The Roman military road still stands out clearly against the landscape. In the foreground is a modern road.

The Via Septimiana (named after the Emperor Septimius Severus 193–211) in the ruins of the Roman legionaries' town of Lambaesis in North Africa.

A Roman post-coach. Relief from second or third century A.D. found at Maria Saal in Carinthia.

King Henry IV's carriage comes to grief on the Seine at Neuilly on June 1606.

Der Pflasterer.
Lebt ohne Eigen Rach, dem, der beleidigt nach.

Early road-makers. *The Plasterer* from Chr. Weigel's *Book of the Estates* 1698.

The Via Mala,
Switzerland (steel
engraving, about
1725).

The Mont Cenis
road, Savoy Alps
(steel engraving,
about 1830).

Peru. A well-preserved road bridge from the Inca period.

Tibet. A ferry on the Sinkang-Tibet motorway.

Venezuela. The costliest motorway in the world (6 million dollars a mile). One of the enormous bridges in course of construction.

conquest, out of public funds. The Romans had to rely to a large extent, like modern art and science, on special collections or on legacies, and many a well-to-do Roman considered it an honour to make a substantial donation for the completion of a road. At the same time, Caesar was not always prepared to wait for someone to come forward: when he heard of a Senator who had amassed a fortune quickly and easily, he usually made it clear that a 'voluntary' donation was expected....

Contributions to Rome's road-building programme also brought their reward; many a Roman citizen with nothing much else to his credit gained high office by donating money to the roads. Quite frequently the otherwise undistinguished donor acquired a unique form of immortality by having his name linked with a famous road: it is safe to say that barely one in a thousand people who walk or drive today along the Via Appia has ever heard of Appius Claudius!

In so vast a network of roads there were bound to be local variations in the methods employed: the materials available often left a great deal to be desired, so that all kinds of compromises had to be made in order to meet regional requirements. Moreover, in the course of the centuries the Roman technique of road-building underwent a number of changes as the Romans learned by experience. Quite frequently orders came down from above which gave first priority to economic or military considerations; sometimes there was a shortage of funds; and at other times a road was needed quickly which meant that only local materials could be used. So there is no basic pattern running through the Roman roads, no standard measurements or methods of construction. Even the most elementary technical instructions are missing, so we can only study the roads themselves and draw our own inferences.

The first of the Roman roads were built in a style that was later adopted in the Italian Renaissance. Andrea Palladio (1518–80), the famous Renaissance architect, described the method adopted in his *Quattro libri dell' architettura*. First the foundation was levelled and cleared of stones. For this purpose the Romans employed rollers of wood or stone, which are mentioned by Virgil, among others, and which had the great disadvantage of being too light. On the other hand, it was only in cases of emergency that the Romans moved such heavy weights as the fifteen or twenty tons of a modern roller, for, apart from anything else, it took a great deal of time.

The foundation was, therefore, very loosely reinforced with sand or gravel, sometimes with a layer of sand on which a further layer of gravel was superimposed, and often—though not always—the edges were built up with stones. On both sides there were always drainage ditches. Many of these gravel roads have been found in western Germany; they seem to have been the first to be laid by the Roman occupation forces in Germania and were never given a firm surface, as they were quite adequate to serve remote garrisons. In Italy itself this type of road was later replaced by the more solid four-layer road except in places where the traffic was light.

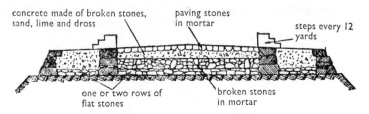

concrete made of broken stones, sand, lime and dross

paving stones in mortar

steps every 12 yards

one or two rows of flat stones

broken stones in mortar

Cross-section of a Roman road

On the busier roads the Romans employed paving-stones, which rested on a layer of sand. The cavities between them were filled up with broken stones, or sometimes even with small iron plates.

Lime mortar, which the Greeks had been using for some time and which they had employed in the streets of certain towns in Sicily and southern Italy, was only adopted by the Romans at a relatively late stage. At that point, however—from the third century B.C. onwards—they began experimenting on a large scale by mixing lime with the different varieties of sand found in the peninsula. They also tried out various mixtures, adding loose rubble or gravel, till they produced the first cement with roughly three parts gravel to one of mortar.

This gravel cement, which the Romans called 'caementum', was very adaptable, for it could be laid at any given depth and filled up any minor cavities in the foundation. A further step forward was taken with the so-called pozzolana, volcanic substances which derived their name from Puteoli (the modern Pozzuoli near Naples), where they were first discovered and 'which cannot themselves be described as binding materials but, when mixed with certain other substances, produce latent hydraulic properties' (Kastl). Experts consider that the mixtures of lime and pozzolana used in the Roman roads—examples were found in the Rhine valley—are almost comparable in quality to modern cement.

The possible variations were now considerable. With mortar to bind them, a wide range of materials could be added: tuff-stone chips, broken lava or tiles, and even cinders (as, for example, in many Roman roads in England). Sometimes only the middle layer was bound with mortar; a Roman road excavated at Trier had a top-surface of gravel and a sand foundation. Elsewhere, however, we find no fewer than three mortared layers. To get a clearer picture we must refer to the two diagrams, but with the proviso that each

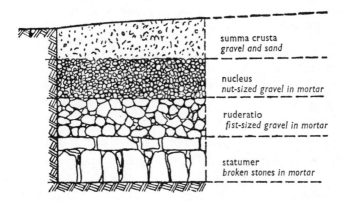

summa crusta
gravel and sand

nucleus
nut-sized gravel in mortar

ruderatio
fist-sized gravel in mortar

statumer
broken stones in mortar

Section of a Roman road

merely represents one of the most common types of road which, in a very short distance, may look quite different.

A German engineer, Artur Speck, in a short but extremely informative study of road-building (Berlin, 1950) sums up the main technical developments in Roman road-making as follows.

1. their skill and adaptability in laying foundations, which in marshland, for example, were laid on pile-gratings;

2. the production of a strong, self-contained bottom layer of broken stones, tile-fragments, and gravel, with the stones decreasing in size as they neared the surface;

3. binding the stones with clay or lime mortar into a cohesive and more or less watertight mass;

4. the provision of a durable paved surface for all their main highways; and

5. the basic uniformity with which these methods were applied throughout the vast area of the Roman Empire, a clear distinction being drawn between main and secondary roads.

These points can be summarized in the following general terms: the Romans took certain known factors in the technique of road-making and evolved a method which they applied with remarkable consistency for the maintenance and advancement of their world empire.

Another feature of the Roman roads which is equally absorbing is their alignment. The course they followed was by no means always dictated by rational principles; specific preferences and prejudices had to be considered which are completely foreign to modern road-building. It is a striking fact, for example, that the Romans never liked travelling in mountainous country; so, wherever possible, mountains were given a wide berth even if it meant passing through marshland. Quite often it would have been both economical and sensible to cross a range of mountains and thereby make a particularly short connection between two towns (as, for example, between Capua and Aternum, the modern Pescara), but the Romans, working on the principle that seas join but mountains divide, kept their roads as near the coast as possible and consoled themselves with the knowledge that coastal roads could at least replace shipping when winter storms and rough seas made sailing impossible.

This deep-rooted prejudice appears to have survived to the present day. Try, for example, the excellent road that runs up the Liri valley from Gaeta through Sora to Pescara and in a day's drive you will meet three or four vehicles at most.

While it was possible to circumvent the Apennines and the Abruzzi, there was no way round the high Alps. The Romans had, it is true, improved the old Etruscan coast road—which, according to legend, was built by Hercules—and made it one of the most magnificent in the empire, the Via Julia Augusta, but, as the traffic to and from Gaul and Germany increased, the coastal road became more and more inadequate.

The reluctance of even intelligent and progressive Romans to travel in mountains has been amply substantiated. Did it originate in the years of bitter fighting against the tough mountain tribes, the Samnites and Volsci, whose villages still seem to threaten the valleys below them? Or should we seek the explanation in the Romans' love of the sea and the kind of landscape that Quintilian, Catullus and other poets immortalized in their verse? Cicero, one remembers, regarded mountainous country with its woods and crags as unsuitable for anything but a very short visit, while Livy considered the Alps downright ugly. When Caesar crossed the Alps with his army, he closed the curtains on his litter and busied himself with reports and accounts.

To understand the Romans' dislike of mountains, one must remember that crossing the Alps two thousand years ago was full of hazards. Of the seventeen Alpine passes in fairly frequent use only two were really safe: the Julia (near St. Moritz, present height 7,500 feet) and the Brenner, which even today reaches a height of 3,500 feet without a single hairpin bend. On the Julia Pass the wide bends built by the Romans have survived to the present day. At that time the steepest gradient was 1½ in 10 (today it is 1 in 10) and the road varied in width from nine to eleven feet.

Major roads of this kind were, however, exceptional. As a rule the Roman mountain roads were narrow and by present-day standards were cart tracks sometimes no more than five feet wide. But their most striking feature was their steepness, even in places where a relatively short detour could have been made. An example of this is the Maloja Pass in the Engadine, today one of the easiest of the Alpine passes with a maximum gradient of 9 in 100 and twelve bends; the Romans, however, climbed this 6,000-feet pass with only three bends, which subjected both vehicles and animals to a tremendous strain.

On Mont Genèvre (between Clavière and Briançon) men and animals even had to go behind the vehicles to prevent them from running backwards; today this same pass has a maximum gradient at one or two points of 1 in 10 and is open all the year round to every kind of vehicle.

The proverbial straight line was a basic principle for the Roman road-builder, although recent research has shown that it was not universal. The Romans preferred it not merely because it was the shortest distance between two points but also because they disliked climbs and dips; a road would frequently be specially built up to keep it as horizontal and straight as possible. Several examples of this can be seen on the Via Flaminia (from Rome to Fano on the Adriatic), on which Vespasian (A.D. 69–79) cut through a whole series of low hills in order to keep the road, even in the Apennines, as free from bends as possible; for the same reason the Via Appia ran dead straight across the Pontine marshes to Terracina.

If this radical method was expensive in Italy itself, it created such enormous problems in freshly-conquered or occupied territories that one is forced to admire the method itself almost as much as the finished product. The technique of measurement was still in its infancy; it was carried out by slaves under the supervision of army officers and was designed from the beginning for use in agriculture, for drawing frontiers and plotting land rather than for building roads. In central Europe with its trackless wastes, its forests and its marshes, road-building detachments frequently had to use smoke signals as a means of communicating with one another.

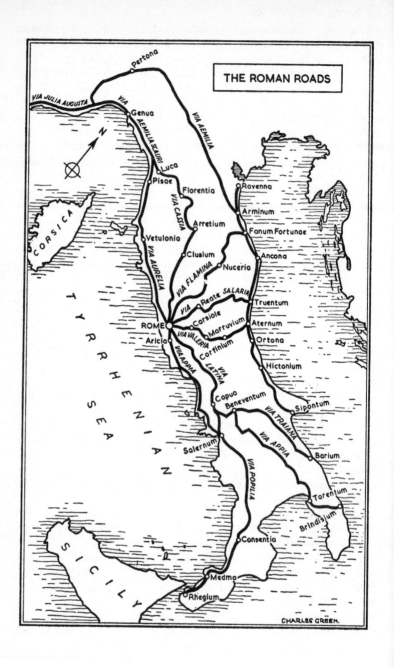

THE ROMAN ROADS

Pertona
VIA JULIA AUGUSTA
VIA
Genua
AEMILIA SCAURI
VIA AEMILIA
Luca
Pisae
Florentia
Ravenna
VIA CASSIA
Arminum
Arretium
Fanum Fortunae
Vetulonia
CORSICA
VIA AURELIA
Clusium
Ancona
VIA FLAMINA
Nuceria
SALARIA
Reate
VIA
Truentum
ROME
Carsiole
Aternum
VIA VALERIA
Marruvium
Aricia
Corfinium
Ortona
VIA APPIA
VIA
LATINA
Hictonium
T Y R R H E N I A N   S E A
Capua
Beneventum
Siponium
VIA TRAIANA
Salernum
VIA APPIA
Barium
VIA POPILIA
Tarentum
Brindisium
Consentia
S I C I L Y
Medma
Rhegium

CHARLES GREEN.

If a valley had to be crossed, the Romans would build a viaduct rather than take the road down into the valley and up again, and in building their viaducts they preferred a series of small arches to a few large ones. In this particular branch of architecture they were much less skilled than, for example, the Etruscans, many of whose impressive bridges are still standing. Very often the Romans built several rows of small arches on top of each other, and the finest example of this is the Pont du Gard, the great aqueduct in southern France, in which two rows of arches, one forty-three, the other forty-five feet high, are surmounted by a row of countless small arches. As bridges of this kind could be built piecemeal, the Roman technique had the virtue of simplicity and of saving timber, for no sooner was one arch completed than the scaffolding was moved along to the next.

The bridge over the Tajo at Alcantara rose to a height of more than 200 feet above the river and had six arches, of which the two in the centre had the largest span, one being 110, the other 117 feet. They were built in the reign of Trajan between A.D. 98 and 106, and in this case we even know the name of the architect: Caius Julius Lacer, who was buried in a small temple on the left bank of the river not far from the bridge.

The bridge, which is entirely in granite without any mortar, is more than 600 feet long and about 25 feet wide. Since it was built 1,900 years ago it has several times been damaged: in 1231 one of the smaller arches was destroyed and was only restored 300 years later (!); in 1809 the British blew up the second arch on the north bank; and in 1836 the Carlists, supporters of the Pretender to the Spanish throne, thought it necessary to try out their gunpowder on this ancient monument. The neighbouring town of Alcantara received its name, which in Arabic means 'bridge', from Trajan's structure.

For the same reasons that motivated their viaducts, the Romans preferred to build half-way up a valley rather than on its floor, for the gradient was thereby reduced and the road was in no danger of flooding. To quote only one example, the old road linking Verona with the Brenner Pass by way of Trient, Klausing and Sterzing was built along the hill-sides. Even mountain ridges, especially in enemy country, were regarded as better suited for roads than valleys. In such a case, however, there were clearly important military considerations: in Gaul with its restless, warlike tribes the Romans diverted the Bronze Age, amber road between the Rhine and Massilia (Marseilles) from the low-lying valleys into the hills.

Unlike the Greeks, who tried as far as possible to adapt their roads to the lay of the land, the Romans with their straight-line principle were in constant conflict with the facts of nature. The Greeks had called the Persians barbarians, and, as evidence of their barbarism, had pointed to the Persians' lack of respect for nature in building their roads. The Romans not only adopted this process of levelling and excavating, bridging valleys and tunnelling through mountains, but made it a basic principle of their road-building

Bridge built in the reign of Trajan

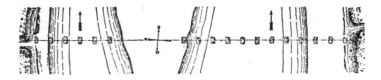

Ground plan of the remains of Trajan's bridge

technique. The result was an unprecedented onslaught by man on nature—a tremendous effort to change the face of the earth. The Romans, it would seem, built their roads not just for utilitarian purposes but to express an almost Promethean sense of power and purpose, the power and purpose of a conqueror bringing his superior knowledge and skill to the most primitive peoples and lightening their darkness.

The Urartaeans and the Assyrians had tunnelled through rock to build aqueducts long before the Romans; the road-tunnel, on the other hand, is a Roman invention. The tunnel under the Posilipo, through which today the whole motor traffic from Naples to Fuorigrotta and Pozzuoli flows, is mentioned by several Roman writers. Not so well known is the fact that the rock of Cumae (the modern Cuma) was pierced by a Roman tunnel, so that both these major works were located almost within a stone's throw of each other in country which is still more redolent of ancient Rome than any other part of Italy, and which fills the traveller with an almost traumatic

sense of remoteness from present-day life. The man responsible
for these and other tunnels was the engineer Cocceius. Those who
commissioned the work had drawn up a splendidly ambitious plan:
the lakes in the Misenum peninsula were to be linked up and
developed into a series of inland wharves and harbours, as Rome's
open harbours were not adequately protected against the pirate
leader, Sextus Pompeius, the uncrowned king of the Mediterranean.
After the murder of Sextus at Milet in 35 B.C., Octavius Augustus
lost interest in the plan; Misenum, being more easily accessible, was
more suitable as a naval base. Today the grottoes and caves, which
had been used for military and ships' stores, are inhabited by
Neapolitans whose box-lid huts were demolished in the city's sweeping slum-clearance campaign.

Although tunnelling through the rock was a tremendously laborious process—the work advanced at the rate of only a few yards each
year—the main problems must have been those of ventilation and,
particularly, of precision planning and measurement. An architect
named Nomius Datus, who was behind schedule with a tunnel near
Lambaesis in North Africa, defended himself in this inscription on
a memorial altar there:

> After leaving my quarters, I was set upon by robbers who
> stripped me of my clothes and left me seriously injured. But
> I succeeded in reaching Saldae, where I met the army com-
> mander. There I found everyone in a depressed and irritable
> mood. They had lost all hope that the two ends of the tunnel
> would meet, because each end had advanced beyond the
> middle of the mountain and they still had not met. As always
> happens in such a case, here too the mistake was attributed
> to the engineer alone, as if he would not have taken every pre-
> caution to ensure the success of the work. *What more could I
> have done?* I began by demarcating the outlying spurs of the
> mountain and traced on the mountain ridge the line of the
> tunnel as precisely as possible. I drew plans and cross-sections
> of the whole work and handed them to the governor of Maure-
> tania. I even took the precaution of summoning the foreman
> and his workmen and in their presence, with the help of two
> shifts of experienced men, I began ... the excavation. *What
> more could I have done?* But during the four years (!) while I
> was absent from Lambaesis ... the foreman and his assistants
> had committed one mistake after the other; both the galleries
> of the tunnel had diverged from the straight, both to the right,
> and, had I arrived a little later, Saldae would have possessed
> two tunnels instead of one.

Nomius Datus, who had been given a hero's welcome at Saldae,

finally managed to sort things out by joining up the two galleries
with a cross-gallery, in other words by a piece of patchwork which
is a clear indication of the difficulties involved in tunnelling at such
an early period.

Much less difficult, but often just as time-wasting and laborious,
was the work involved in keeping roads straight: spurs of rock had
to be carefully hewn down by hand, lesser ridges cut through and
hillocks removed. The Romans knew that all this was pioneer work
—hence the special tablets erected to commemorate many of these
achievements. Nearly always, however, they are in honour of some
emperor or general, hardly ever of the architect or the builders
themselves. A road in Phoenicia, which was chiselled out of the rock,
owes its origin to the Emperor Antoninus Pius (A.D. 138–61), with
whose proverbial wisdom this work of peace was undoubtedly in
keeping, but also in Beirut, near Sesamus (on the Black Sea coast
of Paphlagonia), and elsewhere in Syria, Palestine and North Africa
commemorative tablets of this kind were set up where excavations
had to be made.

So again and again we see the classic straight line in Roman road-
making triumph over landscape and natural obstacles. The advent
of the aeroplane has brought striking evidence of this fundamental
principle of Roman planning, as, for example, in the old Roman
road, which can still be seen, from Castell Colon through Brecon to
Cardiff like a taut ribbon across the fields of Wales with here and
there only a slight deviation from its straight course, or Dere Street
in the Tweed valley between the old Roman fortresses Bremenium
and Tremontium, which runs so straight, up hill and down dale,
that the fields are still bounded by it.

From these examples one can see that the Romans were still ob-
serving the same basic principles in Scotland more than five hundred
years after they had applied them in Syria, Spain or Anatolia. We
can easily visualize how such a road was built: legionaries, prisoners
of war, or slaves first drew two parallel lines with the surveyor's
chain, which gave the direction and the width of the road. Then the
ground was dug till something like a shallow canal-bed had been
made, into which sea- or river-sand was poured and rolled. Then
between rows of sharp-edged stones which had been set up along the
edges the actual building of the road began in layers such as have
already been described and which reached a depth, hard to imagine
today, of seven to eight feet.

It was only in the width of their roads that the Romans were apparently prepared to make concessions. A country road which was
in regular use was usually about four feet wide, so that the peasant

could walk beside his horse or ox. It was called an 'actus' and was also used for cattle. The old common roads, on the other hand, which were used by livestock going to and from their pastures in the hills, were more than ten times as wide. A minimum width—7¾ feet —was laid down for public roads, but although it may seem very narrow to us, even this limited width was not always possible, especially in the Alps. Even the narrowest of Roman mountain roads required an enormous amount of manual labour.

Later, as transport increased, roads had to be eleven and even thirteen and sixteen feet wide to admit two lanes of traffic; the major long-distance roads in Gaul (where land was cheaper than in Italy) and in Asia Minor were as much as twenty-seven feet wide. Roads of this size naturally raised enormous problems in the towns, and more than one emperor made himself unpopular by simply tearing down his subjects' property where it impeded traffic.

At first glance the Roman roads appear to have been made to last for ever: they had to be dead straight, so that the Roman vehicles with their fixed axles could travel on them just as comfortably as modern fast-moving vehicles with their dislike of tight bends. No expense was spared in building these roads and the amount of material used was enormous; the Via Appia had, at one point, an embankment 250 yards in length, 14 yards wide and 15 yards high, supporting walls up to 48 yards high and tunnels which reached a maximum depth of 40 yards in the Monte San Angelo near Terracina.

But even a colossus has his weak points. The Romans built their roads too much on the pattern of their floors, which only had to carry stationary loads and, apart from human footsteps, were not subjected to any changes of pressure. The road surfaces were thick enough but not elastic enough for the Roman vehicles with their lack of springs and their solid wheels. The hard surface was much more susceptible to wear and tear than a more flexible one and the slightest movement of the foundation through pressure or through flooding caused dangerous cracks. Furthermore any damage to these road surfaces was much harder to repair than the modern pothole, which can be so quickly filled in.

Despite these criticisms, the Roman roads remain a tremendous achievement, which was never equalled in the Middle Ages and surpassed only in our own time. It is, therefore, well worth while taking a closer look at some of these ancient roads, if only to savour the beauty of their names, which sound like trumpet-calls. Via Augusta, Via Trajana, Strata Diocletiana. Throughout the centuries, those who have written about them have been wildly enthusiastic, particularly, of course, authors such as Nicolas Bergier, the French lawyer who lived more than two hundred years ago when public highways were in a disastrous state. Since then Thomas Codrington, at the beginning of the present century, and Ivan D. Margery, fifty years later, have given detailed descriptions of literally all the major and minor Roman roads in Britain. Similar accounts have been given of other former Roman territories with the sole exceptions of Spain and Anatolia.

One of the striking facts brought to light by research is that around A.D. 330 a pilgrim could travel from Bordeaux to Jerusalem entirely on Roman roads—in other words, he could cover more than 3,000 miles on *good* roads (something that is not possible today). An itinerary from the year 334 gives the route: Bordeaux–Arles–Milan–Aquileja–Byzantium–Ancyra–Tarsus–Antioch–Tyre–Caesarea–Jerusalem. At that time a traveller could also travel on equally good roads from Hadrian's Wall in the extreme north-west of the Roman Empire to the frontier of Ethiopia, a distance of 4,500 miles. A round trip was, of course, also a possibility and it is not at all unlikely that at various times throughout the centuries keen Roman travellers undertook them. If, for example, one started out from Alexandria, one could ride, drive or walk to the Scottish border by way of Carthage, Hispalis (Seville), Saguntum, Lyons, Reims, Boulogne, Dover, London and Eburacum (York), then return through Dover, Leyden, Cologne, Mainz, Milan, Verona, Aquileja, Serdica (Sofia), Byzantium, Nicomedia, Ancyra (Ankara), Damascus, Gaza and Pelusium. It is significant that areas like the Balkans and countries which now lie behind the Iron Curtain were much more closely linked by road with the rest of Europe in the first three or four centuries of the Christian era than they are today.

From the beginning the Romans had so planned their highway-system that the north–south roads would not only meet the requirements of the narrow, boot-shaped peninsula but would also supplement the shipping routes. This made the roads that linked up with the Adriatic ports especially important, for they were the overland components of a general network of land and sea routes leading to the Balkans and the Levant.

The natural focal point of this network and therefore of the whole empire was the city of Rome. From it radiated seven major long-distance roads and about half a dozen minor roads; starting from the north-western coast-line, they were the Via Aurelia, the Viae Clodia and Cassia (which joined not far from Veii and proceeded together to Rome), the Via Flaminia, the Via Salaria, the Via

Valeria, and finally the two old southbound roads, the Latina and the Appia.

The Via Aurelia left Rome by the Pons Aemilius, which crosses the Tiber south of the island, unlike the road known today as the Via Aurelia which leaves Rome by way of the Vatican City. Outside Rome, however, the lines followed by the old Via Aurelia and the present highway are almost identical; they run in a general westerly direction towards the coast with the old Etruscan city of Caere (now Cerveteri) on their right and reach the coast near Pyrgi, which is not far from the village of Severa. Even in pre-Roman times this was all cultivated land and Aurelius Cotta, that energetic censor after whom the road is named, undoubtedly found old roads already in existence. In 353 B.C. Caere was finally occupied by the Romans, following an uprising, but another century passed before, in 241 B.C., the first section of the Via Aurelia was built as far as Cosa, near the salt lakes of Orbetello.

Strangely enough, this whole region had reached the peak of its prosperity before the great road was built, perhaps because the road turned it into a mere transit area and brought northern Etruria and Tuscany closer to the crowded capital. In post-Roman times Caere became a bishopric, but the great highway fell into disuse and, with the general decline of maritime trade, the ports also declined. In the eighth century the road was only just usable, and Centumcellae, farther to the north, had replaced the ports of Pyrgi and Punicum (which had always been closely linked with Caere) with the result that Caere also went into a decline.

The present town of Cerveteri has retained its old name (Caere vetus) and is most picturesquely situated around a palace on a hillside, which gives the Princes Ruspoli the right to call themselves 'Princes of Cerveteri'. The famous Etruscan necropolis was discovered as long ago as 1536, but as little or nothing was known of the Etruscans then the discovery passed almost unnoticed.

It took another century and more for the Via Aurelia to reach Pisae (Pisa), which 2,000 years ago was a sea-port and during the Etruscan period was allied with Caere. At that time the Arno flowed into the sea farther to the south-west and large ships could sail right up to the town, so until well into the Middle Ages Pisa remained a wealthy trading and naval port. A steady stream of traffic flowed into it along the Via Aurelia, and from the interior of Etruria goods came partly by way of the Arno, and partly on the Via Cassia, which ran parallel to it and which linked such important places as Clusium (Chiusi), Cortona and Arretium (Arezzo) with the coast road. Florence also lay on this tributary road, but in spite of its situation on the Arnus (Arno) it was still unimportant. It was too young and it had been founded by the Romans, whereas the towns between Pisa and Caere, which flourished with the expansion of old Etruria, bore names which have come to life again during the last few decades: Tarquinii, Volci, Volaterrae. . . .

It was a considerable time before the Romans and their new towns were able to change a pattern of trade which had existed for centuries. That is why the Via Aurelia remained for many years a sort of foreign intruder—until order was established in the new Roman colonies in Gaul and Spain, when it became one of the main thoroughfares in the whole of the Roman Empire.

The continuation of the Via Aurelia along what is today the Italian Riviera did not, of course, bear the name of Aurelius Cotta (who had long since died) but the melodious name Via Julia Augusta, and in the year 13 B.C. it was paved as far as Arles in southern France. But to the traveller who set out from Rome it remained the Via Aurelia, however far he travelled along it.

In the country between Genoa and Marseilles lived tribes who had been active traders many centuries before the Romans. They had transported their goods from the Mediterranean to the north, either up the Rhône or even across the Alps, returning to the Ligurian coast with salt and amber. It was no easy matter to impose a new, strange trade route upon these worldly and self-conscious peoples—a route which seemed to them quite superfluous. It was only after eighty years of fighting and hard bargaining that the Romans succeeded in obtaining the same status for their new road as had been enjoyed by the old, winding trail which, according to legend, Hercules had laid. A strip thrice five hundred paces wide was recognized as extra-territorial, making the road and the land bordering it safe for travellers. The Massilians, following the example of the Ligurians, even agreed to be responsible for maintaining the road.

Like the present road, the Via Julia Augusta wound its way between the Alps and the sea. A few miles west of Ventimiglia, the Roman Albintimilium, the Augustus monument still stands as a reminder of the bitter fighting that took place. This monument was erected more than 1,300 feet above the sea in the year A.D. 5 to commemorate the defeat of the Ligurians. The village of La Turbie, where it stands, has remained to this day one of the sights on the Grande Corniche.

At Frejus, the Roman Forum Julii, the road left the coast and, like the present road, skirted the wild hilly country of the Maures— by so doing it avoided all the small bays and was also easier to patrol. Those who have travelled along the Corniche des Maures, as the present coast road is called, will admit that the Romans knew how to plan their highways. On the other hand, it was probably with considerable reluctance that they decided to leave the familiar coastline and plunge into the interior. Behind the ancient Massilia they founded a veterans' colony at Aquae Sextiae (Aix-en-Provence), where retired legionaries found in the warm springs a cure for the rheumatism which they had contracted in the raw climate of Gaul and Germania.

At Arles the new Roman east–west road joined the old trade route from the north. The Celts had given the place the unattractive name of Arelas, or Arelate (the place of the swamp), while the Ligurian bronze and amber merchants called it Theline; Caesar made it one of his largest military colonies in Gaul. Thanks to its strategic position at the junction of two roads and the Rhône, Arelate soon replaced the old town of Massilia in importance. Under the Emperor Constantine (306–37), who was particularly attached to the town, it acquired some magnificent new buildings and became the official capital of Gaul. It remained very dependent on its roads, prospering from the trade that passed along them through the south of France, and in 880 it was still Arelat, the proud capital of the kingdom of Burgundy.

The fact that it retained its name and its important position so long is an indication of the enduring effects produced by the Roman roads. One such remote effect was doubtless the eventual absorption in 1032 of Arles and the Burgundian territories around it into the Holy Roman Empire; another two and a half centuries passed before they became part of the kingdom of France.

At Arles the Roman road crossed the Rhône and ran up to Nemausus, the holy city of the Celts, known today as Nîmes. At Narbo Martius (Narbonne) a road branched off from the main highway to the west, linking Tolosa (Toulouse) and Burdigala (Bordeaux) with the Mediterranean port of Narbo, where the Romans built merchant ships and galleys of wood from the near-by Cevennes.

Tarraco (Tarragona) did not derive its importance from the Roman road to the same extent as Arles; it had already become established as one of the main ports in the Mediterranean. But, after Spain became a Roman province, the hinterland was opened up: gold, tin and lead came down the Ebro and along the secondary road which ran from the great Asturian mining area through Caesaraugusta (Saragossa) to Tarragona and crossed northern Spain from Lucus Augusti (Lugo) through Asturica Augusta (Astorga).

The coastal road, which was called the Via Augusta, but was in

effect a continuation of the Via Aurelia, also passed through Saguntum—the ruins of which are still to be seen—and on through
Valencia and Ilici (Elche); it reached its southernmost point at Nova
Carthago (Cartagena). And here, in effect, is the end of the Via
Aurelia. The Via Augusta, the main Spanish thoroughfare, turned
inland south of Valencia, passed through Cordova and Seville and
finally reached the port of Gades (Cadiz).

Spain played a very special role in Caesar's life: it was here that
he became rich, that his soldiers first hailed him as Imperator, but
here too—at Cordova—he suffered his first epileptic fit. Caesar knew
the great coastal road better than almost anyone else. 'For the most
part', writes Plutarch (A.D. 50–125), 'Caesar slept in his chariot or in
litters, so that he could still be active even when he was resting. . . .
He travelled with such speed that he needed no more than eight
days to reach the Rhodanus [Rhône] from Rome.' Caesar also
travelled from Obulco in southern Spain to Rome in twenty-seven
days. It is clear from this that travelling on the Italian section of the
road was easier than in Spain. Caesar's daily average on his journey
to Arles was considerably higher than for the entire journey to
southern Spain.

At one point only the Via Aurelia was bested by a younger rival:
the road across Mont Ginévre, which proved a great deal more
comfortable because, instead of the frequent ascents and descents
with which the Via Aurelia made its way through the Maritime Alps,
only one steady climb was necessary. This particular pass, which
was not turned into a first-class road until 1957, is roughly three
times the height of the highest point on the Via Aurelia, the so-called
Alpe Summa in the Maritime Alps. But the Roman road which ran
from the Po valley through Susa to Brigantio (Briançon) was definitely superior to the coast road. In 77 B.C. Pompey is reported to
have led an army over this pass, which subsequently became the
main link between Rome and her western provinces and gradually
took the place of the road over the 6,800-feet-high Mont Cenis. At
Susa, originally called Segusio, the roads forked just as they do
today, and the Dora Riparia valley can fairly be described as one of
the oldest trade routes across the western Alps.

After the Aurelia the most important of the northbound roads
from Rome is the Via Flaminia. It bears the name of the tribune
and censor, Gaius Flaminius, who intended it to be a link between
Rome and the rich wheat-growing provinces in the Po valley, which
had been wrested from the Gauls (220 B.C.). Between Foligno and
Fano (on the Adriatic) one can still follow it through Nocera,
Gualdo Tadino and Fossombrone. These peaceful Umbrian hills are

a part of Italy which seems eternally asleep. There are innumerable small hills and bends to break the monotony, but the villages are silent and traffic only begins near the coast. The mountains cast their shadows early and one's thoughts wander all too easily to the unfortunate tribune who met his death in a Carthaginian ambush on Lake Trasimene, not far from the road that bears his name.

The Emperor Augustus and Pope Julius III (1550–55) made improvements on the road; the final stretch leading into Rome, the Porta Flaminia and the Via del Corso, is probably the finest and busiest of Rome's modern roads.

As a coastal road along the Adriatic the Via Flaminia has continued to be important right up to the present time. As the Romans feared the sudden storms that still blow up in the Adriatic, they preferred land to sea travel, and the road ran dead straight from Ariminum (Rimini) along part of the Via Aemilia to northern Italy.

The Via Aemilia, laid in 187 B.C., branched off at Ariminum from the coastal road, which continued as far as Ravenna, and followed more or less the same course as the present motorway through Cesena and Forum Popoli (Forlì), Bononia (Bologna) and Parma to the Po, which the Romans called Padus. At Placentia (Piacenza) it reached the river (which was important both as a trade route and for its many tributaries) and then curved to pass through Dertona— which was a much busier trading centre than the modern Tortona— and join up with the Via Julia Augusta, the extension of the Via Aurelia.

This impressive twin-track conception had the effect of lightening the burden on the stretch of the Via Aurelia that passed through the densely-populated areas of Etruria: a second road ran due north from Rome (whereas the Via Aurelia ran north-west), turned west-north-west at Rimini and rejoined the Via Aurelia this side of the Alps.

The network, which was as scientifically planned as any existing today, was completed by short transversal roads running across to the Adriatic. The ancient Via Salaria had led to Reute (Rieti). In 117 B.C. the Via Caecilia was built as an extension of it, skirting the Gran Sasso mountains to the north, while the Via Valeria (started in 305 B.C. and completed in 154 B.C.), like the present motorway, ran through Carsoli to the river Pescara (the old Aternus).

The Via Appia leaves Rome in a south-easterly direction and it is still possible to drive along it. The section of the Via Appia Antica between the third and eleventh milestones, which is open to traffic, is like a corridor leading into the past. It is saturated with the stillness of the Roman Campagna, and the ancient, half-ruined tomb-

stones and villas on either side have an air of timelessness which
even the modern cars that pass slowly along the paved road cannot
destroy. One cannot help wondering what sort of impression this
road and the surrounding country made on the traveller who had
just left ancient Rome.

There were many more trees than there are today: in the reign
of Augustus, Greek travellers were delighted by Italy's forests, and
Pliny the Younger refers to the abundance of game in the area between the Tiber and the Alban hills. The Via Appia, quiet though
it is today, is still a reminder of the extent to which the ancient
Roman lived on and with his roads. He loved their trees as much
as if they were in his own garden, and the wells and springs at the
roadside were almost as important to him as those in his own villa.
The Via Appia, which had already been famous for three hundred
years before the Roman Empire, is a striking example of a road
which was aesthetically conceived and planned—not merely a ribbon
of stone, but a living artery in which even the tombs were not out of
place.

We must also remember that the Romans, like the Greeks, frequently travelled on foot. When Cicero retired to his estate near
Pompeii, letters were brought to him from Rome by runners, who
covered the distance along the Via Appia in four to five days; they
slept under the pine trees or in the shadow of the tombs, if shelter
was not available. They *lived* on the road, which brought new life
to that once deserted area, the Pontine marshes.

As the speed of travel increased, the character of the road
changed. Modern roads tend to discourage loitering; in fact, the
most up-to-date are usually studded with 'No Stopping' signs. The
masterpieces of road-building in the ancient world, the Roman
roads, were like channels through which the Roman way of life
flowed into the open country. Wherever there was a Roman road,
there was Rome herself; that is why they were not simply laid, they
were built like houses and temples. . . .

The country through which the Via Appia passed on leaving
Rome was, at the time of the Volsci, fertile and well watered. Within
an area of some 300 square miles there were thirty towns and cities.
But frequent wars ruined the crops, the population dwindled, and
before long work on the canals had to be abandoned. Appius
Claudius (around 315 B.C.), who built the Via Appia, was compelled
to combine road-building with work on the canals, and from then
on the fortunes of the road, or at least of its oldest part, were in-
separable from the marshes. Under Caesar, Augustus, Trajan and

Theoderic (456–526) extensive drainage work was done as part of the maintenance of the Via Appia. In later centuries the popes, as the sole relatively permanent authority in those parts, assumed the responsibility for the queen of roads and the country around her. But neither Bonifacius VIII (1235–1303) nor that famous builder Martin V (1368–1431), neither Sextus V (1521–90) nor Pius VI (1778) succeeded in completely draining the marshes and freeing Rome from fever. Even the old Via Appia was bordered by abandoned and dilapidated settlements, and the modern traveller can picture those scenes of desolation when he sees the small ruined town of Ninfa, north-east of Latina, overgrown with ivy—a memorial to the dire poverty that forced several hundred families to abandon their homes.

After running dead straight for a good sixty miles, the Via Appia (from which the present motor-road only deviates in the Velletri area) reached the Roman spa, Tarracina (Terracina), called by the Volsci, Anxur. Remains of the walls of this ancient town, which was occupied by the Romans in 388 B.C., can still be seen on the 600-feet-high hill above the modern part of the town; to the east of the town, at the Pisco Montano, is the spot where, on Trajan's orders, a rock was removed with enormous difficulty and expenditure of manpower to make an improvement in the Via Appia.

Terracina marks the end of the marshes, which have now been sufficiently drained for new towns like Aprilia and Pontinia to arise in the middle of what was once a malaria-infested area.

From Terracina the Via Appia continued on to Capua, which in those early times was one of the wealthiest towns in Italy, for it lay in one of the great wheat-growing areas and was therefore in a position to supply Rome with two essential commodities: vegetables and grain. The link with Capua, the natural terminus of the Via Appia, and Campania was particularly important. The morale of Hannibal's army is said to have been so undermined by its stay in this prosperous, luxury-loving town that it lost all its warlike virtues; for the same reason two hundred years later Caesar allowed only his veteran soldiers to settle there.

Early in the third century B.C. the Via Appia was extended eastwards beyond Capua, which by then was losing its importance. In 291 B.C. the road reached the Samnite town of Maluentum, the Roman Beneventum. After the fourth Samnite war, work on the road was continued to carry it in a south-easterly direction through the thinly-populated Apulia to Tarentum, where, as far as traffic is concerned, it might well have stopped. But the Romans, who did nothing by halves, took the queen of roads a stage farther across

the heel of Italy to Brundisium (Brindisi), where she met the Via
Trajana at the end of its journey down the Adriatic coast.

Thanks to the Via Appia and the Via Trajana, and also to the
trade with Greece and the Orient, Brundisium became one of the
largest and richest cities in Italy. At its peak it had a population of
100,000, a figure which has never been reached since. But Brindisi
was not only the terminus of the oldest and most famous road in
the Roman Empire, it was also the place where Rome's greatest poet
died: in the year 19 B.C. Virgil died here on a journey from Greece
to Rome.

Another famous poet, Horace, who was born in Apulia, describes
the Via Appia almost cynically in one of his satires in the first book
of the *Sermones* published in the year 30 B.C.

> Leaving great Rome, my journey I begin,
> And reach Aricia, where a moderate inn
> (With me was Heliodorus, who knows more
> Of rhetoric than e'er did Greek before):
> Next Appii Forum, filled, e'en nigh to choke,
> With knavish publicans and boatmen folk.
> This portion of our route, which most get through
> At one good stretch, we chose to split in two,
> Taking it leisurely: ....

So according to Horace, it was possible and, in fact, customary to
travel about forty miles a day on the straight Pontine stretch of the
Via Appia and to spend the first night in Forum Apii, a small
market town about eight miles from the sea. The journey then continued (at least at the time referred to) by water, in a long transport
barge towed by mules. This is borne out by contemporary accounts
of travelling conditions on the Via Appia, which was frequently
closed to traffic, but on which, even when in use, the vehicles set up
thick clouds of dust and the animals attracted swarms of insects.
After Terracina (which Horace still calls by its old name Anxur)
and Campania came a restless night at Beneventum,

> ... where our host,
> As some lean thrushes he essayed to roast,
> Was all but burnt: for up the chimney came
> The blaze, and well nigh set the house on flame:
> The guests and servants snatch the meat, and fall
> Upon the fire with buckets, one and all.

In a hostelry near Trevicum (the place itself lay a short distance
away from the Via Appia), where Horace stopped for the night after
an exhausting journey through the bare country of Apulia, he was

confronted by fresh hazards: the wood smoke made his weak eyes
smart, but his chief concern was with one of the host of young
women who lived on the great highways earning rich rewards with
very little effort. But the poet waited half the night in vain.

> Then four and twenty miles, a good long way,
> Our coaches take us, in a town to stay
> Whose name no art can squeeze into a line,
> Though otherwise 'tis easy to define:
> For water there, the cheapest thing on earth,
> Is sold for money, but the bread is worth
> A fancy price, and travellers who know
> Their business take it with them when they go.

Shortly before he reached Venosia, where he was born the son
of a freed slave, Horace and his companions turned north-east and,
'after traversing a long road which had been spoiled by rain',
reached Barium (Bari) by way of Canusium and Rubi and proceeded
from there to Brundisium. This appears to have been quite a common alternative route, for the final stretch of the Via Appia between
Venosia and Tarentum was poorly supplied with hostelries and
villages were few and far between.

The 320-mile-long Via Popila—which was built in the year 132
and owed its existence to the energy with which the two Gracchi
(about 130 B.C.) flung themselves into road-building—ran up to the
toe of Italy where Reggio di Calabria lies today. Gaius Gracchus
fought to free overland travel from control by regional authorities
—at that time a bold innovation—and, when land was being distributed, he always kept a watchful eye on the roads and their proper
maintenance; he not only built new roads but also improved the
existing ones and opened up a number of subsidiary roads. After
the Gracchi the Senate appointed special officials for road-building
and maintenance in the peninsula; this example was soon followed
by the confederate states with the result that, even at this early stage,
something like an organized road-system throughout Italy began to
emerge.

To the weary traveller, especially if he arrived on foot, Rhegium
(Reggio di Calabria) was more a haven than just a destination. This
ancient harbour town at the southern tip of the peninsula had finally
been conquered by the Romans about five hundred years after its
foundation by Greeks from Euboä and Mersenia. More than a
thousand families from Campania settled there and the traveller
from Capua could be sure of meeting friends or relations who had
crossed the barren wastes of Lucania before him and found new
homes within sight of Sicily.

Chapter 9

WENCHES, ROBBERS AND SOLDIERS

Quintus Horatius Flaccus has given us our first glimpse into the immorality and abuses to which the traveller on the great roads of the Roman Empire was exposed. Horace was not the only tired traveller who complained that frogs and crane-flies kept him awake and that the donkey-driver proposed a substitute for sleep by 'praising loudly the charms of his daughter'; Lucian, Seneca, Plutarch and many other writers gathered similar impressions on their journeys, but, as we have not the space to quote them individually, we must attempt to summarize.

Even if one covered forty miles a day, the long stretches of the road still took a considerable time, so the Roman's first concern was for company. Failing that, he was accompanied, wherever possible, by servants or slaves. The more important the traveller, the more imposing the train, and when Poppeia, Nero's wife, travelled across country with gold-harnessed draught animals and five hundred female asses as itinerant boilers for her baths, there can have been little room left for other traffic on the roads she used. Seneca, though a wealthy man, tried once to get away from Roman luxury travel and to travel across country with only two carriages—one for himself and his friend Caesonius Maximus, the other for the servants. With all his powers of philosophic self-persuasion, he had to admit that he felt wretched. Others spent so much money on their travels that, while still on the road, they considered paying their debts by appearing as gladiators, or fighting animals in the arena. In view of the length of the journeys, it seems natural that many carriages were equipped for sleeping and that travelling scholars or politicians had acquired the habit of dictating en route. Travel-reading consisted of parchments bound together in book form, which was much more convenient than the customary rolls of papyrus; these 'books' were, so to speak, the paper-backs of the ancient world and, at the same time, a tribute to the quality of the Roman roads—even in a well-sprung car it is difficult to read on a bad road!

So most wealthy Romans travelled with all their servants and plenty of baggage: the servants were slaves who had to be fed and who were kept very busy on the journey. For the well-to-do Roman was always most reluctant to put up in the public hostelries; he was accustomed in his own villa to hygiene, peace, luxury and privacy and, rather than spend the night with the riff-raff of the roads, he preferred to sleep in his carriage or in a tent put up by his servants. After all, the weather was mild enough. So we have the rather surprising picture of ladies and gentlemen, whose names remind us of so many painful hours from our schooldays, travelling across country as campers or in ancient safari-carriages, forerunners of a camping movement which has spread throughout the centuries wherever good roads and a favourable climate are found. Both these prerequisites existed in the greater part of the Roman Empire.

Here and there, of course, excellent hostelries existed which were sufficiently expensive to exclude the common run of travellers. The much-travelled Greek, Strabo, recommended to his readers several hostelries where the food was particularly good, and Epictetus hinted that many travellers were less concerned to reach their destinations or return home quickly than to enjoy the good living in this or that place on the road. It has not so far been established whether the ancient world, which produced quite a number of reliable travel-guides, also had a guide-book with a specifically gastronomical flavour (such as is quite common today). We shall never know which people first discovered the gastronomical charms of travel. . . .

One group of people in the ancient world was certainly as dependent on hostelries as it is today on hotels—the commercial travellers, who are constantly on the move and who can charge everything to expenses. This was a privilege they also enjoyed in ancient Rome, so that there was no hostelry too small, too dirty, too hot, or too crowded for them. In certain trading centres like Lyons, for example, there were hostelries two thousand years ago which specialized in commercial travellers, who used them in preference to others. There they found a second home, and the female staff were usually so willing to stand in for absent wives that a whole series of imperial

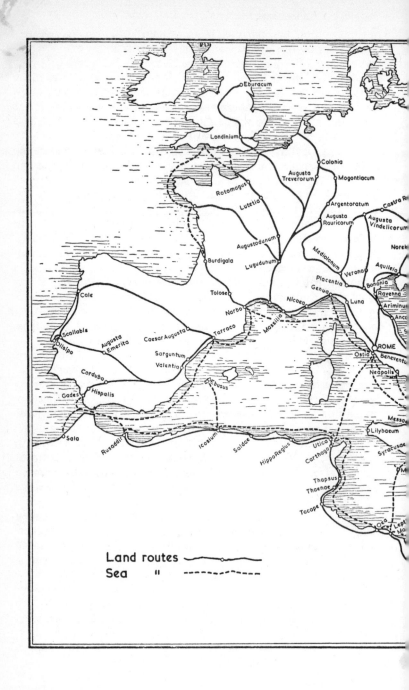

Land routes ———o———

Sea   "   ---------o---------

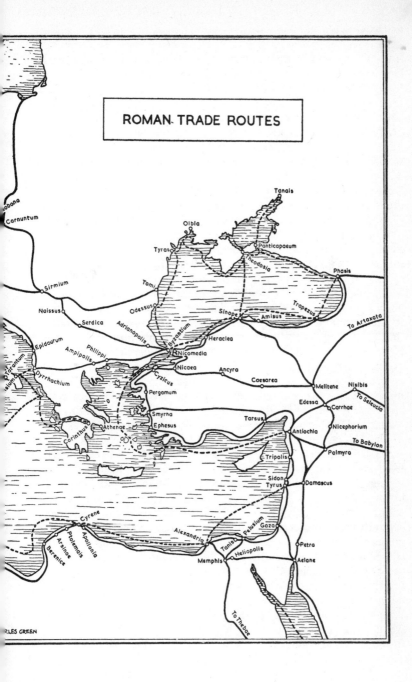

ROMAN TRADE ROUTES

Tanais

Olbia

Tyras

Panticapaeum

Theodosia

Phasis

Vindobona

Carnuntum

Sirmium

Tomi

Trapezus

Naissus

Odessus

Sinope

Amisus

Serdica

Adrianopolis

To Artaxata

Epidaurum

Philippi

Byzantium

Heraclea

Nicomedia

Ampipolis

Cyzicus

Nicaea

Ancyra

Caesarea

Melitene

Nisibis

Dyrrhachium

Pergamum

Edessa

Carrhae

To Seleucia

Smyrna

Tarsus

Nicephorium

Corinthus

Athenae

Ephesus

Antiochia

To Babylon

Tripolis

Palmyra

Sidon

Tyrus

Damascus

Cyrene

Apollonia

Gaza

Ptolemais

Alexandria

Pelusium

Petra

Arsinoe

Tanis

Heliopolis

Aelane

Berenice

Memphis

To Thebae

RLES GREEN

edicts were issued condemning these places as brothels. It is significant in this connection that, according to Roman law, adultery
simply could not be committed with women and girls employed in
hostelries (!). It was only in the reign of the Emperor Constantine
(306–37), when traffic on the Roman roads was beginning to decline,
that the mistress of the house was excluded from this ban and intercourse with her became adultery. The Emperor Alexander Severus
(222–35) had previously decreed that female slaves, who were not
allowed to be sold as prostitutes, should also be prevented from
working in hostelries—a striking instance of the way road-houses
and public brothels were considered identical. Innkeepers had the
worst possible reputation, and the police kept as close a check on
them as on habitual criminals. Innumerable reports from ancient
times make it clear that the traveller was completely at their mercy
and that they were not slow to use their power; whereas there were
many roads, most of them long, accommodation was extremely
limited, and this lack of competition was fully exploited.

Among those who shared in the proceeds of these establishments
were, quite frequently, prominent citizens of the Roman Empire.
They built the hostelries on their land near the road and put in slaves
to run them and hand over the profits. The State not only tolerated
this state of affairs but even encouraged it; State hostelries built by
Nero, Hadrian and other emperors were reserved for officials—
ordinary mortals either had to sleep in the open or resign themselves
to being fleeced in the public road-houses, to say nothing of the
insect life that was so prolific and so varied that a special book could
be written merely on the linguistic terms coined by Pliny the
Younger, Dioscorides and other authors to describe these creatures.

The famous, much-travelled doctor, Claudius Galenus (131–201)
—the first surgeon to carry out a resection of the breast-bone—
lived up to his own prescription that a doctor must also be a philosopher. His numerous writings are a gold-mine of contemporary
history and customs, all the more valuable because they were written
with an integrity that inspires complete confidence. So it is almost
certainly true, as he reports, that various innkeepers would offer their
guests human flesh in place of pork, and that one of his travelling
companions once found the joint of a human finger in what was
otherwise an excellent dish of stew. According to Galenus, one innkeeper and his family were even caught in the act of preparing a
human victim for the pot and were handed over to the police.

Anything that was left of the traveller's belongings when he left
the inn was usually taken by highway robbers, who were either
tipped off by the innkeepers or by their own spies. At the turn of

the third and fourth centuries Heliodorus of Emesa wrote a romantic novel *Aethiopica* which has since become famous, but of which
he was later just as ashamed when he became a bishop as Pope Pius
II (1458–64) must have been of writing the erotic story of Euryalus
and Lucrecia under his own name, Aeneas Sylvius Piccolomini.
Heliodorus invented his plot, but the background was taken from
real life and gives us a vivid picture of an age which to the robbers
was undoubtedly golden.

The robbers there [in northern Egypt] live either in huts on
small hills above the water or on house-boats in the water
itself. The women also live in these floating dwellings, where
they beget their children, feeding them at first with their own
milk, later with fish dried in the sun. As soon as the little one
begins to move about on all fours, it is tied by a short leather
strap round the ankles, which enables it to crawl as far as the
side of the house-boat. These straps are the robbers' nurse-
maids.

People who have grown up beside and on this lake love it
as their home. It is a proper robber stronghold with water in
place of walls and a forest of reeds to serve as ramparts.
Through the rushes they have beaten out a whole network of
winding footpaths, which they know by heart but which make
the water-fortress inaccessible to any stranger. They need fear
no surprise attack.

Another and no less famous robber encampment in the Roman
Empire was in Asia Minor, where, in consequence, the important
roads between Ephesus and Sardes and between Antioch-Palmyra
and Damascus were never safe. This encampment was named after
a small and very old hill-town, Isaurien, was first mentioned in the
fourth century B.C., and was a constant headache to the republic
of Rome. Time and again the Romans invaded this small robber-
State but it always re-emerged, and about the middle of the third
century A.D. the robbers became so powerful that they set up their
chief Trebellianus as a rival emperor. In the wild mountainous
country, in which each encampment was a small fortress, he managed to 'rule' for some time, holding court at Isaura and minting his
own coins. In the fifth century the robber hordes of Isaurien occupied the wealthy Seleucia, so that it can be said with some justifica-
tion that Isaura outlived the Roman Empire. The relations between
these robbers and Rome, whose empire completely surrounded
them, have been compared by Jacob Burckhardt with the position
of the Cherkess in Czarist Russia. The Emperor Probus (232–82)
alone succeeded in imposing his authority on them for a few years,
and the difficulty he had in achieving this makes us realize how wild

these mountain people were and how ruthless they were in their treatment of travellers:

> In Probus's reign one of their robber captains, Lydius, made Lykia and Pamphylia unsafe; he had defied all attacks by not merely withdrawing into the impregnable fortress at Kremna but also guarding against starvation by judicious sowing and harvesting; the unfortunate inhabitants, whom he had driven out and whom the Roman military commander tried to send back into the town by force, were thrown down from the walls into the gorges below. An underground passage led from Kremna under the Roman camp to a remote, secret spot beyond it; this was used from time to time by the men of the beleaguered garrison to bring stolen cattle and food into the town, till the Romans tracked them down. From then on Lydius found himself compelled to reduce the number of his men to the absolute minimum by killing them, and a few women were also spared though as common property.
>
> (JACOB BURCKHARDT)

It was only after Lydius, who could well be regarded as the inventor of total war, had himself fallen that Kremna surrendered; he belongs, therefore, to a long line of great robber barons, which began with Amyrtäos, the king of the marshes, and still persists, even in Europe, at the present time. The modern bandit, however, has a much shorter life than his counterpart in the Roman Empire, and whereas there were whole tribes of robbers in the Nile Delta, Asia Minor and Dacia, today, even in Sardinia and Sicily, there are only small bands, who are constantly obliged to change their hide-outs.

In Italy itself highway robbery reached astonishing proportions, even under powerful emperors, and at times traffic on some of the major highways was brought to a complete standstill: in the third century A.D., for example, the Via Appia was completely at the mercy of the robber captain Bulla and his 600 men for two years. Bulla was kept informed of every more or less important traveller who landed at Brundisium or left Rome, and what he was carrying with him in the way of valuables. It was not until his mistress betrayed him to the imperial cavalry and he was captured that the band broke up. Most of them were runaway slaves; Bulla himself was torn to pieces by wild beasts in the circus.

Another robber leader, who was much more famous than Bulla, though much less popular with his people, appeared on the Via Appia about a thousand years later and also lies buried beside it. His name was Robert de Hauteville, but he was popularly known as Robert the Crafty (Guiscard); when he followed his half-brothers from Normandy to Apulia, they had already shared out the country between them and fobbed him off with one small town. Robert Guiscard used it as a base for his raids and robbed travellers and merchants till he had enough money and men to carry out his own ambitious plans.

When Robert Guiscard died in Corfu (1085), the Norman fleet brought his body back to Apulia; a sudden storm blew up in the Adriatic and the ship sank, but, as if by some miracle, the body of the notorious Norman baron was rescued and in accordance with ancient Roman custom it now lies before the gates of Venosia—the birthplace of Horace—on the fateful Via Appia.

In the third century the road to Gaul and Spain was also preyed upon by a band of robbers which numbered more than two thousand armed men and had its headquarters in the town of Albenga, the ancient Albium Ingaunum, on the Via Julia Augusta. The tribe to which the leaders of this band belonged was at one point so powerful that it put up its own claimant to the throne. He was called Proculus, and he made a serious effort to take over power in the whole of the Roman Empire. Had he succeeded, he would, of course, have been compelled to wrest the Via Julia Augusta out of the hands of his own relations. . . . Other classic hideouts for large robber bands were the Pontine Marshes, where, for health reasons, no garrisons could be maintained; the forests round Cuma, which still seem wild and deserted; and even the outlying districts of the capital itself, where the robbers could always go into hiding, feeling safer than in the open country. When we learn from an author of ancient Rome that it was regarded as highly dangerous to travel by night from Rome to Tibur (Tivoli), we see the whole, gigantic network of Roman roads in a very different light: created by man, it was abused by man, and the traveller, who listened anxiously in the flickering light of the torches for any suspicious sound, would presumably have preferred a safe country road to the hazards of the paved Via Tiburtina.

In his famous work on the period of Constantine the Great, Burckhardt raises the question of the social background of these highway robbers: in his chapter on the herdsmen-robbers of the Nile Delta he writes: 'We would find many such old, oppressed peoples caught up in a new form of barbarism throughout the empire as a whole, if only the history of the provinces were not so sparse.' This puts the situation on and around the great roads in its true perspective: the innumerable racial groups in the vast empire had their own culture and organization before the Romans came. The Romans conquered them, but could not fully occupy the various countries they had conquered (Egypt under the Ptolemies is one of the most striking examples and Cleopatra herself conclusive proof). This explains how in areas close to such great centres as Alexandria and Tarsus, which the Romans took great pains to develop, the population reverted to conditions of extreme poverty and primitiveness and, as they could not set up States of their own, lived in a state of anarchy. In large areas of the Roman Empire the great roads which had been built to last for ever were, in fact, no more than causeways running through an invisible swamp in which the subject peoples were the masters. Even the robber bands on the Apennine peninsula cannot simply be dismissed as mere criminals, but must be regarded as a social phenomenon. A key witness to this is the robber captain Felix Bulla: a centurion who had been sent out to parley with him was returned to his base with shaven head and the following message: 'Tell your masters they should look after their slaves better, then they will not come to me and become robbers.'

If the road-house keepers were despised for fishing in troubled waters and, without risk to themselves, robbing or defrauding defenceless travellers, the writers of the ancient world show a great deal of sympathy for the real master of the highways, the robber. As Apuleius, Heliodorus and others served as examples to writers for many centuries after, became popular again in the Renaissance, and even influenced Cervantes and the Spanish picaresque novel, it is fairly safe to say that the romantic picture of the robber originated in the contemporary accounts of conditions on the Roman roads.

From all this there emerged on the Roman road a strange and noteworthy microcosm of Latin life. Freed from the ties of communal life in the towns, the Roman traveller revelled in this age-old mode of living which gave him a greater sense of freedom and in which his restless Etruscan, Phoenician or Greek ancestry could find expression. And what of the Roman women? They were borne along in litters, the wind brushing gently against their cheeks, the peaceful landscape unfolding before their eyes. Caesar allowed only mothers and women over forty to use litters because he wanted to discourage luxury travel, but still more in order to relieve congestion on the roads. According to Clemens of Alexandria (the philosopher and writer who was eventually converted to Christianity), women, for the most part, regarded a journey by litter as a sort of fashion parade, and Seneca tells us that any man who opposed such a journey was liable to be condemned as mean and boorish and even as a tyrant. . . .

The open road, which today is frequently a symbol of the moral no-man's-land between law and violence, had obviously ceased to be within the jurisdiction of Roman law; highway robbers and prostitutes turned what were once holy pilgrim ways into a haunt of anti-social elements. Even those in positions of power merely aggravated the confusion and the amorality by their luxurious tastes and their megalomania: their mistresses were borne half-naked through starving crowds, who were driven back with sticks into the ditches. When Julia, the wife of Agrippa, the Roman general, and daughter of the Emperor Augustus, got into difficulties with her litter-bearers because the river Skamander was unexpectedly high, Agrippa imposed on the simple inhabitants of the next village in Asia Minor (who had no inkling of Julia's arrival), the enormous fine of 100,000 denarii for failing to lend assistance. King Herod had to intervene to prevent the fine being levied.

The vast empire managed, nevertheless, to take all these abuses in its stride, built more and longer roads and set up connections which no travel agency today would find in any timetable. The simple explanation is that neither of the two main driving-forces in the life of the empire—trade and war—could do without roads.

It is still common practice today for the consumer to pay more, and often a great deal more, for a given commodity than it costs in the country of origin, even though in many cases the margin of profit is greatly reduced. In the ancient world transport took much longer and therefore cost considerably more than it does today, moreover freight space was much more limited, so that the retail price of a commodity was often a hundred times the cost of production. So it was important to find a good transport route, for, even if the Italian peasant could not compete with the luxury goods from the Far East, the silk from the Séres province of Macedonia, and the spices from Arabia on which the fancy ladies of Rome spent a substantial part of their incomes, his foodstuffs still fetched as much as five times in large towns what they were worth in the nearest market.

The most famous flock of geese in ancient times is undoubtedly the gaggle that woke the guards on the Capitol, when the Gauls attacked it in 387 B.C., and so helped to repulse the raiders; but almost as remarkable is the performance of a flock of geese which an enterprising peasant drove from the mouth of the Rhine to Rome in A.D. 50 in order to obtain a better price for them. Herds, large and small, of swine, cattle and poultry could be seen almost daily on the Via Aemilia, which linked the Po fortress of Placentia (Piacenza) with the Adriatic port of Ariminum (Rimini). It ran dead straight past the foot of the mountains, just like the present highway which has replaced it, and from every valley alongside it came agricultural produce on its way to market in the towns. It has been said of the Via Aemilia that no other road had ever played such an important part in spreading culture: it brought the peasants out of their self-sufficient, primitive way of life in the Po valley, but at the same time it aroused the trader in them, and with higher rewards for their labour came increased demands in the outlying areas where they lived. Before the Via Aemilia was completed, those same peasants had to sell their corn and their wine at about a tenth of the price that Egyptian corn and Greek wine fetched in Ostia; now a stream of agricultural products flowed down the Via Aemilia from about fifty valleys to the richer areas of central Italy and in return new customs, new people, and the invisible products of civilization and town life flowed northwards (an exchange which is typical of many road-systems and which also applied to the railways in the nineteenth century).

The economic advantages of the Roman roads to the mother country and the metropolis need no elaboration. But such a vast network would hardly have arisen if the Romans had not been faced with a problem that confronts any imperial power, but which was particularly complex in ancient times—that of moving large detachments of troops sufficiently quickly to forestall or at least crush local unrest. The empires of the ancient world consisted of a large number of conquered territories which were kept in subjection by a small local garrison with a large, but remote military power in reserve. Roman troops which had conquered Gaul, Spain or Britain did not remain there; they were sent—sometimes even in the midst of a battle, or immediately after it—to other centres of unrest, possibly in Asia Minor, in Egypt or on the Danube. So it was of vital importance to Rome and to the Roman imperium to build good roads in the conquered territories while the campaign was still in progress, roads along which the legions could move quickly to fresh battlefields.

From 162 to 165, when Lucius Verus finally defeated the Persians after a long and bitter campaign and plundered the royal palace at Ctesiphon, his troops included legions from the Rhine Army and units from the Danube. Nero transferred a legion from Britain to the Caucasus. In order to deal with the rebellious desert tribes in North Africa troops were transferred not only from Spain but also from the area known today as Hungary, and Marcus Aurelius moved garrisons from North Africa to fight the Marcomanni. Even the snowbound Alpine passes had to be crossed, when Vitellus (born

A.D. 15) ordered the Rhine legions, which were still loyal to him, to march to Italy. Their forced march across the Great St. Bernard was in vain: Vespasian (9–79) arrived first with the eastern legions and caught Vitellus in Rome, where he had taken refuge.

Although there were other occasions when troops arrived too late, as, for example, the legions which Cleopatra sent out against Brutus and Cassius in Syria, nevertheless, the system as a whole was impressive, and the omnipresence of the Romans often came as an unpleasant surprise to some rebellious prince who had never heard of lines of communication. ... It was a system that worked as long as there were legions, and thereafter the roads were at the service of the conquerors, for roads as such are neutral—they are designed for travelling in two directions!

Not a few of these roads were built so specifically for marching soldiers that it seems unlikely that any civilian vehicle could ever use them: the Via Egnatia, for instance, which ran for close on 700 miles from the Adriatic port of Dyrrhachium (Durazzo) by way of Lake Ochrida and Salonica to Byzantium, crossed an area which is still virtually devoid of roads, along the familiar Roman straight line with gradients which were much too steep for draught animals.

Yet the history of the Roman roads is a series of tremendous pioneer achievements and, given the space, one would like to enumerate them. There is, for example, the Gabine Road, which ran inland from Salonae across trackless mountain country, or the road-system in Asia Minor through the wilds of Anatolia. Is it not a shattering thought that Claudius Galenus, the most famous physician of his time, could travel overland from Pergamon to Rome and return by the same route, in other words the whole length of the Via Egnatia and back, while we today, 2,000 years later, need a Land Rover to travel to Greece? Even the Aurès mountains in North Africa, which for thousands of years had been more or less inaccessible and certainly unsafe for travellers, were surrounded on all sides by Roman roads: in the north a traffic route linked three garrison-towns; in the west there was a well-guarded road, with a chain of sentry-posts, which ran from Lambaesis through the oases known today as El Kantara and Biskra, to the foothills; another Roman road ran along the southern slopes of the mountains; and in the year A.D. 145 the Emperor Antoninus Pius even built a military road in the mountains themselves, with well-supplied garrisons to guard it against raids. Robber bands had gathered so often in the Negrin oasis that Trajan decided to occupy it, and the military road he built for this purpose ran even farther south to the edge of the steppe country where Bir Mohammed Ben Yunis stands today and where the ruins of a Roman fort can still be seen.

The Franco-American Hoggar Expedition in the 1920s, on which Count Khun de Prorok completed his Carthaginian research, found clear indications that the road through Biskra into the Hoggar area —a stretch of more than 1,000 miles, starting from the Mediter- ranean coast—had already been in use in pre-Roman times. It was probably one of the routes by which the Phoenicians in the fifth century B.C. brought slaves, gold and hides from the interior of Africa. There must also have been a considerable flow of traffic in the opposite direction, for in the so-called grave of Tin Hinan (at Abelessa), which belongs to the fourth century B.C., chains with gold stars were found (of a kind which is quite common in the Punic graves of Carthage and Utica), as well as cornelian jewellery and amber beads, which had made the long journey from the Baltic to the North African desert—a striking testimony to the area covered by the Phoenician traders.

The Roman roads stretched across forty degrees of latitude, over the highest mountains, sometimes dead straight, sometimes in bold curves, and the Roman architects and generals even mastered the great rivers of Europe and Asia, although bridge-building (which we can only deal with cursorily) does not appear to have been the strong suit of these indefatigable road-builders. The masterpieces of the Roman engineers must be regarded as feats of strength rather than works of art, as roads thrown across rivers rather than bridges. The men who built them were not artists but brilliant tacticians, whose workmen were not skilled stone-masons or experienced builders but legionaries, who were all too often called upon to pick up their swords while they were busy felling trees or chiselling stones.

The most famous of these bridges is undoubtedly the one Caesar built in ten days for his first Rhine crossing: in this short time the entire building materials also had to be prepared and transported to the site. The account he himself gives in his report on the Gallic campaigns is interesting in several respects, but above all for the remark that it 'would have been beneath his dignity and that of the Roman people' to cross the Rhine by boat (as the riparian tribes had been doing for a long time). From this it is clear that the Romans felt they had a civilizing mission to fulfil, which, once the fighting was over, required them to build roads and bridges. Their building was done not merely for practical but for ethical reasons.

The style of the Rhine bridge is as simple as it is meaningful; it consisted of a centre-piece, which rested on sloping stakes and which carried the causeway, while further props were inserted at an even wider angle up-stream and down-stream to concentrate the force of the current still more on the mainstays. As a result, the current itself pressed the stakes deeper and deeper into the bed of the river instead of loosening them. Moreover, the struts up-stream served to stave off tree-trunks which the Huns threw into the Rhine in an attempt to damage the bridge.

We know that even at home the Romans showed an almost superstitious preference for wooden as against stone bridges, for a wooden bridge can be quickly and easily destroyed by fire. Caesar demolished his first Rhine bridge, when he returned to the left bank, probably with an eye to the powerful Suebian army, which had cast a spell over all the tribes on the Rhine. Caesar's second Rhine bridge, near Bonn, was also, at least partially, destroyed. A four-story tower was erected and a garrison of twelve cohorts remained behind to demolish the remainder of the bridge should the Huns attempt to invade Gaul.

From the constructional point of view the Emperor Trajan's Danube bridge, which spanned the great river near the town of Turnu-Severin, not far from the so-called Iron Gate, was more important. The site was chosen not merely for military purposes but also for transport in general, for beyond the gorge to the north of the Danube lay the fertile Wallachian plain, and the highway from Singidunum (Belgrade) ran to the south of the river. On the other hand, while this road remained on the south bank, the military road which ran northwards from Serdica (Sofia) and which joined up at Naissus (Nisch) with a route from Salonica, continued on the other side of the Danube in the form of strongly-fortified feeder-roads. These led on the one hand across the plain to Trajan's frontier-wall and to the river Alutus (Oltul) which had long marked the frontier, and, on the other hand, right into the heart of the Transylvanian mountains, from which the Romans extracted copper, gold and iron.

Trajan was undoubtedly the greatest bridge-builder among the Roman emperors; his bridges spanned not only the Danube but also the Tejo, the Tormes and other rivers. He owes his fame to his architect, Apollodorus of Damascus (whose Trajan columns are known to everyone who has visited Rome), who also built the Forum Trajanum (near the church of S. Maria di Loreto) and the splendid semicircular markets, which can still be reached from the Via IV Novembre.

Apollodorus also built the great Danube bridge for his beloved master, but, as his written account of the work has been lost, it is impossible to say with certainty whether the famous bridge was of

stone or, like Caesar's Rhine bridges, of wood. Dion Cassius (160–
c. 230), the Greek writer, did not actually see the bridge in course
of construction but he appears to have seen it later. He at least
throws some light on the piers, for he writes: 'There are twenty piers
of hewn stone; the height of these, not including the foundations,
amounts to a hundred and fifty feet [?], the width more than sixty
feet. The piers themselves are a hundred and seventy feet apart and
are joined together by arches. They were erected in the swirling
water and on the clayey soil, for the river could not be diverted
anywhere.'

From this contemporary account, the technical details of which
have aroused considerable scepticism in modern engineers, one at
least realizes how extremely difficult the whole enterprise must have
been. A bridge of this kind was not built to be demolished again;
it was a work that demanded every ounce of skill from even such a
brilliant architect, compelled him to improvise and forced him to
invent where previous experience was completely lacking. The piers
could only have been of stone, or, more precisely, of stones and
binding materials. To sink them in the river-bed, considerable digging had to be done without such things as divers, caissons, air-
pumps, etc., being available. The normal practice in ancient times
was to divert the river into a new, specially-dug bed, but here this
was not possible. Moreover, on the Danube at least, Trajan did not
have such unlimited manpower as the Pharaohs and the Babylonian
kings had at their disposal. So Apollodorus had enormous boxes
made, several hundred square metres in size and open top and
bottom. They were pressed down into the water until they rested on
the river-bed where the water flowed round them. Workers were then
able to go down and create a firm foundation on which the piers
could stand. One can imagine how often this laborious process had
to be repeated from the fact that, according to the remains that have
been found, the total length of the bridge was about 3,600 feet, while
the distance between the piers—115 to 125 feet—was unusual at that
period. Not all the twenty piers to which the contemporary writers
refer were anchored in the river-bed; a narrow flat island made the
work a great deal easier, although the width of the river at this point
(which has presumably remained more or less the same to this day)
is much greater than at the Iron Gate.

On these piers, however, a wooden construction or a wooden frame-
work filled with stones or cement may have rested. An oak beam
covered with mortar, which projected from the river-bed and was
therefore fairly easy to trace, suggests a mixture of stone and wood
throughout the construction. At all events, the Roman soldiers de-

picted on Trajan's column in Rome are seen to be engaged in a great variety of jobs while building the Danube bridge: some are felling enormous oaks in the Transylvanian mountains, others are breaking stones, while others again are digging in the river-bed, making bricks and building walls. Trajan had made peace with the Dacians, but obviously only in order to renew the war in more favourable conditions: in 101/102 he had three times defeated Decebalus, the Dacian king who in 103 submitted to the Emperor, but Trajan did not trust him and began at once building the great bridge which was completed by the end of that year. In 104 Trajan's army crossed it and marched northwards to Sarmizegetusa, Decebalus's capital, in what is today Transylvania. Defeated in the mountains at the very heart of his country, which until then had been regarded as impregnable, Decebalus committed suicide: Dacia became a Roman province. . . .

Trajan's finest bridge was built in his native country, Spain, but the largest and the most important was the one that gained Rome a whole province, at the other end of Europe in the Wallachian plain. Trajan was not the son of an emperor but only an adopted son of Nerva's, so—in accordance with Roman tradition—his successor Hadrian, who was himself Trajan's adopted son and eventually destroyed the Danube bridge, was not allowed to rest on his laurels. Hadrian is said to have destroyed the bridge without any military pretext, in other words without any threat of attack by the tribes in the north. However that may be, the bridge was certainly destroyed; Constantine the Great found only the piers remaining and built a new bridge on them.

The fate of Apollodorus of Damascus is also shrouded in mystery. He is believed to have criticized Hadrian's plans for the Venus and Roma temple in Rome and to have been banished and later even condemned to death by the hot-tempered and moody emperor.

Trajan and Hadrian were both great builders and wise rulers; Antoninus Pius, like Marcus Aurelius, may have had a less spectacular reign but he was certainly not lacking in wisdom. Although there were several outstanding achievements in road-building in the third century A.D., it was during the reigns of these four rulers that the Roman road system reached its peak, and its supreme virtue lay not so much in the area it covered as in the standard maintained on individual roads.

During this period, when the roads were actually the property of the empire and its peoples, most of the itineraries and guide-books appeared which, together with excavations, are the main source of information on the Roman roads. These guides were presumably

intended for envoys on missions abroad, and in later centuries new
editions appeared, in which (as the text was edited and expanded)
copyists' errors and false information crept in. The original routes
with the respective distances in Roman miles were, as far as one can
judge today, surprisingly accurate. To take only one example, the
Itinerarium Antonini Augusti for Britain gives no less than fifteen
routes. Each one has its own heading, as in a modern motoring
guide (e.g. Iter a vallo ad portam Ritupis=from the frontier wall
to Richborough Port) and the total mileage is given, with the individual staging-points and distances below. Another itinerarium from
the year 333 describes the route from Bordeaux to Jerusalem and
back, touching on Milan and Rome and giving a detailed account
of the holy places.

Apart from these written itineraries, which listed up to 3,000
stations on some 300 roads, there were also road maps or, to be
exact, sketches of routes in the form of graphs. A copy of one of
these, which seems originally to have been the work of a cartographer
named Castorius, has survived and has become known as the Tabula
Peutingeriana (Peutingerian Table). Its eleven pages are stuck together in the copy to make a single long sheet which shows military
and trade routes as far as the eastern limits of the known world and
gives three and a half thousand names of stations in neat calligraphy.
The rivers too are marked, though in a somewhat comic, almost
childish perspective, and villages or towns are represented, as in
some modern relief-maps, by characteristic buildings.

The century in which Castorius recorded for the last time in his
maps the impressive expanse of the Roman road-system was the
last century of an undivided Roman Empire; on August 24th 410,
Alaric conquered Rome and allowed his soldiers to plunder the city.
It is a regrettable fact that neither the Picts nor the Saxons, neither
the Vandals nor the Goths really knew what to do with the Roman
roads. They made no attempt to maintain the roads which now
belonged to them and could have been of great use to them. So a
rapid process of deterioration set in throughout the known world;
this was in its way as monstrous as the original work of construction
had been momentous.

The first to fall into decay were the wooden bridges, which were
never repaired, and the roads suffered accordingly, for the rivers had
once more to be forded and, apart from one or two exceptions
(Zeugma on the Euphrates and a few Roman towns in Germany),
the fords were some distance away from the Roman roads. In the
wooded areas trees fell on the roads and were left lying, and no
attempt was made to repair the damage done by flood-water, so that

the Roman flagstones subsided and even pedestrians found the going difficult. Traffic on the short stretches which were still usable was confined to local transport—peasants' carts on their way to market —but soon they too were reduced to mere piles of stones which were fair booty for anyone who cared to remove them. Near the towns they disappeared completely, while in the country they were used to mark the boundaries between fields and private estates.

Today that gigantic network of roads, which could have stretched twice round the equator, has almost disappeared; but the modern road-builder is constantly stumbling on remains in the most remote areas. When the Grossglockner road was built in the Austrian Alps, fragments of a Roman road were found more than 6,300 feet up, and, since air-photography came to be used by the archaeologist, one can see the clear lines of these ancient roads, as if they had been drawn in the grass by some ghostly hand, for in dry weather the grass over the stones withers, exposing the road beneath.

Chapter 10

FOURTEEN HUNDRED DECADENT YEARS

The core of Europe's traffic-system was, and still is, the area between Scandinavia and the Alps, between the Rhine and the Vistula. Yet it was precisely in this area that the Roman network was at its thinnest.

The Danube formed a secure frontier. It had been crossed by the Romans only in its upper reaches west of Regensburg. The frontier-wall, or 'limes', turned northwards between the rivers Kocher and Neckar, but immediately to the north of the river Main it turned westwards again towards the Rhine. About the beginning of the Christian era the Romans made several astonishingly daring sorties through the great forests between the Rhine and the Elbe, but, as the Germanic tribes put up a fierce resistance, the Romans had to content themselves with holding the Rhine and the 'limes' and to abandon all idea of extending their fine roads into the territory of these ferocious tribes.

The ancient traffic routes—the Rhine, the Danube, and even a few Alpine passes—were already in use in pre-Roman times. Such improvements as the Romans made to the general traffic situation were sporadic; their chief concern was to link up their Alpine roads with the main trade routes in the German provinces, as, for example, at Augsburg and Salzburg. For centuries the inhabitants of Germania had been using a few rough tracks from the coasts of the North Sea and the Baltic to the Danube, and from the estuary of the Elbe and Trave to the middle Rhine. Roads as such did not exist, for, like the Anglo-Saxons, they seemed almost to have an aversion to them. They had certainly little use for them. Unlike the Romans and other Mediterranean peoples, they had no towns; they lived in small villages and their modest wants were quite adequately met by a few itinerant traders. Anything more spacious than those beaten tracks would merely invite an invading army. . . .

This is all very far removed from the sacred roads of Greece or the much-honoured art of road-building under the aegis of some Roman senator or emperor. The Greeks and Romans considered it an honour to be buried by the roadside, and the Empress Nitokris was even laid to rest over a gateway! The crossroads, where the Greeks erected altars to Theseus and the god of travellers, Apollo, was an accursed place to the Germanic peoples. It was here that they set up their gallows, that men were tempted by the devil, and that suicides were buried.

Roads between villages, and above all between the villages and the fields, were just as wide as was absolutely necessary—and no wider. In the Middle Ages a church path had to be sufficiently wide 'to let a man pass with a dead corpse on a cart'. But an even more frequent wayfarer was the 'knight in full armour carrying a spear crosswise'; even in this awkward position, he had right of way, and if his spear touched a house it was liable to be demolished.

Many such regulations were in force throughout Germany. In some places the road had to be as wide as three horses abreast, in others there had to be enough room for a peasant woman to walk beside a cart without dirtying her cloak. How strictly these rules and regulations were applied depended, in the last resort, on those who owned or tilled the land along the roadside, and their attitude in turn depended on the landed gentry, the local nobility or the relevant prince.

In the Rhine district and in Flanders the situation was comparatively good, because, thanks to the temperate climate, the Roman roads could be kept in a reasonable state of repair for several centuries. The most extensive improvements on these roads were carried out by the Duchess Brunehilde of Flanders, and there is many a long, straight road on medieval maps, and even later, which is called a Brunehilde road. In Germany itself, however, the picture was a very different one. Road-building was given particular impetus under Charlemagne, for whom, as for all rulers of large empires, good lines of communication were vital. Wherever possible he restored the Roman roads, and he created the first east–west roads which could be used all the year round and which linked up with the main rivers.

His plan for a Main–Danube canal (of which all that remains today
is the so-called 'Fossa Carolina') shows how concerned Charlemagne
was with traffic problems in central Europe. But it also shows how
even in the ninth century the natural roads were superior to the man-
made roads, and how they re-emerged after the Romans had completed their magnificent network of roads.

The island in the river Main at Frankfurt soon proved to be more
important than the great Roman road on which Mainz lay; Vienna
arose from a small fort at the gateway to the Alps, while Carmuntum
on the Roman amber road was declining. The German roads bore
names which reflected their natural origins (in contrast to the Roman
roads which for centuries were named after their builders): the Wine
Road ran from the lower Main to the Taurus mountains, the Kinzig
Road to northern Thuringia, the Nidder (or Lower) Road to Fulda,
and the important High Road straight across Saxony to Silesia. As
early as the year 900 merchants were travelling by this road from
Kiev to Frankfurt, and shortly afterwards traders from Kiev and
Novgorod were visiting Vienna. The crusaders followed the Danube
down-stream through Hungary, which had just become a Christian
country, while the Knights of the Teutonic Order started out from
Vienna towards the north-east, where they founded their own State
on the Don and the Vistula. On ancient tracks which had been used
for thousands of years salt was transported to Germany from the
mines at Hallein and Reichenhall. The Isar was usually crossed at
Föhring, till Henry the Lion quarrelled with the Bishop of Freising
and destroyed the bridge; a new crossing was provided a short distance up-river, where the monks of Tegernsee had some property.
Within two years—in 1158—the settlement at the new crossing had
become so prosperous that Duke Henry set up a mint and a town
began to emerge from the salt trade—it became known as Munich.
This is a particularly striking example of the influence of roads on
town development, which began, in this case, with a concentration of
vehicles waiting to cross a river and ended with the establishment of
an important centre of communications.

Even more striking is the example of Nürnberg. Not much older
than Munich (the first recorded reference to it was in 1050), its
emergence as a key trading centre was also due to the increasing
importance of road traffic and of trade between the various parts
of Germany.

As the centuries passed, individual village communities became
less and less isolated. The monasteries maintained regular contact
with each other and, even under the weaker of Charlemagne's successors, prevented heathen princelings from laying their hands on

large areas of the country which lay between the natural highways. No peasant enjoyed meeting one of the monastery's bailiffs and paying his road tax, but in return he knew that he could make his way to market without undergoing any more serious risks. The king's highways acquired a special significance of their own; they were virtually extraterritorial and particular care was taken to see that foreign travellers were confined as far as possible to these roads, on which they caught only fleeting glimpses of local life or people. The road was still regarded as a thing apart from local interests and local life, but it was no longer scorned and neglected; on the contrary, it was the visible symbol of royal power, for the king had every reason to keep his military roads outside the jurisdiction of his nobles.

The roads themselves benefited very little by their privileged position. The princes and bishops were, in fact, better situated to maintain the local roads than a king or emperor, who was constantly on the move, all too frequently in Italy and sometimes even in the Holy Land. In 1235, at the Reichstag in Mainz, the Emperor Frederick II promulgated his famous 'Landfriedensgesetz' (Peace Law), which was the first in the Holy Roman Empire to be issued in German. It was an attempt to link road-tolls with road maintenance: whoever collected the toll was to be responsible for maintaining the road, and anyone who levied an illicit toll was to be treated as a highwayman. The obligation to use specific roads was abolished.

Although this all sounds very progressive, the last provision in particular proved quite impracticable. Local road laws carried much more authority than imperial decrees, and they stipulated that vehicles must continue to travel on certain roads and must not attempt to evade those points where tolls were levied. If anything, merchants were even more strictly controlled: they were obliged to offer their wares at their local town before going elsewhere, and if they used the main highway they had to display their goods for sale for three days in any village or town with a recognized market. Some towns, like Cologne, would allow pilgrims or apprentices to pass through but never merchants. On the 7th of May 1259, Archbishop Konrad of Cologne issued a decree: 'Any merchants attempting to pass through Cologne on their way from Hungary, Bohemia, Poland, Bavaria, Suabia, Saxony, Thuringia and Hesse or from Flanders, Brabant and the other Low Countries . . . can be taken into custody by any citizen of Cologne who catches him . . . and punished according to an old custom known to the people as "hausen". . . .'

There was no danger to life or limb, but a substantial fine was involved. The German Hansa towns exercised many such prerogatives, which had a far-reaching influence on trading not only by sea but also by road.

While the ordinary citizen, who was inured to the guild system, was inclined to accept these customs without grumbling, the nobility regarded them as impositions by the shopkeepers whom they despised, and made a point of ignoring any local regulations governing markets, boundaries and roads. The economic history of the Middle Ages in Germany is full of angry protests by the towns, which were constantly complaining to the princes and bishops.

Frederick II undoubtedly had good reason to condemn abuses on the roads as tantamount to highway robbery; it would have been difficult otherwise to check the arrogance of the nobility, who considered it almost an act of chivalry to rob the shopkeepers. It was, however, not merely impoverished noblemen but also simple wayfarers, deserters from the army, or unemployed labourers who made the roads unsafe throughout Germany. Many a tragic story is told in the unpolished yet strangely moving language of the contemporary records. There was, for example, the case of the merchant Mattes Krafft, who invested everything he had in purchases for the Polish court, only to be robbed in 1510 near Bunzlau. 'Mattes Krafft was thereby made a poor man', wrote his burgomaster in a report to the relevant authority, but whether the unfortunate man received any redress is not known.

The few newspapers that appeared in the sixteenth and seventeenth centuries reported only the most sensational robberies and it is clear that the population had grown more or less resigned to highwaymen and stray bandits as unavoidable evils.

In 1732 the *Vossische Zeitung* reported from Cölln (Berlin).

> A band of five to six hundred robbers are making the flat country around the town very unsafe and causing great damage; a number of troops have been sent out against them and in the past few days some have already been captured and brought into Brüel.

Robbery must have been profitable, however, for the number of recruits increased. There were even reports of women wearing trousers, carrying pistols and competing with the men. As late as the end of the eighteenth century a band of robbers two hundred strong crossed the Rhine from Belgium and settled in the Westerwald. But the *Vossische Zeitung* gave an account of an incident in Europe in 1797 which reads like a romantic melodrama:

> One evening a nun arrives at an inn and begs for shelter for the night, for, as she has no money, she has nowhere else to go.

The innkeeper, moved by her sad plight, shows her to one of his own rooms and provides her with light. Shortly afterwards a group of Frenchmen who have been lodging at the inn return from the town, notice a light burning in the room and inquire after the newcomer. One of them, overcome by curiosity, decides to visit the nun and goes up to her room, but, when he tries to engage her in conversation, she dismisses him curtly and continues to read from a prayer book lying in front of her. He leaves her and tells the innkeeper that he cannot believe she is a nun. The innkeeper refuses to entertain such a suspicion, but the Frenchman hurries back to the room, finds some pretext to come near her, uncovers her bosom and finds there two pistols and a small whistle. He holds the struggling nun fast and calls the innkeeper, who is not a little astonished to find dressed in the habit of a nun a sturdy fellow with such suspicious instruments and at once has him arrested. About midnight the Frenchman climbs to the roof of the house and whistles with the small whistle he had taken from the nun. It is not long before twenty-six men are swarming into the court-yard. But twenty soldiers who have previously concealed themselves opened fire on them, brought down most of them and carried the others off to Cologne.

At least one moral of this story appears to be that the French were highly experienced in the ways of robbers. . . .

To have sacrificed Germany's forests—as the English sacrificed theirs—in order to keep highway robbery within bounds would have been both pointless and fruitless, for the German forests were much vaster and denser than those in England, few of which survived the nineteenth century. Deforestation on the same lines as in England and France was, therefore, extremely rare. A more serious threat to Germany's forests was the practice of repairing roads not with stones or gravel but with wooden beams and branches. For some five hundred years this wasteful practice continued, despite the fact that wood was clearly not strong enough to carry heavy vehicles. In the year 1571 such a deep hole had been worn in the road from Marburg to Frankfurt that three wine-carts in succession came to grief in it, and a farm labourer even lost his life in the quagmire that had formed at the bottom of it. The official in charge of the road gave orders for the hole to be filled with five hundred bundles of brushwood, reinforced with stones.

In 1665, during the war with Holland, Bernhard von Galen, Bishop of Münster, had a road built across the Bortanger Moor, which consisted not only of brushwood but also of window-frames and doors, which the warlike bishop's well-trained army collected from the surrounding villages. This road, which was about four miles long, was wide enough for three mounted men or five foot-soldiers to march abreast.

It was not until the middle of the seventeenth century, following the appalling havoc wrought by the Thirty Years War, that the impoverished Germans began to appreciate the value of their timber, and in 1651 Duke Christian Ludwig von Braunschweig issued a decree for the protection of his forests, which set an example that was soon followed in other parts of Germany.

It is hardly surprising in the circumstances that people were reluctant—and more particularly women—to undertake long journeys in the sixteenth century. In countless letters, Mothers Superior and other ladies (both spiritual and worldly) complain that they cannot visit their friends because the roads are so bad and so unsafe; even such a powerful individual as Archbishop Peter of Mainz, Archchancellor of the Holy Roman Empire, had to apologize in a letter to the Archbishop of Bremen for failing to keep an appointment: the roads were too unsafe and a sufficiently strong escort was too expensive. Yet conditions in Germany were no worse than elsewhere, as we know from accounts given by foreigner travellers. Monsieur Michel de Montaigne, who was by no means uncritical, was favourably impressed by almost everything he saw in Germany in 1580 (although his travels were confined to the southern part). He found that the inns were not cheap, but they were extremely clean. Travellers were well received and treated in accordance with their station (the City Council of Augsburg sent Montaigne and his companion fourteen flagons of wine!), the food was excellent and plentiful, and Montaigne was particularly impressed by the panelled walls and the gleaming pewter plates. His only complaint was of the women. 'Among the women we saw not one was beautiful,' he remarked once, and the following day he made this entry in his journal: 'On Monday in the Liebfrauenkirche we attended the splendid wedding of the rich and ugly daughter of a local citizen with a manager of the firm of Fugger in Venice. We did not see a single beautiful woman.' The road across the Brenner Pass, however, brought an even more serious complaint; Montaigne suffered from a congestion of the kidneys and took to riding horseback.

This was apparently the only way to cope with the bad roads. Even for women, riding was the customary form of travel until well into the seventeenth century, and Duke Julius of Brunswick (1528–1589) made great fun of anyone who chose to have his bones rattled in a carriage. The bridle-paths, which ran for long stretches alongside the Roman roads, were often in much better condition than the roads themselves.

Germany's bridges were not much better than her roads. The skill and artistry of the Romans had long since been forgotten and their bridges for the most part destroyed. A wooden bridge which was built across the Rhine at Mainz in the Carolingian period only lasted a year. Naturally there were many places, particularly on smaller streams, where the Roman bridges survived; at other points, where the building of a bridge was a fairly simple matter, new bridges were constantly being erected when the old ones were demolished during the all too frequent wars. The wooden bridges at Regensburg, Passau, Coblenz, Meissen and other places were greatly admired. But the fact remains that until well into the fifteenth century the most popular method of crossing a river was by ford. Ferries were also in regular use and were subject to innumerable rules and regulations, the most common being that if there was a threat of invasion, the inhabitants of the nearest village or town took precedence over strangers. If a fugitive and his pursuer were in the same ferry, then the ferryman must stand between them—the fugitive in the bows, the pursuer in the stern—for a ferry gave the same right of asylum as the roads of ancient Greece.

The German Romantic poets and writers are the last sources to draw on for descriptions of the roads; any dry, matter-of-fact merchant who had rumbled his way across Germany by coach could have given a more accurate picture of the roads, the tolls and the inns. But at least the Romantics have provided us with valuable evidence how people at that time reacted to road travel.

From Ludwig Tieck (1773–1853) we can guess why the general public of his time showed so little interest in the condition of their roads. Travelling as a young man into the Fichtel mountains, he was so absorbed in the beauties of the landscape that he made only one observation on the road itself: 'It is four miles from Erlangen to Streitberg . . . but how very different from the road between Berlin and Potsdam, where one yawns and falls asleep and sees only sand and small firs and Prussian coats of arms.' The highway from Berlin to Potsdam was undoubtedly much better than the road from Erlangen to Streitberg, but that did not worry him unduly. As a true Romantic he had his own image of reality complete in his mind before he set out. That is why in another passage he could again paint a most improbable picture: 'In Ebermannstadt everyone was very friendly, particularly the women, who in the Catholic part are almost all blonde with blue eyes and a certain warm Madonna-like expression; almost all the men have black hair and look like Peter and Judas in the Old Masters. . . .'

Ernst Theodor Amadeus Hoffmann (died 1822), the great *fantaisiste* in German literature, appears on the other hand to have been a highly introvert traveller who actually saw the roads in terms of symphonies. Opportunities for such flights of fancy were all too frequent. Wherever the road was too bad or too steep, the romantic travellers were only too happy to climb down and have an opportunity of breathing in their beloved Nature.

Even to the Romantics, however, travel could be an unpleasant experience. In November, 1809, Joseph Freiherr von Eichendorff ventured on a journey to Berlin. The fact that he started out on the Oder shows how frequently even passengers chose the slow riverboats. But they had barely been a quarter of an hour under way when the boat ran on to a sandbank and, after three days packed with similar incidents and a great deal of physical discomfort, Eichendorff and his friends decided to try the much-despised public highway. They found a country inn where they could spend the night and catch the stage-coach in the morning:

> [We] consumed that night an enormous dish of vegetables and eggs, conversed with the entire family over a pipe of tobacco round the stove . . . and finally about eight o'clock stretched out on the straw, on which we spent a dreadful, sleepless night. For to begin with we were wakened by the discordant singing of Protestant hymns at the family's evening service (the innkeeper's wife in her nightdress) and the children spent the rest of the night crying.
>
> 19. 11 [1809]: After cats, a whole family of hens, etc., had walked over me, I arose a little refreshed and towards 9 o'clock we set off. No sooner had we reached the village than we had to cross the Oder, from where we caught the last glimpse of our boats plunged in the unfathomable solitude of a snow-driven bay near by. It was a strange crossing. Two small boats were lashed together and first the horses, then the carriage and ourselves were rowed over on planks laid across the boats . . . Some time after seven in the evening, in bright moonlight, we finally arrived at Frankfurt-an-der-Oder, half dead from frost, hunger, thirst and bruised ribs, and put up at the good Golden Lion inn just outside the town. Here we amused ourselves somewhat . . . and for the first time for almost fourteen days we undressed and went to bed.

At the end of this unhappy journey (which seems, however, to have been nothing unusual) Eichendorff and his friends reached the outskirts of Berlin only to be confronted by a drunken toll-inspector who could not stand up, so all the baggage had to be carried indoors where he could go through it sitting down. . . .

Incidents of this kind were all too common, but travellers at that time appear to have been remarkably long-suffering and resilient. On a journey through Bohemia, Eichendorff had this to report:

> Immediately behind the town [Iglau] we had to make a daring leap out of the coach to escape almost certain damage to life and limb. A sad, monotonous, stony country, and a shameful road. In this way we swayed, staggered and crashed through an endless series of shabby little towns, which for me at least are wretched beyond description, till we crossed the Bohemian border. But this truly diabolical road so disarranged our post-chaise, that we had to have it caulked in a Bohemian town.

Just short of Linz a wheel broke and Eichendorff had to enter the town on foot. But as usual his spirits are quickly revived: here by the inn, there by the theatre, in a third town by a pretty innkeeper's wife. The road was simply an unavoidable evil—there was no alternative. . . .

The Romantics have also invested the postilion with a certain glamour; his contemporaries called him simply 'brother-in-law' and were not nearly so enamoured of him as the poets would have us believe. In fact, the sound of his horn must have got on many a traveller's nerves.

Ever since 1616 a German postal regulation had required the 'brother-in-law' to blow his horn continuously from the city gate to the post-station. A further regulation in 1812 obliged the postilion to 'blow industriously and well'.

> Anyone who does not possess a breast of iron, innards of copper and a posterior of platina would be well advised not to travel by the so-called ordinary stage-coach, for it is nothing if not ordinary.
>
> The old box rests immediately on the axis, and the seats are so hard they remind one of English steel; made-up roads are only to be found near the capital and if one travels by the ordinary stage-coach on the other lamentable roads in the country, one runs a grave risk of breaking a few ribs.
>
> Anyone who does not have a carriage of his own will not fare much better with a post-chaise; for the vehicles into which one is frequently bundled are exactly like penitents' carts.
>
> The ordinary stage-coach moves forward indescribably slowly, one has to wait hours at each stage, and I have personally had the experience of travelling a bare eight miles in

twenty-four hours. None the less the postal system is said to
have improved enormously under its present chief, the old and
revered Seegebart; in what sort of condition must it have been
before!

This question which Adolph von Schaden posed in his *Lighter
and Darker Sides of Berlin* a century and a quarter ago was highly
relevant to the fate of Germany's roads. As long as road traffic was
a more or less private concern, and drivers and merchants had to
make the best of it, then bad roads were inevitable. Officers and
nobles rode, while the rulers on their rare journeys seldom travelled
over dangerous stretches of road. With the introduction of a postal
system, however, of regular lines of communication on the Persian,
Roman and Mongolian patterns, Germany too began to take an
interest in improving her roads.

The history of the German postal system is linked from the outset with the Taxis family, who came originally from Bergamo. In
1504 a certain Franz von Taxis entered into an engagement with
Philippe Le Bel of France to maintain a regular postal service between the court of Maximilian I, the Low Countries, and the royal
court of France; the Spanish court was also to be associated with this
new system. In 1516 it was extended to cover Rome and Naples, and
the first postal service from Brussels to Italy by way of Vienna had
special branches to Paris, southern France, Nürnberg, Frankfurt,
Schaffhausen, Hamburg and other towns. To begin with, a coach
travelled on these lines once a fortnight, and only court officials or
travellers on imperial business were allowed to use it. But before
long a weekly service was introduced and the range of passengers
was widened. For a distance of six hundred miles the stage-coach
took seven to ten days (previously it had taken about forty days!).

Frederick William, the Great Elector (1640–88), was able to
benefit by the experience of others when he introduced the Prussian
State postal service. In his time the main line ran from Kleve right
through northern Germany to Memel. At every stage the travellers
had to change, for it was not until the eighteenth century that
coaches were introduced which could cover several stages. Even as
late as 1820 the journey from Frankfurt to Stuttgart took thirty
hours and the stops totalled more than ten hours. From Berlin to
Hamburg, which takes about three hours today, then took thirty-
six, not including the time spent in overnight stops.

Despite the wide publicity that was given in Goethe's time by
authors and letter-writers to the lamentable state of the postal service and the roads, improved methods of road-building, which had

been especially developed in France, made little progress in Germany. The division of the country into small States made any large-scale development virtually impossible. So it was in Austria that the first moves were made towards better roads, for at that time Austria was a relatively large country with a well-developed economy.

Charles VI (1711–40) built highways with a foundation of stones in the first half of the eighteenth century. The gaps between the stones were filled with slack, then came a layer of broken stones and a top-surface of metal. When Silesia became part of Prussia, Maria Theresa built a long cattle road from Cracow through Moravia to Bohemia for the migration of Polish cattle (similar to the Danish-North German road from Viborg to Hamburg, on which in 1611, for example, no less than 52,000 head of cattle were driven to Germany).

In Germany, as in England and France, the first improvements came in the towns, where more and more regulations were introduced to make the streets cleaner: for example, the dumping of refuse in the lanes was forbidden. Street-lighting spread throughout Europe: Paris had the first street-lamps in 1658, London in 1668, Amsterdam 1669, Berlin 1679, Vienna 1687, Frankfurt 1707. In 1814 gas-light was introduced in London, and by 1882 Berlin had its first electric light. Johann Friedrich Reichardt, author of books on music and travel, wrote in 1809 in his *Confidential Letters* that Vienna was the city with the finest paved streets, 'which are most scrupulously maintained and great effort and care is taken to keep them comfortable and clean throughout the year. A large number of men and vehicles are employed year in, year out, often day and night, in sweeping and cleaning, in removing all refuse and in watering the streets and promenades. The city and its main suburbs are abundantly and completely illuminated by many thousands of lamps ... constantly throughout the year, even by moonlight.'

Vienna, on the other hand, was a royal capital which was just entering on the most brilliant period in its history; the rest of the country had to wait some time before its streets and roads were given the same attention. The public highway was still the poor relation on whom economies always fell when money had to be saved. In 1728 the newspaper *Hamburgische Korrespondent* gave a revealing account of a visit by the Emperor to the Semmering Pass, where the road had apparently been improved:

Vienna, June 30. On his journey over the Semmering mountain, which hitherto could only be crossed by a strong team of oxen and in bad weather was almost impassable, His Illus-

trious Imperial Majesty expressed his deep satisfaction with
the new road, which now enables vehicles with two horses to
pass in comfort, and was graciously pleased to reward the
workers, who completed the road in the short space of forty-
eight days, during which time they really worked at it. [!]

For centuries innumerable merchants had been obliged to hire
special teams of oxen in order to cross, with immense hardship and
at great risk, what was the only Alpine pass before the Brenner: in
the Middle Ages vehicles could only cross the Col di Tenda, the
Brenner and the Semmering. Yet forty-eight days were sufficient
to lay a comfortable road for ordinary vehicles to use. This fact in
itself is a sad reflection of the interest shown by so-called gracious
and illustrious monarchs in roads and public transport.

As even Napoleon built only two roads in Germany—one from
Metz to Mainz, the other from Wesel to Hamburg—constructive
proposals for improving the general situation had to come from the
road-users themselves. As in England and France, it was the road-
builders who finally took up their pens in sheer desperation and
tried to arouse the interest of the general public in something that
immediately concerned them. For, particularly in an industrious
country like Germany, the state of the roads was in blatant contrast
to the country's economic development. Ever since the Crusades
German merchants had played a leading part in Europe's trade. The
Fuggers had branches in Lisbon, Cairo and Seville, and the Welsers
sent special expeditions to Venezuela. Yet in Germany itself merchandise could be confiscated merely if it happened to touch the
ground, and on one occasion at Höchstätt a whole ship's cargo from
Regensburg was seized merely because one cask dropped into the
water. . . .

In addition to these hazards, the lamentable political situation in
Germany compelled vehicles to cross one frontier after another, and
by no means all of these were land frontiers, for every so-called
convoy stage had its barrier at which road-tolls had to be paid. In
nineteenth-century Saxony, for example, there were more not less of
these toll-gates than there had been three hundred years before.
Drivers sought detours when the weather permitted, but none became a permanent highway.

The main difficulty in publicizing this appalling problem was that
for a thousand years the Germans had treated their roads with con-
tempt. Anything that aroused disgust was thrown on to the road. If
Montaigne on his journey through southern Germany was struck by
the large number of pest-houses, the explanation was quite simple:
they were not only kept well clear of the towns, they were even

erected, where possible, at road-junctions, so that the unfortunate inmates—cripples, lunatics and lepers—could make a living from the travellers! On the left bank of the Rhine between Mainz and Kranenburg—a distance of 180 miles—there were no less than thirty of these pest-houses. Not surprisingly, the roads became hot-beds of infection. Plague control also interfered with traffic and sometimes brought it to a complete standstill. In the eighteenth and nineteenth centuries, for instance, so-called 'Kontumazhaüser' (pest-houses) were set up, mainly on the roads leading to the Balkans, and in many places the roads were patrolled by hussars, who rode up and down with drawn swords turning travellers and vehicles away from the towns!

Another prejudice that had to be overcome was the general assumption that time was unimportant and that nothing would be lost by arriving a few days later. However much one may deplore the pace of modern life, the extremely leisurely approach did not stimulate any demand for better roads or faster and smoother travel. If an official was required by his sovereign to travel by express coach, he regarded it as a sign of disfavour. Precedence on the roads was given on grounds not of urgency but of social status. The ultimate criterion was the Almanack de Gotha. . . .

To the merchant, however, time was still money and it was this class of society—together with more far-sighted military circles—which gained a wide hearing for the complaints of the civil engineers.

The outstanding figure at this decisive stage was Christian Friedrich von Lüder, whose name is still associated with his plan for a national network of roads. But Lüder was not only a prophet, he was also brilliantly methodical. His main work actually gave a 'complete survey of all problems arising from road-building' (1779). At the same time he was the author of several anonymous polemical pamphlets, in which he particularly criticized civil engineers for their lack of training and skill—most of them only had experience in building fortifications and knew nothing about the special problems of road- or bridge-building.

Not only engineers, however, but also skilled workers were in short supply. In Prussia and Austria, the largest German States, general conscription had not yet been introduced, but, on the other hand, those who joined the army remained in it for virtually the rest of their lives. And it was the working class that provided the recruits —precisely the class which would otherwise have supplied skilled labour for the roads. In Bavaria and Austria soldiers were used for this purpose, but this was an emergency measure which did not greatly contribute to the quality of the roads. The employment of

forced labour (which the Emperor Joseph I, for example, reintro-
duced in Galicia) and of prisoners also failed to produce the kind of
results one could expect from specially trained workers.

A new awareness came with the economic crisis which hit almost
all countries in Europe after the Napoleonic wars. It became a question of sheer necessity to improve communications between the
various centres of production; Europe could no longer afford, for
instance, to allow the surplus agricultural production in eastern
Austria-Hungary to remain isolated for want of proper roads. In
spite of its very considerable size, Austria in 1816 had only 5,500
miles of made-up roads; within twenty years the figure had risen
by 50 per cent, but by present-day standards it was still absurdly
low. The Bavarian engineer Wiebeking (who bore the strange title
of 'Head of the Secret Canal- Water- and Roadbuilding Office)
built about 120 miles of new highways and another 3,000 miles of
old roads were improved. In Brandenburg the first metal road, from
Magdeburg to Leipzig, was laid in 1789, to be followed in 1794 by
the first of the so-called State roads from Berlin to Potsdam.

In East and West Prussia up to 1830 there was nothing that could
be described as a public highway; road-building only began there
when the first railways were already running in England. The same
was true of Saxony, where a series of spendthrift kings had emptied
the State coffers, and of Mecklenburg, where an English company
began laying the first road in 1821.

In Switzerland modern road-building only started in 1836 with the
South Tyrolean engineer, Alois von Negrelli, who later became
famous through his association with the Suez Canal and who was
responsible for the important road-system from Altstätten over the
Ruppen to St. Gallen. He followed an ancient trade route and
spanned the Trogener Tobel with a bridge 180 feet high. Among
Negrelli's later works in Switzerland, the road from Teuffen to St.
Gallen is particularly worth mentioning because its steepest gradient
was 4 in 100. His road from Wil along the river Thur through Wild-
haus to the Rhine was still cited a century after it was built as a
masterpiece of road-making.[1]

A race had begun between those who were determined to save
the roads from extinction and those who were captivated by the
shrill whistle of The Rocket, the first locomotive in regular service,
which attained a speed that was clearly far beyond the capacity of
any road vehicle. Wiebeking, Lüder, Negrelli and others championed
the road, although they undoubtedly realized the enormous poten-

[1] See Birk, who, apart from his book *Die Strasse*, has also written a special
monograph on Negrelli.

tialities of the railway; Friedrich List (1789–1846), the great exponent of a united Germany, was one of those who favoured steam.

The outcome of the contest between rail and road was not a foregone conclusion: the Roman road had already emerged victorious from the challenge of the Greek and Illyrian groove-roads. Moreover, the few railway lines that were laid in the nineteenth century would not by themselves have influenced the fate of the roads. The conflict lay not between lines of communication, but between rival types of conveyance. And the decisive moment was reached in 1834, when, following the introduction of short railway services between Nürnberg and Fürth and Berlin–Potsdam, two cities—Leipzig and Dresden—were linked by rail.

The situation to the east and south of Europe was no better than in the heart of the continent itself. Russia's roads suffered from the almost insuperable competition of the long waterways, which in such a vast country were clearly much more economical than overland routes on which, by medieval standards, a single journey could take months. Travelling by boat was more comfortable, inns with all their hazards could be dispensed with, and the danger of physical injury—which was all too frequent in a stage-coach—no longer existed. During his travels Peter the Great became familiar with Holland's waterways and canals, and when he returned home he linked up the great rivers—and to some extent the lakes—with a number of canals, thereby creating a fairly efficient transport system. As the Russians enjoyed this form of travel, in any case, it did not occur to them to improve their roads.

Catherine II, the restless Czarina from the German princely house of Anhalt-Zerbst, was the first to take an interest in roads—partly under the influence of certain members of her court, partly because she was impressed by what had been done in France. The target she set herself, however, was too ambitious for her time: the Siberian military road, which was begun in 1781, was to run from St. Petersburg via Moscow to Perm, then on to Tobolsk and Irkutsk, the remote Cossack settlement which lies on Lake Baikal near the Chinese frontier. Technically, this immense project was perfectly feasible, for only a few years later Napoleon built his famous Alpine roads, which raised much more difficult problems. But on a purely administrative level, to say nothing of the tremendous material obstacles to be overcome, Catherine's plan was impracticable, and Siberia remained more or less virgin territory until it was invaded by the railway.

On the other hand, some of the old Russian trade routes (which had been in use for many centuries) played quite an important part in the country's economy: the fur roads and the tea road.

Many Russian towns grew rich on the fur trade, particularly the great Hansa town of Novgorod, which lies on both banks of the river Volchov and was also within reach of the sea by way of Lake Ilmen. As early as the twelfth century merchants from Germany and Gotland had permanent branches there, and even before that, from the ninth century onwards, Greek and Arab traders came in from the south. They did not come in summer, as one might have supposed, but towards the end of the winter, when the nights were growing shorter, in dog-drawn sleighs. The country was flat and the marshes were still frozen, so travelling by sleigh was much more comfortable than by coach. While the Germans and the Swedes were able to bring linen, metal goods, lead, sulphur, wine, and later on ammunition by ship, which they traded against Russian furs, leather, eiderdown and hemp, the Arabs in their small sledges had to manage, for the most part, without barter-trade and pay in cash. This explains some of the surprisingly large deposits of Arab coins found in Russia and round the Baltic Sea (many of which, however, may have been left by the Normans on their raiding expeditions).

This trade route, seen geographically, suggests a feeler which the Pontine world or Black Sea area put out to the north and north-east. Its first port of call was the famous and mysterious town of Bolgar, which reputable scholars like Alexander von Humboldt (1769–1859) and Christian Gottfried Ehrenberg explored. It lay in southern Russia on the right bank of the Volga near the influx of the river Kama, which the fur traders followed to reach the hunting country near the Urals. Trade with Bolgar appears to have started in pre-Christian times—at least there are references in Herodotus to suggest this, and Hellenistic relics of various kinds have been found—and to have continued up to the fourteenth century after the Mongol invasions. In the eleventh century the Arabs had already pushed northwards beyond Bolgar, reached the town of Cherdyn, and even crossed the Yekaterinburg Pass in the Urals as far as the Siberian fur country of Pechova.

Bolgar, which at one time was the capital of an independent State, certainly survived longer than the old town of Perm. Today, not far from the village of Bolgary, one can see what remains of the walls of the old commercial town, and countless gravestones covered with Arabic, Armenian and Tartar inscriptions. There are in fact quite a few indications that Bolgar was not merely a trading centre but also an Arab colony on Russian soil. In the tenth century, a ruler of Bolgar by the name of Almus wrote a letter to the Caliph Mulchtadir, in which he asked not only for builders but also Islamic teachers to be sent. The delegation which was sent in 921 in response to this letter was led by a Mohammedan Greek called Ibn Fadlan, who wrote an extremely interesting report on his journey.[1] He touches on the traffic situation and mentions three forms of travel: on the Volga, which was only possible down-stream and took a considerable time; on horseback across the steppes; and by dog-sleigh. Kiev could be reached from Bolgar in twenty days, but only by remaining all day in the saddle.

The interesting fact is that, in spite of these difficulties, fur-traders and merchants from the north (and even from the Arctic coast) came as far as Bolgar and there made contact with the Arabs. From them Ibn Fadlan learned things which left him in no doubt that he was dealing with men from the Polar zones; they described the Polar summer, in which the sun never sets, and a 'fish from whose teeth knives and sword-hilts are made', which could only mean the walrus.

In the Carolingian period these intensive trade relations must have penetrated deep into Europe: in the tenth century in the town of Mainz, which was called Magansha in Arabic, dirhems were in use which had been coined in Samarkand between 913 and 915. More than ten thousand of these coins were found at Muron in the Vladimir gouvernement and thirteen thousand in Gotland. In Sweden and Finland as many as two hundred different caches have been discovered!

Access to the Pechova country was mainly by water, using the rivers Kama, Kolva and Vycherka, Lake Tuchussovsk, and finally the small river Vogulka. The final lap to Pechova was covered by a hill-track across the 700-feet-high watershed. There are still a number of timber structures, principally bridges, marking the way. Here, of course, payment was seldom made in coin, but with Arab wrought-ironwork, swords and other utility goods; the trade was conducted in silence, the Arabs laying out their wares and retiring to wait for the natives to display their skins.

The last eyewitness account of the fur road came from Ibn Batuta, the great Arab traveller, who in the fourteenth century spent twenty-four years travelling the world (and trading) and who visited Bolgar. The town must have recovered to some extent from the first Mongol wave of terror, for in 1340 Ibn Batuta found a small but industrious Mohammedan colony there. Unfortunately, he was dissuaded from travelling on into the heart of the fur country. He writes simply: 'I am renouncing my plan on account of the great difficulties attending the journey and of the small profit it would have brought.

1 See Markwart, also Hennig.

One travels in these areas only in small carts which are drawn by strong dogs ... Only rich merchants, each of whom takes a hundred vehicles with him, are wont to travel in these wastes. The carts are also laden with food, drink and firewood ... In exchange for their own goods they are offered skins of sables, white squirrels and ermine ... Those who travel to these places do not know whether they are demons or men to whom they sell their goods and with whom they trade; for they never see them face to face.'

Two or three centuries after the Arab fur trade had ceased, the first Chinese tea reached European Russia through Siberia. Moscow's society ladies were now in a position to appreciate how superior this brand of tea was in taste, aroma and bouquet to all the other varieties which until then had reached Europe by sea. And one day the same thing happened as with silk and the perfumes of Arabia: husbands, who so far had only been aware that tea went well with vodka, had to pay a much higher price for the next consignment. A 'jour' without caravan tea became unthinkable; the tea road had come to stay.

It ran from Peking over the Nan-kao Pass in a general north-easterly direction through the Gobi desert and reached the Russian border near the town of Kiachta, south of Lake Baikal. From there to the European border of Siberia was still another 2,500 miles!

The town of Kiachta, until then a remote, sleepy little postal station on the so-called steppe service to Peking, blossomed—thanks to tea—into a prosperous trading centre. The road from Kiachta into Russia was famous (in parts at least) for its high quality, and it carried considerably more traffic than many frontier towns in Europe. In the last ten years before the Trans-Siberian Railway was opened, an average of about thirteen million roubles' worth of tea passed through Kiachta each year on its way to Russia (other commodities only accounted for about 700,000 roubles, so that the title 'tea road' was not a misnomer).

Opposite Kiachta and separated from it only by a 70-feet strip of no-man's-land and a wooden fence was the Chinese town of Mai-machin, which the Russians called Kitaiskaya Sloboda (Chinese town). Its population of three thousand was entirely male, for women were forbidden to live in the town, perhaps because the Chinese wanted to protect their women against their fellow-traders on the other side of the border.

The 3rd of November, 1901, was a fateful day for both towns: the longest railway line in the world, which had been started ten years before when the Emperor dug a spadeful of earth at Vladivostock, was completed and opened to traffic. Although for some years the service on the branch lines through Harbin and Mukden was highly erratic, tea never again resumed its long caravan-trek across the Gobi desert. For some time after 1920 the old tea road across the great desert was sometimes used by automobiles, and might have become one of the first motorways inside Asia, if the political unrest in Manchuria and the prolonged conflicts between China and Japan had not made normal traffic conditions in this area virtually impossible.

So Russia was a country without roads, and the railways, which in the vastness of Asia showed up to better advantage than anywhere else, became vital arteries in the great empire. They were fast, economical (water and coal or wood are to be found almost everywhere in Siberia), and powerful enough to carry in one train the load of dozens of caravans and thousands of dog-sleighs.

A mere glance at Italy, noted today for its imaginative road-building, the birthplace of the Roman roads, of Rinaldo Rinaldini and the Camorra, is enough to bring home to us how little talent the *ancien régime* and the Europe of the Romantics had for solving practical administrative problems. From a purely technical viewpoint the road problem had been solved thousands of years before, but as roads are not so simple to build as pergolas and campaniles, they remained at a medieval standard until fairly recent times. This is all the more surprising when one remembers that Italian engineers and workers (who worked on several magnificent Alpine roads in the early nineteenth century) had shown that, by some miracle, the tradition which began with the Romans and was continued in the Renaissance had survived the centuries.

But Italy had always been—and still is—a land of contrasts. Beneath the great dome of St. Peter's, people lived in half-ruined houses and narrow lanes which stretched right down to the Tiber. The Popes had the power to drain the Pontine Marshes, and Pius VI (1775–99) made a name for himself by doing so, but they were not in a position to see to it that the streets of Rome were kept clean. Pope Benedict XIV (1740–58), a man of great culture and tolerance, was painfully conscious of this. He decorated the city with splendid works of art, helped found academies and libraries, reduced the number of feast days and encouraged the small industries, but everything became bogged down in dirt. Then he himself decided to find out the reasons and discovered that the prelate in charge of the funds for street-cleaning was using them for a quite different and extremely squalid purpose. Pope Benedict arranged that his carriage should pass through a lane where the prelate concerned had a regular rendezvous. It was well timed. The horrified priest had to kneel down, as was the custom, and ask the Holy Father for his blessing. The Pope opened the carriage door and gave him a long lecture, which had the effect not only of rousing his conscience but also of making him experience for himself the appalling state of the Roman street in which he was kneeling. From then on there was a marked improvement—at least in Rome.

Outside the capital conditions were no better. The small States of Italy were heavily in debt and economized on the roads, if only because the climate made them just passable even in bad weather. The kingdom of Naples made improvements in two of its main highways (Capua–Aversa–Naples and Capua–Caserta–Naples), but concentrated almost entirely on traffic conditions in the immediate neighbourhood of Naples. A new road was built round the notorious town of Posilipo, which had become a favourite haunt of bandits and was sometimes virtually sealed off by them. The kings of Naples had to wage a full-scale guerrilla war against them. In 1751, for example, according to contemporary reports special commando units were created, each with 100 armed men, an executioner and a priest. They had the authority to pass sentence on the spot, and condemning a highway robber to the galleys was regarded as a sign of leniency, which could only be exercised in very extenuating circumstances.

Twenty years later one of the most notorious murderers of his time was arrested. His name was Grillo and he had remained in hiding for twelve years in a chestnut wood near Naples, during which time he had killed no less than seventy-five people. In 1786 the whole of Europe followed with morbid excitement the adventures of Rinaldo Rinaldini, whose romantic exploits were described by Goethe's brother-in-law, Vulpius, and proved an even more sensational bestseller than *The Sorrows of Werther*.

In the Papal State, a band of thirty villains are at large committing highway robbery and, although they are being hunted, they still evade capture [wrote Berlin newspapers in 1786]. At the end of April the band were betrayed and surrounded near Montebello. Rinaldini, the leader, put up a spirited resistance; he alone was overpowered and lost his life. The bandit Zulini, who betrayed him, has been richly rewarded for his services. The officers of the law obviously had more money than courage, or Rinaldo Rinaldini's reputation really had an intimidating effect, for a subsequent inquiry revealed how the 'victory' over this eighteenth-century Robin Hood was achieved:

22 July. The Count of Carpegna, whose castle suffered serious damage during the capture of the robber Rinaldini, has now decided to prosecute Lieutenant Piccoli, who commanded the papal troops and gave the order to open fire. The damage done to the castle is indescribable, irreplaceable, and without precedent in recent times even at the hands of enemy troops. The entire roof, which covers a considerable area, with all the copper gutters, the most costly furniture, magnificent paintings by old masters, including pictures by Raphael, Michelangelo, etc., and the archives, the large library—everything was destroyed by a fire which was started inside to force five powerless [i.e. wounded] robbers into submission, while a greatly superior body of troops fled, too cowardly to risk an attack.

It is hardly surprising in such circumstances that banditry became more and more widespread in Italy, and that the Camorra not merely controlled all the roads and markets in southern and central Italy, but even had its contacts in the highest government circles.

It is hard to imagine how the nineteenth century with its industrial expansion would have managed without the invention of the steam-engine. Even the achievements of someone as far-sighted as Napoleon were limited in scope, designed for military purposes, and in Italy or Dalmatia were confined to relatively unimportant areas, which merely underlined the chaotic conditions elsewhere. The road resisted—and still resists—the sort of radical solutions so beloved of more progressive statesmen, and any ruler who was not in a position to mobilize a whole nation had to watch his roads expanding literally at snail's pace, while the costs rose to astronomical figures. And when a costly road of this kind was completed, it could only be used by horse-drawn vehicles as of old, and the heavy vehicles demolished it in less time than it had taken to build it.

The end of the nineteenth century was the age of the railway. That was inevitable. What is surprising, however, is that no one appears to have looked beyond the railway. It was, of course, a new and even unexpected development, but even level-headed and open-minded people regarded it as an end in itself, the *ne plus ultra* which reduced to absurdity all attempts to improve on it. People were obsessed by the railway, lived for it, and built their politics round it—although thousands of automobiles were travelling on the roads of America and Europe. Yet on the eve of the First World War international traffic projects were drawn up which solely concerned the railways. The mere mention of the Baghdad railway was enough to excite people—on one side of the Channel with pride, on the other with anger.

'About 1915, when the difficult stretches of tunnel in the Taurus and Amanus mountains have been completed, the Baghdad railway will run continuously from the Bosphorus to beyond the Euphrates, and by about 1917 the slogan "Berlin–Baghdad", which once aroused so much controversy, will have become a reality. Even serious political upheavals and obstacles of all kinds should at most interrupt this proud cultural achievement for a short time, but in no circumstances can it now be thwarted.' Dr. Richard Hennig, who wrote these words in 1913, has probably smiled over them himself, since his subsequent work established him as one of the outstanding authorities of our time on international traffic.

In parts of the world like Persia, Afghanistan, Central Africa and Central America, where even today roads hardly exist, groups of engineers made surveys for railway lines. No less illustrious a figure than Ferdinand de Lesseps (died 1894), builder of the Suez Canal, waxed enthusiastic about the gigantic project for a trans-Asiatic railway and sent his son Aimé Victor to Asia to explore the possible routes over the roof of the world. In 1898 the Murgab railway, which ran southwards from Merv, was opened, having been built on the Czar's express orders in the record time of two years across more than 190 miles of Turkman desert. It was in no better position to pay its way, either by passenger or goods traffic, than the railway lines which were to run from Samarkand over the Khyber Pass to north India. Today, plans of this kind merely raise a smile, but in the years before the First World War, when military rather than economic considerations were paramount, they aroused so much heated discussion that it looked time and again as if the British and the Russians would declare war over Afghanistan. The British took the precaution of building a long tunnel through an enormous mountain on the Afghan border, although they had no immediate use for it; but they knew that if war did break out there would be no time to build tunnels. But the world heaved a sigh of relief when the rival powers finally agreed to build no railways, in Persia at least, until 1910.

In Africa it was France and Germany who opposed Britain when she proposed to carry out the Cecil Rhodes plan and build a railway on British territory from Cairo to Cape Town, because this would have involved a trivial exchange of territory with the Belgian Congo!

But there were even bolder projects: James B. Eads, naval captain and hydraulic engineer, submitted to the Mexican Government in 1880 an admirably detailed plan for a shipping railway to cross the isthmus of Tehuantepec in Central America, which would transport loaded ships by means of specially constructed machines from the Atlantic to the Pacific and vice versa. As the highest point on this line would only be about 800 feet above sea-level, Eads was given a concession, but died before he could execute his daring plan. In the meantime, the Tehuantepec railway, which was opened by the Mexican President Diaz in 1907, has become to some extent a competitor of the Panama Canal.

As we have seen, the railway and steam-power were generally believed to be capable of anything. Although world opinion and governments were still highly sceptical in the eighteen-thirties, by the turn of the century no project was too bold to be taken up. In 1913 the road was never mentioned, except to remark *en passant* that some projected railway line or other 'will replace a motor-road at present in existence': a grotesque remark which shows how few statesmen can see even three decades ahead.

Chapter 11

THE INCA ROADS

When soldiers and officers of Christian Spain first saw the fabulous splendour of the Alhambra at Granada and the fountains of the summer palace at Generalife, they thought they were in Paradise; yet they were even more impressed when they crossed the ocean to Peru and saw the streets and roads which had been built by the Inca rulers. At that time there was nothing comparable in Spain itself; all that the Spaniards knew about roads had been gleaned entirely from the remains of the Roman roads, which, after all, were more than a thousand years old. Yet in a country of heathens and idolators, to whom they were bringing the light of Christianity, they found not only a State which was wellnigh perfect in its organization but also a visible expression of it in a network of roads which was magnificently planned and brilliantly executed.

The astonishment of the Spaniards was reflected in a number of contemporary reports by soldiers, monks and government officials, whose testimony, together with the discoveries made by archaeologists, is our main source of information on the Inca roads. The ancient American civilizations, principally those of South America, have left almost no written records. The Roman writers, politicians and soldiers had expressed themselves in such detail on their roads that one could almost retrace them from literary sources alone. Our main source of information about the Inca civilization, however, is the Spaniards, together with a few chroniclers of Indian origin from the generation after the conquest, who had learned to transcribe their inherited knowledge in Spanish or at least in Latin symbols.

There were, of course, plenty of zealots who tried to discredit the whole impressive political structure of the Inca rulers as the work of the Devil, and in Peru, as in other countries converted to Christianity, priceless treasures were destroyed. But accounts given by more responsible eyewitnesses show that Peru had a traffic-system which was in many respects similar to the more or less contemporary State postal service in Mongolia, although it was undoubtedly more efficient.

In describing the Inca roads, modern historians constantly make the mistake of comparing them with the Roman roads, a comparison which can only favour the Romans, for they, after all, built a massive network comprising 50,000 miles of main highways and twice as many secondary roads. The empire of the Incas at its peak, which was about the year 1500, covered a coastal strip sixty to three hundred miles wide, stretching from Quito (Ecuador) in the north to about 35 degrees latitude in what is today Chile. In spite of repeated attempts they failed to expand farther south. In this area of roughly 750,000 square miles lived between seven and ten million people. The savage tribes in the south and the head-hunters in the jungle east of the Andes would have resisted any further advance by the Incas, even if the Spaniards had not appeared. So the Inca Empire remained a great deal smaller than the Roman Empire, which embraced the whole of the Mediterranean.

The very earliest accounts of the Inca roads make it clear that they were systematically planned, that two roughly parallel causeways ran from the north to the south of the long, narrow empire. One was a coastal road, which ran from Tumbes (in the border area of the present States of Peru and Ecuador) through Lima (the present capital of Peru) and Santiago de Chile to Talca, which lies about 120 miles south of Santiago. The precise course followed by the Andes road has proved more difficult to trace and—even after the expedition led by Victor von Hagen which spent two years trying to locate it—there are still gaps. It started north of Quito, passed through the town to the junction Huancabamba and from there, drawing away from the coast, it crossed the mountains to the capital Cuzco. Running south-east from the city to Lake Titicaca, it split in two in order to serve both shores of the lake and joined up again. After a wide sweep eastwards it reached what is today Bolivia, before it passed through the Argentine cordilleras to Santiago. The coast road was about 2,250 miles long, the Andes road 600 miles shorter.

There were many transversal roads connecting these two main highways, which have only been partly explored. The most impor-

The Inca roads

tant of them were naturally in the area round the capital Cuzco in the interior, and ran partly from Cuzco to the sea and partly into the wild mountain country, where the population who had fled from the Spaniards had built fortresses in the Urubamba valley and other places still undiscovered. The branch roads into the mountainous jungle north of Lake Titicaca, where numerous Inca gold mines are believed to have been situated, have also still to be explored.

Heinrich Harrer has compared the exploration of the Inca roads with Sven Hedin's (and others!) search for the silk roads; exploration in the Andes was, however, much more difficult than the crossing of the Tarim basin—more difficult but not more dangerous, for the Peruvians are a peaceable people, whereas even today the Tarim basin is a seething cauldron of conflicting political interests.

The remains found in the Andes country were, on the other hand, more impressive; even where the Inca roads were not paved, they can still be described as made-up roads, which are almost clearly recognizable and, moreover, were equally clearly designated as highways by their staging-points and their flights of steps. About a fifth of the present Peruvian network of roads consists of original Inca roads which have been repaired, or of roads which are in the same state as five hundred years ago when they were built. It is only on the coast, where the sand is constantly shifting in the wind and where the new Pan-American Highway with its four traffic lanes has attracted so many motorists, that the Inca roads have ceased to be a part of the landscape. In the interior, where ancient mountain passes are used almost entirely and the valleys are populated, one can still find Inca roads; there is not a single traveller from Humboldt up to the present time who has not spoken of them.

The Inca rulers were no more inventors of roads than were the Romans, nor were they the first cultured people in the area which they later occupied, but their centre at Tiahuanaco on Lake Titicaca enjoyed a high standard of material culture, as did also the coastal resort Nasca. In the northern part of the Inca empire the Chimu had developed a large, well-organized and prosperous State, from which —according to several modern American authorities—the Incas borrowed essential features of their own political system. In any case, roads were part of both the Nasca and the Chimu cultures. In fact, the Chimu highway, which was sixty-five feet wide, was appreciably wider than the Inca roads; on the other hand the Andes passes required narrower roads.

Whether the ancient American civilizations had discovered the wheel is a question over which scientists are still at variance. If the toy with wheels which was found in certain graves is genuine, then we are faced with the problem why this invention by or for children was not also used by adults. At all events, the Inca roads could only be used by pedestrians, litters and, if need be, by herds of llama. Even the Spaniards' mules were unable to climb the steps with which the Inca engineers overcame differences in height of as much as 2,000 feet in one flight.

Travelling in the Inca Empire was, therefore, fairly difficult, and indeed it was intended to be so. The fascinating organization of this highly centralized State, with its ruthless consistence that reminds one of Orwell's *1984*, has a Utopian rather than historical appeal to the twentieth-century student. The road, like everything else, was in the service of the State and no one who was not on any official mission dared use it. It served the armed forces, the State officials and—the couriers. The ancient Greek institution of running messengers had been developed to a fine art under the Incas—mainly for the transmission of news, but also sometimes for the transport of small and particularly precious commodities such as fish for the Inca's table at Cuzco. Different Spanish authors have given different accounts of the achievements of these runners, but whether the twelve hundred miles from Quito to Cuzco were covered in five or seven days is unimportant—either of these is a remarkable achievement and implies superb organization.

The runners, who were called Chasqui, were stationed along all the post roads in the empire. They spent the daytime in small rest-houses known as 'tampus' and when not on duty could run a little farther and spend the night at a larger tampu. Each tampu was a relay-station and the courier had to run about two miles to the next where he handed over the so-called 'kipu'. One man stood before the tampu keeping watch in both directions. When a messenger appeared (in brightly coloured costume like a medieval herald), he ran to meet him and then ran beside him. Once the oral message was transmitted, the kipu was handed over, and the man who had been relieved stayed at the tampu to rest. The kipus, or small packets tied with coloured and artistically knotted cords, were far from adequate substitutes for written script. They were aids to memory, especially for numbers and dates, but without the oral message were usually incomprehensible.

In this way the Inca in Cuzco was kept fully informed of the Spanish invasion, and the Europeans were particularly puzzled by the speed with which news travelled. This did not, however, save the Indians, who had apparently become so much creatures of logic and organization that they had lost all imagination. They simply could not conceive that any harm could come to them from a few hundred men—the more so as these men had arrived by sea and not from the impenetrable jungle forests in the east.

In such an extensive and almost infinitely elongated empire, mobile troops were just as important as an efficient news service. Most of the roads were built in preparation for some military campaign. The regional governors received precise instructions about the projected road and the course it was to follow, and work was immediately started in all areas through which the troops were to pass. In any case, Inca peasants had no private life in our sense. Once instructions had been issued how many men were needed to work on the road, the remainder was mere routine. The main work in the fields (which could not be neglected) was done by the women, while the men had to carry out forced labour on such public works as road-building, fortifications, temples and palaces.

Road and rule were one—as with the Romans. Each new area, after it was subdued and incorporated, was at once given its military road; in fact, sometimes conquest and road-building were more or less simultaneous.

The last of the Inca roads, on the other hand, were laid in flight. This is a phase of their history which has only come to light in the last few decades: the period when the ruling family of the Incas, having recovered from the shock administered by the Spanish conquest, withdrew to what the Swiss would call a *reduit*. Under the supreme command of an Inca named Mancu Capac II, new towns were built in the trackless Vilcabamba territory, which even today is almost inaccessible. Nearly four thousand feet up, these so-called 'hanging towns' cling to saddles and escarpments in a mountain range that reaches heights of 13,000 feet and more. Far below them raged the waters of the Urubamba Gorge. These towns, the best known of which was Machu Picchu, are today either abandoned ruins or overgrown by the jungle; some, like the fortified capital Vilcabamba itself, have defied all attempts to find them. What one did find everywhere was the road which also linked this area with Cuzco, the capital, long after it had been occupied by the Spaniards.

In 1537 the Indians launched a counter-offensive; along the road which thrust its way through the wild mountain country they marched into the occupied territory, attacked settlements, seized food supplies and surrounded Spanish patrols. They carried on a guerrilla war (as the Spaniards themselves did against the French three centuries later) which lasted for several decades. It was not until 1572 that a Spanish officer, Tupac Amaru, a nephew of Ignatio de Loyola, succeeded in capturing the last Inca of Vilcabamba and bringing him to Cuzco, where he was beheaded before a silent, kneeling crowd.

The road survived Mancu Capac II and Tupac Amaru. Narrow but secure, it winds its way along the steep slopes, its supporting walls built without mortar, as are all Inca buildings. It is paved with large blocks of stone, which are roughly fitted together in the soil and which give less trouble to pedestrians than to animals.

The Inca gold roads also ran into remote and almost inaccessible country—the high valleys and plateaux north of Lake Titicaca, where the tropical jungle creeps up the slopes and the rivers tumble down to join the mighty Amazon. To reach this watershed one has to cross a series of passes, almost all of which—marked by little pyramids of stones—lie more than 13,000 feet up. Naturally, even without these 'apachetas', no pass is hard to identify: they are not really road-signs like the stone cairns in the Norwegian highlands, but the result of a typical form of Indian self-deception. When an Indian begins the ascent, he takes a stone with him: at the highest point of the road he lays it down, convinced that he has thereby thrown off his fatigue, and continues, lighter both in body and spirit, down the other side.

In ancient times, when gold was still being dug and washed, men and animals were much too heavily burdened with their precious load to think of the stone of self-deception. Merely to pay the ransom for Atahualpa, one of the Incas captured by the Spaniards, gold to the value of five million pounds was brought to Cuzco from every corner of the country. The Spaniards took it and strangled Atahualpa (for they had promised not to spill his blood . . .).

As a rule, the Inca engineers kept their roads well clear of watercourses; the sudden tropical downpours filled the narrow gorges with raging torrents of water in a matter of hours, and any low-lying road would be immediately in peril. Victor von Hagen, who almost lost a fully-laden truck in a tropical storm on a modern road near the river Mantaro, wrote with considerable feeling in his *Military Roads of the Sun God* (1957):

> Had an Inca engineer planned his road in this way, he would have forfeited his life . . . As they [i.e. the Incas] realized that they would never be able to maintain a road along the Mantaro canyon, they made a fork at Mayoc, built a suspension bridge and cut steps up the opposite slopes to the plateau . . . and so on through the mountains. The builder of this modern road had done nothing to protect it against water, which streamed down from the high rocky walls carrying great

boulders with it down to the river. Wooden bridges crossed the larger streams ... They were a daily nightmare to us.

Where no other solution was possible, the Inca engineers built bridges in the road itself. They had stone bridges, which they constructed by the archaic method of pushing stone flags forward from both sides till they were able to close the remainder of the gap with carefully hewn stone blocks up to twelve feet long. Here again no mortar was used.

A pontoon bridge on the Rio Desuguadero, the only effluent from Lake Titicaca, was in use for eight hundred years. It shows how clever the Inca administrators were in exploiting the skill of the various tribes in their great empire. Lake Titicaca is known to be the home of a people that is undoubtedly very old and in the course of thousands of years has developed a strange, amphibian mode of life. The 'native land' of these people is artificial islands of rushes, their means of transport tiny kayaks made of reeds, and their food and clothes also consist to a large extent of reeds.

This tribe was obliged to renew the pontoons on which the bridge rested every year, for the rushes slowly absorbed the water. In 1864 an American diplomat and student of Peruvian antiquities gave a detailed description of the bridge and made a sketch of it, and in 1953 Victor von Hagen's expedition, in exchange for a few bunches of koka leaves and some bottles of cognac, were allowed to watch the Indians re-erect the rush pontoon-bridge within a few hours, working on instructions given by a very old man. The actual road-surface of the bridge was not made of planks but of rushes woven into thick mats—as no vehicles had so far used it, it probably made little difference.

The suspension bridges seem to us today just as unsafe. The Spaniards both admired and feared them, particularly when the wind blew them to and fro over some yawning abyss. This enterprising method of building is presumably as old as the art of weaving and tying knots, and therefore considerably older than bridge-building as such. Suspension bridges with anchor ropes, ropes, and bamboo poles were known in the island of Celebes and in several parts of India, China and Japan as long as men can remember— the same is doubtless also true of Peru.

The most famous of these bridges was across the Apurimac Gorge between two walls of rock in which the anchor ropes were fixed. It lay to the north-west of Cuzco in a very narrow valley which runs more or less parallel with the Urubamba Gorge, the gorge of the hanging towns. On the way from and to Cuzco the Apurimac bridge had to be crossed. The Spaniards dreaded it because of its swinging motion, while the Inca's subjects feared the controls that were posted there. So it is not surprising that, remote as it was, this bridge fired the imagination of poets from the time it was seen by the Spaniards. How it became associated with the French King St. Louis (San Luis), whose name it bore, no one knows, but since Thornton Wilder made it the subject of his famous novel, *The Bridge of San Luis Rey*, it has become known throughout the world. The part it may have played in the consciousness of a whole enslaved people is the subject of another novel, *La Chute du grand Chimu* (Paris, 1955), by Lucien Marchal. He too shows what a profound impression individual roads and bridges can make on the human mind and imagination, particularly where the nature of the country is such that its roads are forced to run always through the same valleys or over the same mountain passes.

The almost mythical significance of certain roads and bridges in South America reminds us of the part played by roads in ancient Greece. Like the Romans, the Inca engineers built in straight lines, but their method of ascending mountains by means of flights of steps is reminiscent of the steps across the Attic mountains. The road-builders of the Inca State had great respect for fertile land; fields must not be damaged, and even in legend there is mention of the earliest roads in connection with Bochica, ₌ie divine hero: 'From Bosca he journeyed to the places Fontivon, Bogota, Serrezuela and Cipacon, whence he returned northwards along the slopes of the mountains, blazing trails through woods and thickets wherever he went.' Bochica—who is associated with an Atlas saga of an evil-doer who had to carry the world on his shoulders—stands between Hercules, the maker of roads, and the hero Theseus, who fought to make them free, while the more obviously divine figures of Quetzalcoatl (Mexico) and Uiracocha (Lake Titicaca area) are described as makers of roads, but in the saga they also fulfil a number of other functions.

Road, road-tunnel and bridge seem with the Incas to have been much more closely linked with nature and the gods than is the case with European peoples. In the Andes with their steep peaks, their great heights and deep gorges, roads were also ways of life: a road could mean food and prosperity, and if a pass or mountain road became impassable an artery was cut. So if these roads were given the names of rulers, this was no sacrilege but the contrary: the Inca was no king or emperor in our sense, but a god in the full meaning of the word.

.   .   .   .   .

The civilization of the Inca State, as seen by the modern European, has so many archaic features that it is hard to imagine it on the threshold of our present age—yet, purely chronologically, that is where it lies. To make the picture still more confused, one only has to realize that in many respects the ancient authoritarian State of the Inca rulers was superior to the contemporaneous States in Europe (though no more so than, for example, the Roman Republic at its peak by comparison with the feeble empires of the twelfth and thirteenth centuries). The American Middle Ages lasted not much more than a hundred to a hundred and fifty years. In 1531 Pizarro's soldiers set foot for the first time on an Inca road; in 1651 the first colonial road was laid in North America—the so-called 'Road to the Woods', which ran westward from Fort Casimir on the river Delaware and was the first instalment of a transcontinental road known today as the US40.

The period of decadence, which lasted up to fourteen hundred years in Europe, was a great deal shorter in the New World—which explains why the Inca roads are much better preserved and much more widely used today than the Roman roads. And, as the importance of the railways was appreciated much earlier in the United States than in Europe and therefore expanded much more quickly, it took barely three hundred years for the road to pass through all stages of its development—from its first appearance as a finished product in an ancient civilization to its apparent demise in the unequal duel with the railway. As early as 1840 the U.S.A. had no less than 178 steam railway-lines covering some 3,000 miles, which represented about twenty-five per cent more than the whole of Europe.

The Andes, with peaks rising to 23,000 feet, separated the Pacific coast area and its road-system from the remainder of the South American continent much more completely than is the case today. The Andes form the longest mountain belt in the world, some 4,500 miles, and they cover an area of roughly three-quarters of a million square miles—eight times the area of the United Kingdom. At their narrowest point the Andes are still 110 miles across; at their widest, twenty degrees south of the Equator, almost 600 miles. In the far south of this mountain chain the Valdivia Pass is only 2,500 feet high, but it has never been of any importance as a traffic route: it leads to the wilderness of Patagonia, which up to the present has failed to attract either traders or travellers. The other passes, however, all lie at a height of 13,000 feet (the Uspallata Pass is 12,800 feet up, the same height as the Grossglockner!) and over, in fact some reach 15,000 feet which is on the same level as passes on the 'roof of the world'. Before roads were carried down into the plains of Brazil, the most daring railways in the world were crossing the Andes: the line from Atequipa to Puno in southern Peru crosses a pass 14,800 feet high, while the Oroya railway even climbs to 15,500 feet, the height of the Matterhorn.

One thing that clearly emerges from all this is that in the remote, almost inaccessible areas of America (and particularly of South America) the medieval stage in the development of road-building was completely lacking; the mountain roads of the Incas were directly followed by mountain railways, and it was only a century later—in the immediate present—that the first motorways began to wind their way up into the South American mountains.

South America already had almost 20,000 miles of railways when the first roads were built in Brazil and the Argentine which would compare with the roads of the same period in Europe: the excellent road from Juiz de Fora to the 2,700-feet-high Petropolis, a town to the north of Rio de Janeiro, founded by German colonists; the ten-miles-long mountain road near Valparaiso, built by an Austrian engineer named Lindacker; and several other shorter roads, most of them near the coast and larger townships. And a common feature of these roads has always been a wire fence separating each one from the adjoining land. On this strip of up to 130 feet people were free to drive, ride or walk as best they could.

In the South American plains the modern period of road development was also brief. The metal roads of the Jesuits were excellently planned: they fulfilled their purpose; they were exactly what one expected a road to be in the eighteenth century. Then came the period of the speculators. With a great deal of drive, shrewdness and skill, working-parties were organized and plots of land acquired; the route planned for the road was bargained over and even the building of it was not, in the early stages, entrusted to engineers. Vast areas of South America are still suffering from these hastily and crudely built roads, and in Mexico the situation only changed for the better after the long and bloody civil war between Maximilian with his handful of followers and Benito Juarez, the Indian President, ended in 1867. On the bare tableland, which drops steeply down to the coast, long overland roads which had only minor physical obstacles to overcome appeared comparatively quickly. It was here that Hernando Cortes's invading army had found several well-laid and often straight roads, although they were too few to be compared with the Maya roads on the Yucatan peninsula (still less with the magnificent network of roads built by the Inca rulers). Under

President Porfirio Diaz (1830–1915) a long-term plan was set in motion to improve Mexico's roads—after centuries of exploitation which had harmed both the country and the people. Expensive metal roads were laid up the steep slopes from the sea to the highlands, and railways connected up the country's forty ports with the metropolis in the hills where fierce battles had once been fought between Spaniards and Aztecs on the ancient causeways. After a number of setbacks under corrupt presidents such as Lerdo de Tejada and Gonzales, who seriously jeopardized the work done by Juarez and Diaz, Mexico's transport system is now rapidly being modernized; it has close on 40,000 miles of roads. Due to political instability the development of a railway-system started rather late and it only covers some 15,000 miles. Following the example set in the United States, Mexico has decided to give priority to road transport and to the construction of motorways.

Standing on the threshold of the present age and looking back, one realizes what a strange period the century of steam was! Science progressed at a breakneck speed, one discovery following the other so rapidly that their true significance was overlooked. Steam had changed the face of the world. Up to the end of the nineteenth century the earth was one vast single arena, in which there were only two rivals, equally matched: the railways and the steamship. All other contestants had long since been eliminated.

Safe and cheap transport of large quantities of goods by sea has given the shipping companies almost complete control of intercontinental trade. The caravan roads are deserted, even the Alpine passes are seldom used, and much greater quantities of goods pass through the Suez Canal than ever passed through near-by Petra on the incense road. Steamers, independent of seasonal winds and immune from dangerous currents, circle continents with cargoes that once required thousands of camel caravans.

But if canals have been cut for the ships, bridges and viaducts on a similar scale have been built for the railways. In 1869, long before the Panama Canal was completed, the first railway line was opened for through traffic from the east to the west coast of the United States—from the Atlantic to the Pacific. The Uspallata railway across South America also links the two oceans, the highest railway in the world was built across the Bernina Pass, in Hamburg the Elbe Tunnel was opened, and in New York the Manhattan Bridge across the East River.

People waxed enthusiastic over railway lines that were never built because a single oil pipeline rendered them superfluous; and while the great European powers were waging war in China in desperate opposition to the Trans-Siberian Railway, the Wright brothers were sending their first dragons into the air—light, mysterious harbingers of a new form of transport, which needed neither rail nor road, neither canal nor tunnel. The road was forgotten.

Chapter 12

THE IRON ROAD

In the mild English autumn of 1830 a new chapter was opened in the history of world transport: on September 15th of this memorable year several thousand people gathered beside a new kind of iron highway between Manchester and Liverpool. This was the opening of the first steam railway to go into service. An experimental journey had already been made at Darlington but without attracting a great deal of attention; the journey from Manchester to Liverpool was the crucial test. George Stephenson's (1781–1848) locomotive, The Rocket, reached a speed of nearly thirty-five miles an hour on this occasion, and the fact that a Member of Parliament called Huskisson carelessly crossed the track and was knocked down and fatally injured merely served to impress on the public still more that a new force had entered the world: speed. Suddenly there seemed to be two conceptions of time: the leisurely tempo of the post-chaise and the thundering rush of iron monsters called locomotives.

The tremendous revolution which now set in is reflected in the questions put to George Stephenson before this momentous occasion. These questions were put not by farm labourers or coachmen, but by men of culture and education—in fact by members of the British House of Commons. They were anxious about the crops, about the game in the forests, about the carters, stage-coachmen, innkeepers and bartenders, and finally about the passengers themselves who would risk their lives on this new form of transport.

By the end of the same century, only a generation later, England had 20,000 miles of railways, Germany 30,000, France 25,000, Austria-Hungary 17,000 and the United States 170,000—an enormous railway network, in which a substantial proportion of the national income of each State was already invested.

Up to the nineteenth century, the 50,000 miles of roads built by the Romans across Europe, North Africa and Anatolia had remained the most comprehensive traffic system ever known. Then, with the discovery of a new kind of track—the railway line—a new form of transport had taken over.

The nature of the English landscape, particularly the absence of any high mountains, would have made the creation of an efficient road-system comparatively simple. Instead, the population allowed the Roman roads to deteriorate to such an extent that they were soon no better than the tracks used in the Bronze Age. Tracks which had been in existence since the Early Stone Age again became widely used in the Middle Ages, when they were known as 'green ways': the road from Dover to Cornwall, which passed over the oldest bridges in England; Icknield Way through Wiltshire and Berkshire to Norfolk; Fosse Way from Dorset through Salisbury to the Humber; and the old roads linking the ports of Kent with London and Chester, along which the Romans had transported gold from Ireland.

The Saxon settlers cleared tracts of forest for their villages, but far from these roads, in order to keep a safe distance from the robbers and marauders who haunted the highways. And as the Saxons did not use the roads, they deteriorated more and more.

There was a slight change for the better from the seventh century onwards as the power of the Church increased. The English landed nobility in the Middle Ages were far removed from what the world today understands by English landed gentry. They were rough barons, who often lived far from virtuous lives. So it was not uncommon for an English baron to seek salvation on his death-bed by bequeathing his property to the Church, and before long there were hundreds, even thousands of monks living along the country roads of England and Scotland, for the Church's extensive properties had to be administered, the tithes collected and the tenants watched.

The monks with their well-filled pouches attracted another category of road-user: the highwayman. During previous centuries while a mere handful of Saxon peasants on their way to market were to be seen on the roads, the robber had become more and more of a rarity. The country roads were so bad that no one travelled for pleasure. But by the twelfth century the situation was already beginning to change; highway robbery became profitable again, until it reached its peak with several notorious highwaymen whose fame has never been surpassed even by the most colourful modern gangster.

Adam Bell, Clym of the Clough and William of Cloudesley, to mention only three of the romantic-sounding names, lived in Englewood Forest, kept the whole north of England in a state of constant anxiety, and inspired a large number of ballads, some good, some bad, some indifferent. In one of these poetic fancies they are even pardoned by the King, when William performs the feat of shooting an apple from his son's head. . . .

It is with the next generation, however, that the romance of highway robbery reaches its peak with Robin Hood, the legendary prototype of the gentleman bandit who takes from the rich to give to the poor and never harms a lady—as long as she is pretty. The Robin Hood of history is as elusive as Dr. Faustus, but at least the date of his death is known: 18 November 1247. As various sources give 1160 as the year of his birth, Hood may well have died a natural death instead of, as legend has it, dying by the hand of a nun who betrayed him and let him bleed to death. It is also known that the summit of his career was reached in the nineties of the twelfth century, that he operated mainly in the Midlands and came of a noble family. In fact, contemporary sources are fairly unanimous in claiming that he was the Earl of Huntingdon. . . .

All the ingredients were there to make Robin Hood a popular idol and a favourite theme of writers and poets. From the year 1230, when an unknown chronicler mentions a 'Robertus Hood fugitivus', he inspired a succession of works by Tennyson, Walter Scott (*Ivanhoe*) and the modern 'Wirtshaus im Spessart'.

But if Robin Hood represented the high-water mark of England's highway robbery, he was by no means the last of his kind. A good five hundred years later the newspapers were full of stories of highway robbery in the Scottish Highlands and in the countryside around London. One brave Scotsman, who deprived a robber of his pistol and forced him to cut off one of his companion's ears, then to submit to the same punishment himself, became famous not only in England but also on the Continent for his rough-and-ready justice. On the 20th December 1735, not far from London, a rich butcher was held up at pistol-point by an elegantly dressed female bandit, who took all his money and his watch. And in its edition of 27 August 1728, the German paper *Vossische Zeitung* reported from Cork that a preacher's wife had been imprisoned 'as a foot-pad'.

She has for some years consorted with thieves unbeknown
to her husband, in that these same thieves came frequently to

the house in women's clothes, purporting to be her relations. From time to time she took a few of these relations to bed with her, leaving the poor husband to sleep on the sofa. She was in the habit of going out with the band dressed in a man's clothes, to rob on the road, and she was caught in these clothes with her comrades. Following this, the husband was murdered in his house by some of the band, to prevent him from betraying one or other of them.

It is interesting to note that this took place in the same year in which John Gay's *Beggars' Opera* was first produced. . . .

A statute of Westminster in 1285 laid down a regulation width for public highways and prescribed that there must be room for two carriages to travel abreast—presumably for military purposes. The hedges and bushes by the road had to be burnt down to leave a clear two hundred feet on either side—the object being to deprive highwaymen of cover. A further attempt was made to improve conditions on the roads with the Highways Act of 1555, which obliged the parishes to maintain them and to elect highway inspectors. We know, however, that in the Tudor period (1485–1603) most English roads were rendered impassable by a mere downpour of rain.

In such circumstances—and centuries before Stephenson—the traveller had only one consolation: the famous English inn. The more inclement the weather and the worse the roads, the more popular the inns. When one reads the paeans of praise from travellers who had been welcomed at some inn or other with a glass of hot grog, one realizes how different England was from Italy. Whereas in the cold and rainy North the inn was a place of refuge, in the warm South it was a den of vice.

The English roads blended so completely into the landscape that even the most detailed travel-guides were of comparatively little use. Neither John Leland's *Itinerary* (1533–39) nor William Harrison's account of the common ways (in his *Description of England*, 1577) was of much more value to a foreigner, who was compelled to take a guide, as if he were crossing a desert or high mountains. The inns, however, flourished, if only because, once the traveller had reached one, he was loath to leave it: The George at Glastonbury, the Pilgrims' Hostel at Battle, the Hostel of Godbegot at Winchester have remained famous for more than five hundred years up to the present time.

The speed at which one could travel in those days on English roads was, of course, not to be compared with the speed of Stephenson's

Rocket. When the last Saxon king, Harold, galloped from York to London in the fateful year 1066, he took four days to cover about 190 miles, although he was able to use an old Roman road.

Shakespeare, writing in Elizabethan England, uses the verb 'to post' as synonymous with 'to hurry':

> 'O most wicked haste, to post
> With such dexterity to incestuous sheets'

says Hamlet of his mother, and, in fact, travelling at that time was a great deal faster than the gallop of the unfortunate King Harold. When Queen Elizabeth I died in 1603, Sir Robert Cary took only three days to carry the news to James VI of Scotland, which for the stretch from London to Edinburgh represents an average of about 125 miles a day. This record was broken, however, by a highwayman named William Nevinson, who, hotly pursued, rode in one day from Rochester to York, more than 200 miles.

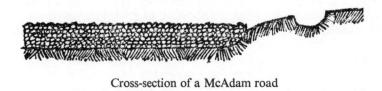

Cross-section of a McAdam road

But such a speed was exceptional: a fully-laden carriage had to have as many as ten horses to get it under way, and in 1663, when the Turnpike Act introduced the toll system, travelling and transport costs immediately went up, but the promised improvement in the roads was slow in coming.

A marked change for the better set in with John Loudon McAdam in the last quarter of the eighteenth century. He was a conscientious but by no means brilliant engineer, and his idea of making a top surface of stones was, for a country like England with its high rainfall, fairly obvious. What earned him his great name was his talent for organization. It was as a result of his tireless publicity and administration that the British Government finally set aside large funds to provide all the main roads in the British Isles with good foundations, on which a ten-inch layer of broken stones was spread. (Contrary to popular belief, which associates McAdam with some kind of asphalt, this was his entire formula.)

When McAdam died in his Scottish home in November 1836, he had many active and productive years behind him, and his writings had found an echo far outside England. At the same time it looked as if they were outdated, for the news of McAdam's death coincided with the apparent demise of the public highways to which his life had been devoted. Stephenson had buried what McAdam tried to resurrect, and the invisible cortège included in England alone 700 mail-coaches, 3,000 privately-owned stage-coaches, postilions and coach-owners: even McAdam had been unable to save them.

In France the situation was not much better, despite the fact that the Romans had built many more roads there than in England— including the secondary roads, they probably covered about 12,000 miles—and the fact that the magnificent Roman roads were much easier to maintain in the French climate. But the common people showed almost as little appreciation of their heritage as the Anglo-Saxons. Unfortunately, the Roman roads were made of extremely useful materials, and the peasants did not hesitate to remove the stones to build a stable or a cowshed. They covered up the holes with brushwood or, at best, with clay; *they* knew where the weak spots were and if a private coach came to grief, breaking a wheel or an axle, the parish did not stand to lose by it; on the contrary, the stranded travellers needed food and shelter.

France was certainly more united politically than the Holy Roman Empire, but she was not, for a long time at least, as united as England. Innumerable provincial nobles, large and small, extracted dues, large and small, from travellers on the most unlikely pretexts: there was a road-toll, a bridge-toll, a dust-toll and, in many places, taxes were levied on the coaches, the horses, or the shafts—in fact special payments even had to be made for travelling over grass or along river-banks. All this was bad enough, but it might at least have made some sense if these funds had been devoted to building and maintaining the roads. The sad truth is that nothing was even done to prevent the Roman roads from falling into disrepair, and a new road was only built when some very special emergency demanded it.

One of these emergencies was the unhappy adventure of Prince Philip Augustus II, a son of Louis the Fat; while out riding in Paris, his horse shied at a pig and he was thrown on to the muddy street. The King thereupon forbade pigs to appear in the streets. But even without pigs the streets of Paris still stank in the delicate nostrils of Philip Augustus II, who, in 1185—five years after he had succeeded his father—had the street paved in front of his castle. Later, enough private funds were collected to pave the main boulevards in Paris.

The medieval pilgrimages had also benefited some of France's main highways. A number of pious fraternities, the Church herself and the various orders of chivalry all saw to the welfare of the pilgrims and—what was still more important—kept the roads safe. So travelling merchants naturally preferred to use the main south-bound highways. They had always followed the river valleys, so that crusaders, pilgrims and merchants all used the ancient amber road, which the Romans later improved. It ran northwards alongside the Rhône, branching off on the one hand to the Seine basin and on the other to the Rhine valley and eastern France.

From the early thirteenth century onwards the French kings began to assert their authority over the unruly barons and counts, who until then had collected road-tolls without doing anything for the roads. The 'Charte de Melun' in 1222 turned an old Roman road, which linked up several extremely beautiful estates in the surrounding of Paris, into the Via Regalis, France's first royal road. But it is significant that before taking this step the King had to obtain the approval of the Bishop of Paris!

However, a start had been made, and, as an increase in central authority has always stimulated road-building, more and more roads throughout France were freed from local tolls and placed under the direct jurisdiction of the throne. A special official was appointed to supervise the entire road-system (sometimes it was the King's Treasurer) and detailed instructions were issued for the removal of any buildings that impeded traffic, for the protection and safety of the roads, and to some extent even for keeping them clean.

But the French kings, as we know, were kept so busy with other things than roads that few of these instructions, formally sealed and signed as they were, ever materialized. Added to this was the fact that the French kings remained, for the most part, in their capital, unlike their German cousins who had to hold court in quite a variety of towns. Towards the end of his reign, Louis XII, 'le père du peuple', expressed grave concern at the state of France's roads, and neither François I nor Henri II, for all their good intentions, was able to achieve much.

About 1550, however, Henri II did build a section of new road, which was so rare an achievement that it is worth recording: the Paris–Orleans road was extended in the direction of the Loire châteaux, which were then the favourite residences of the great nobles. Neither the ordinary traveller nor the national economy derived much benefit.

One of the regulations of that period which is of particular interest today concerned the width of the roads. Whereas even the busiest highways in France, both in towns and in the country, were the same

width as the old Roman roads—sixteen to twenty feet—wherever a
road passed through forest it had to be seventy-eight feet wide. As
there was so little to distinguish the actual road surface from the
verges, what this meant was that a strip seventy-eight feet wide had
to be cleared through the forest to protect travellers against highway-
robbers.

In spite of this, France also had her 'romantic' highwaymen. On
November 10th 1727, the *Vossische Zeitung* reported from Paris
that a plan had been put forward to fell a large part of the forests in
Alsace in an attempt to stamp out highway robbery, and in 1736,
long after the Middle Ages, there was much talk of a robber captain
who called himself 'The Night Prince'. He appears to have had a
lively sense of humour, for he threatened with dire punishment
anyone who ventured out on the roads after ten o'clock at night
without an adequate supply of ready money. A hundred and twenty
livres, or roughly the equivalent in jewels, was the minimum, although in the case of artisans he was prepared to settle for thirty
livres. This arrogant declaration was publicly displayed in Paris,
and one can well imagine that Monsieur Herault, the Commandant
of Police, was not particularly pleased by the comments of the
Parisians.

Even on dangerous roads, however, it was possible to complete
one's journey safely, as the Markgräfin von Rogersweil relates in a
letter of May 8th 1752:

> I arrived safely at Perpignan, and, because I had to pass
> across the Pyrenees mountains, I was warned by all and sundry
> to beware of bandits and to arm my servants. I had no other
> suite than my chambermaid, two postilions and my two
> lackeys. So at Perpignan I bought these two brave fellows a
> pair of pistols and for each one a good sabre. I myself and the
> chambermaid armed ourselves as if for a battle and bought a
> pair of light swords ... I also equipped the two postilions and
> the mule-driver with pistols and the latter carried in addition
> a heavy stick. Thus armed we continued our journey from
> Perpignan to Madrid.
> I had barely completed a day's journey in the Pyrenees when
> suddenly twelve to thirteen bandits ... appeared in the dis-
> tance. I had of necessity to remain on the highway and could
> turn neither to right nor to left, and furthermore the mule-
> driver added to my fears by saying that these were the villains
> we had been warned against. These bandits took to the road-
> side about forty paces away from me, in order to give me the
> impression that they wished to make way; which I could well
> have supported, for they were all on foot, had I but known

that they were carrying firearms. As my mule-driver assured me, however, that many bandits are wont to attack with no more than a pistol and a bandit's knife, I had no hesitation in attacking them with my few people rather than waiting for them to do it.

I saw them take to the roadside some thirty-five paces from me. From my pistol I discharged the first shot: the chamber-maid had joined my two lackeys behind the coach and, follow-my example, they too opened fire on the bandits, so that we four brought down three of these knaves. The robbers also shot at me and my people and killed my lackey Laurant. On the other hand, the two postilions, the other lackey and the chambermaid hit another two robbers. Now my people still had six shots, and, as the enemy attacked us with their knives, they were thrown into confusion by the next salvo; two were shot down, two others were disabled by sword wounds, and yet another was killed by the mule-driver's club. We, for our part, had no more than three wounded and were still faced by two unharmed bandits. I left the wounded lying and ordered the two bandits to be tied to the coach horse, so that I could hand them over to the judge at the next staging-point. I suffered a slight wound on my hand and my chambermaid had a slight wound on the left arm. . . .

The young Maria Leszinska, daughter of the King of Poland, who in 1725 was betrothed to Louis XV (seven years younger than herself), was exposed to dangers of quite a different kind. Her journey to Paris was not unprepared; thousands of peasants had removed the major obstacles and hazards on the roads she was to use. And yet, as we know from the brilliant René Louis, Marquis d'Argenson, who subsequently became Foreign Minister, it was a journey fraught with fear and terror, which served to some extent to prepare the unfortunate princess for the sad fate that awaited her with her dissolute husband.

'The aid of the peasants had been enlisted,' writes D'Argenson, 'to repair the roads . . . but they were made no better; indeed so bad were they that the Queen was frequently terrified of simply sinking into the morass, and on many occasions members of her entourage had to remove her by the arms from the coach which had become firmly bogged down.'

Nevertheless, under Louis XIV a start had been made with improving conditions on the roads. His brilliant Minister, Colbert, took a particularly active interest in the roads as vital arteries of the national economy, but the major handicap was simply lack of experience. The generally accepted idea was still that a road was

merely a track which could in special cases be covered with faggots
—here and there.

But Colbert appointed a man by the name of Gautier to take
charge of roads and bridges, and he and the twenty-two engineers
under him introduced certain innovations which made France's
road-system, in spite of all its defects, an example to her neighbours
and particularly Germany.

Gautier still accepted the view that rain and travellers must make
the road-surface firmer and thicker, but at the same time he used
ditches to drain off the water, cambered his roads and saw to it that
the major highways were sufficiently wide. Paris had so obviously
become the focal point of France that, apart from the old Roman
roads, new roads had to be built which radiated out from the capital
and, in combination with the old traffic routes, gave the country a
comprehensive road-system.

About the middle of the eighteenth century France had about
twice as many first-class roads as at the time of the Romans (15,000
as against 8,500 miles), although today they would not even be
regarded as third-class. In 1681, before the King could set out on a
journey, the worst stretches had to be hurriedly covered over with
faggots and a number of ditches had to be filled in. The Roi-Soleil left
Versailles on April 26th and arrived at Bourbon l'Archambault, the
famous watering-place, on May 5th, which meant that in spite of
Colbert, Gautier and the hurried repairs, it took him almost ten days
to cover 160 miles—the daily average of an ordinary pedestrian on
the roads of ancient Greece and Persia.

Modest efforts made by Gautier to repair the roads had little or
no effect. The century and its ruling sovereigns were not in favour
of such a practical and economical—though far from spectacular—
method of improving the roads. They aimed much higher and, in
so doing, overshot the target. . . .

Voisin, the famous poisoner, was said to be responsible for the
deaths of no less than 2,500 children, in order to extract from their
bodies the ingredients of the love potions with which the ageing
Madame de Montespan, among others, hoped to retain the affections
of her royal lover; the notorious 'Régence' saw Philip of Orléans
dissipating his powers night after night in the most extravagant
orgies, and Law's financial swindle plunged the whole of France
from dreams of untold wealth into bitter disillusionment. In such
an age of wild expenditure, there was naturally no question of saving
money on roads. On the contrary, road-building became almost a
form of architecture, as it had been to the Romans. What was lacking in experience, both as regards foundations and routing, was

partly made up for by the knowledge that bankruptcy was in any case inevitable.

It was in these circumstances that eighteenth-century France produced its astonishing State roads: mostly short and too wide, they were designed not to serve the nation's economy but primarily for the Court, and accordingly they were laid without regard to expense or public convenience. Marshlands were no obstacle; causeways were simply built across them. Mountains were ideally suited for wide, generous curves from which one could admire the straight highways below.

These roads, the last to be built in pre-revolutionary France, were from a technical viewpoint simple and quick to make: hewn stones or broken flagstones were laid on a layer of sand and held together by regular cross-sections of larger stones. The carriages rolled majestically along these roads, and long strips of paving enhanced the buildings on either side.

To begin with—until the Revolution—the nation had to foot the bill. The villages had to do most of the work, and the peasants had to leave their fields which, though not their own, were still their only source of livelihood. Moreover, they soon realized that, as today, the increase in road traffic encouraged the invasion of the countryside by the towns.

The damage done to the peasants was considerable, for, quite apart from the working hours they had to spend maintaining the highways, their own country roads were neglected. In many areas where for centuries the bad roads had provided the peasants with an extra source of income, either through supplying spare horses or through storing goods in transit, the improved travelling conditions had disastrous consequences. One example was the so-called pass over the Vosges at Zabern, where the old road, which called for an extra pair of strong horses, was replaced in the eighteenth century by a new road on which the steepest gradient was a mere 3 in 100.

The forced labour on the roads, which has been widely quoted as one of the main causes of the French Revolution, was only abolished in 1791, and the Republic was only able to take this step because in the second half of the eighteenth century new economic principles had emerged to expose the extravagance of the 'royal' roads. The main credit for this must go to the Ecole Nationale des Ponts et Chaussées, which was founded in 1747 and had two enlightened directors, Perronet and Trésaguet. As a base they used pyramid-shaped stones which were laid point upwards so that the next layer of gravel was firmly embedded in the foundations. In this way the surface pressure was much more evenly distributed over the foundations, and these roads, with their top-surface of fine gravel and sand, lasted much longer than their predecessors.

This new French technique was widely copied in other parts of Europe, above all in the German States and in Austria. Many a German princeling on the far side of the Rhine, who had aped the Bourbons in their extravagant road-building, trimmed his sails to this new and less expensive wind; the tyrannical Karl Eugen von Württemberg (1728–93) was one of them.

As so often happens, the Revolution brought with it so many new and ill-considered regulations that the result was chaos; Napoleon, the great genius of nineteenth-century road-making, found when he came to power that France had some 30,000 miles of roads, but they were in a lamentable state. The *Journal des Défenseurs de la Patrie* in the eighth year of the new era reported, for example, that travellers on the road from Bordeaux to Bayonne had to pass whole rows of broken-down carriages, and, according to a police report from the year ten, the road from Valenciennes to Cambrai was so bad that passengers on the regular stage-coach had to get out and walk at some points—if they wanted to avoid broken limbs. Both in the north and in the south the picture was the same.

A Prefect by the name of Beugnot, whom the new government had appointed to the Département Seine-Inférieure, had his new duties brought home to him in a particularly forceful way. While he was en route to take over his new post, the shaft of his carriage broke and he had to continue on foot. Covered in mud, he eventually met two gendarmes, who asked if he had seen the Prefect's carriage, which was long overdue. Beugnot had the greatest difficulty in convincing the worthy officers of the law that he was the man they were looking for. . . .

Bonaparte himself was involved in a similar accident on the road to Lyons. His carriage capsized, two members of his suite were injured, and he himself had to be dragged to safety through a broken window like a sack of flour. Fortunately, at that time Napoleon was still a fairly thin man.

Josephine Beauharnais, the dignified Laetitia Bonaparte, Queen Hortense, and other members of Bonaparte's family have all left accounts in their letters and memoirs of adventures on the roads—of the excruciating cobbles between Sedan and Bethel, of brushes with death at Feulen, of a near-plunge into the Moselle, and other such incidents. 'And so we travelled on, growing visibly thinner with every mile,' writes Hortense in one of her letters. Yet she belonged to a select circle which had no need to economize and could well afford to travel in comfort!

It was only under the Empire, with the introduction of lighter carriages, that travelling times were reduced and by that time a certain number of Napoleonic roads were also in use, so that around 1810 one could drive from Paris to Milan in ten days. But two further handicaps were not so easily overcome, and they illustrate how (up to comparatively recent times) Europe was still living by medieval standards: accommodation for travellers was still extremely scarce, and almost all the main highways continued to be unsafe. The country which today is famous for its 'auberges' and its 'cuisine', not only had very little to offer, under the Empire, in the way of accommodation and meals, but the food was dull and badly served, while the few hostelries that existed were swarming with vermin. It was the rule rather than the exception for complete strangers to share a room regardless of sex, and the result was seldom so agreeable as in the case of a certain Madame Nouaillé, whose experience is described by Lenôtre, author of the French *Petite-Histoire*.

The lady arrived from Niort at a road-house, in which she had booked a room. She was taken upstairs, only to discover to her surprise that a young man was preparing to spend the night in her room.

'I intend to sleep in this bed, Madame,' he said bluntly.

'I have no intention of telling you to do otherwise,' replied Madame de Nouaillé, calmly, 'but I also propose to sleep in that bed.' And so it was . . . It was situations of this kind that Casanova enjoyed on his journey from Naples to Rome and described so vividly in his memoirs.

The other problem—lack of security on the roads—sometimes produced more serious results. In the year 1805 Talleyrand, Napoleon's Foreign Minister, was attacked by robbers near Strasbourg. The map of Europe, which Talleyrand was to help draw up ten years later at the Congress of Vienna, was very nearly changed that day by a handful of cut-throats.

The same fate that befell the ugly statesman, Talleyrand, also befell the beautiful singer, Grassini, on a journey from Milan. Her coach was attacked by four bandits in the centre of France, and the singer, who was robbed of all her belongings, also had the painful experience of hearing her assailants speaking in her native tongue. When they were captured a week later, they were found to be Italian deserters.

Incidents of this kind were, of course, of secondary importance to Napoleon. He took to road-making—as to so many other pursuits in life—on the grand scale, and he proved to be far in advance, if not of his times, at least of his fellow-monarchs in Europe. He was not content to issue decrees; he himself drew up plans and compelled the responsible officials to do likewise.

While he was still a junior officer in the Revolution army, Bonaparte had realized how seriously an army's movements can be impeded by mountains; as an artillery officer, long before he became Emperor, he came to appreciate the value of good mountain roads, and it is not hard to imagine that plans for the great pass roads which are today associated with his name were already maturing in his mind during those campaigns in northern Italy which made him famous.

One indication of this is the fact that he gave instructions for the Simplon and Mont Cenis roads to be built while he was still Consul. And no less significant is the impatience with which he followed the progress made on his first great Alpine road, the Simplon. When one reads today of the mistakes that were made and the disasters that took place—inevitable results of Napoleon's impatience—one is reminded how young Alexander besieged and conquered the almost impregnable Tyre with the same grim determination.

The engineers whom the Corsican employed to build the Simplon Pass were allowed no time for preliminary surveys and there was no old road there to help them. There was a mule-track which had been used infrequently ever since Roman times and which apparently dated back to the second century B.C. The only maps available were useless for survey purposes. Complicated but precise measuring instruments were in existence, but very few engineers knew how to use them, and these few very seldom ventured into the mountains. Surveyors' chains, pedometers, spirit-levels and compasses were poor substitutes for the instruments available today. It is therefore not surprising that work had to be stopped in spring, 1801, by which time it was clear that the road both on the north and on the south side was quite unusable.

But Napoleon was not one to give up easily, and, not for the first time, he found the right man for just such an emergency: Nicolas Céard, who was not merely a good engineer but also an excellent leader of men. Anyone else, in fact, would have found it difficult, sometimes even impossible, to hold together this motley collection of men with their inevitable unruly elements, and keep them working when, following a particularly serious accident, they flung down their picks and shovels and refused to go on.

There were many accidents, more than enough to earn a modern engineer a charge of criminal negligence. The precise number of fatal accidents in the course of this gigantic operation will never be known; estimates vary between four hundred and seven hundred. But we do know that the uninterrupted shift-work, day and night, in the Gondo gallery, as it pushed forward through the rock, took a toll of more than a hundred lives.

Céard, on the other hand, was a trained engineer who took every possible precaution. He had made a careful study of the whole massif and surveyed the terrain as best he could. In February 1802, eleven months after accepting the commission, he completed the survey for the stretch from Glis to Domodossola. Speed was the essence of the whole project, explosives were to be used to an extent never known before, and Céard had six thousand workers at his disposal—a small army of men, who were not easy to control in such awkward terrain and, in fact, had only one thing in common: a complete lack of experience in building mountain roads. No one, not even Céard, had any such experience, for in the whole of Europe not a single Alpine road had been built for 1,500 years!

Céard overcame all these obstacles, including the administrative problems (as, for example, when the supply of gunpowder ran out, or, what was even more dangerous, money for the wages was not forthcoming!), and even today experts are agreed that the overall planning of the road was excellent. 'Anyone crossing the Simplon by road today,' says Franz Wallack, builder of the Grossglockner road, 'is forced to admit that its construction, even in our time, would be no easy task, but on the contrary extremely difficult, and that its layout has become a model for subsequent Alpine roads.'

The road was opened on September 25th 1805, having been built in what is even today almost record time; and yet, practically the entire work was done by hand, the shotholes were bored not by machines but by long hand-drills, and there was naturally no question of setting off the charges by electricity. On the other hand, the traffic that passed over the new road was a great deal slower than it is today. On a roadway that was anything from sixteen to twenty feet wide horse-drawn carriages were able to pass in comfort almost everywhere. The gradient, which never exceeded 9 in 100, also presented no problems to a good team of horses, and yet it still took several days for a fully-laden vehicle to climb one side of the pass and make the descent on the other. Lodging facilities were, therefore, absolutely essential, particularly as even in summer the nights could be bitterly cold at 6,500 feet above sea-level; so ample stabling was provided and a number of smaller shelters were scattered along the roadside. These, however, were mere accessories to the road itself and to the bridges—more than six hundred of them, some in wood, some in stone—which formed an essential part of it.

It was not until 1825, twenty years after the road was opened, that the Simplon Hospice was completed a few hundred yards south of the main pass. Since then the monks of St. Bernard have become associated with it.

The Simplon road must be regarded as a turning-point, for it halted—at least in the countries which Napoleon dominated—the steady and almost continuous decline of the European roads since Roman times. In fact, if one considers the boldness of much of the construction, one is forced to the conclusion that the Simplon road was the first in Europe to surpass the work of the Romans.

Some stretches of the roadway had to be hewn out of the rock and this was naturally easier with explosives; the bridges form most impressive arches over deep gorges. For the historian there is particular interest in the fact that, apart from Céard, an engineer named Gianella from Milan played an important part in building this famous road. In the sector entrusted to him, which lies between the Algaby Gallery below the village of Simplon and Domodossola, he appears to have clung to his native traditions and modelled himself on the Roman roads, whereas Céard in the stretch from Glis to Simplon applied up-to-date French principles.

Bonaparte's second great achievement in the art of road-building was the road across Mont Cenis (6,800 feet) between Lanslebourg and Susa, a pass which had been used in prehistoric times but neglected by the Romans in favour of the Mont Genèvre. Napoleon spent even more money on this pass than on the Simplon: twenty million francs, which at the present value of the franc would run into milliards. Both passes together cost nearly a seventh of the total amount Napoleon spent on roads throughout Europe up to the time of his abdication.

Napoleon regarded the Mont Cenis pass as the main gateway into Italy, and, as such, it was much better situated than the Mont Genèvre pass which debouches into the southwards-running Durance valley. The new road was so wide that up to the thirties of the present century, more than a hundred years after it was built, it was still the widest Alpine road between Vienna and Nice. As the difference in height between Lanslebourg and the top of the pass is at most 2,300 feet, Napoleon's engineers were able to complete the climb in six great loops with a maximum gradient of between 8 in 100 and 1 in 10. The descent to the Italian plain also presented no problems, although for horse-drawn artillery it could be even more hazardous than the ascent.

On the Mont Cenis, as on the Simplon, Napoleon naturally had the greatest interest in the maintenance and safety of roads which had been built at such enormous expense. He not only erected a hospice on the Mont Cenis, which lies on the Lac du Mont Cenis 6,200 feet up, he also made generous tax concessions to encourage people to settle there, with the result that, apart from the hospice, about forty houses were built along the pass.

In order to be able to use the Mont Genèvre pass as well, Bonaparte had to improve the approach roads from the interior of France, so he turned the Col de Lautaret into what for that period was a modern highway, linking Grenoble with Briançon (the French terminus of the Mont Genèvre road). The Col de Lautaret, like the Simplon and Mont Cenis, is just over 6,500 feet above sea-level. The total length of the road between Vizille and Briançon is about sixty miles, the gradient never exceeds 1 in 10 (today 7 in 100), and deep gorges keep large parts of the road in permanent shadow.

In the Maritime Alps there were only two passable roads before Napoleon's time: the old Roman Via Aurelia, about eight feet wide, which ran over the mountains above the French Riviera from Mentone to Fréjus and then on to Arles, and a coastal road in the eighteenth-century style, which a Prince of Monaco built between Nice and Mentone so that his residence could also be approached by land. (Landscape pictures in the castle at Monaco show how delightfully unspoilt this coast was in the early eighteenth century before the road was laid. That an area which is so popular today should once have been so wild is as hard to imagine as the fact that Goethe had to travel along the coast by boat, whereas now thousands of cars stream along the famous Gardesana road every day.)

With characteristic boldness and vision, Napoleon decided to modernize the Via Aurelia, which in his time was popularly known as 'lu camin aurelian'. This road still provides some of the most impressive views in Europe. It is 1,800 feet above sea-level at its highest point near the Col d'Eze in the village of La Turbie, where the Augustus column (Trophée des Alpes) stands. Known today as the 'Grande Corniche', it runs about 1,300 feet above the Principality of Monaco. The existence of a Ligurian fort, which can be reached from Le Vistaero by means of a series of steps, proves that the Via Aurelia was originally an old trade route, which Ligurian and Etruscan travellers must have used many centuries before the Roman occupation. The Grande Corniche, the importance of which Napoleon quickly appreciated, is therefore around 3,000 years old.

Europe could only be conquered if the Alps were conquered: this simple fact had compelled the Romans to pit their skill and resources against the mountains. With no less determination, though on a somewhat narrower front, Napoleon launched an attack on these massive mountains. Within a few years he had added to the already existing passes four new routes for his invading armies.

It is interesting in this connection and essential to any assessment of Napoleon as a road-builder that he spent roughly twice as much money on roads between 1804 and 1812 as on military fortifications. If one includes the 31 million francs he spent on bridges, then his roads cost more than the numerous buildings he erected in Paris and the official buildings in the French provinces. But, if by so doing he set a magnificent example, an equally impressive achievement was the legal reforms he introduced for the acquisition and State ownership of land. By these statutory innovations he swept aside abuses which for centuries had made road-building a form of privilege which was detested throughout France.

Chapter 13

A CURIOUS VEHICLE

It all began in the most harmless way.

'A certain mathematicus has invented a carriage for 4 persons,' wrote the correspondent of the *Vossische Zeitung* on August 4th 1727, from Paris, 'with which he will drive without horses through its own internal motion fourteen French miles in two hours and this in the deepest sand.'

So a desert coach, a special vehicle for deep sand, was the first precursor of the automobile; unfortunately, nothing more is known of its 'internal motion'. The ambition of the inventor seems to have remained unfulfilled, for six years later another inventor receives honourable mention, this time in the *Hamburgischer Korrespondent* 10 May 1733:

> In Berlin, a certain distinguished person, who is in the service of the King of Prussia, has invented a curious vehicle which, as soon as anyone seats himself in it, moves off quickly and, according to one's wishes, continues to move slowly or more rapidly, also to right or to left, and turns in a small circle; at the same time it is equipped, unlike other such vehicles, with a spring, in consequence it remains constantly in motion as long as one pleases.

Unfortunately, the inventor was apparently too distinguished to take out a patent and this phenomenon too was heard of no more.

This brief report does at least indicate that even at that early stage the use of a spring to propel an automobile was not entirely unknown. They may even have used two springs, so that the passenger could wind up one while the other unwound—bigger versions of the toy cars which modern children tend to look down upon as old-fashioned.

Here, too, it was steam that brought a revolution. When England's roads were finally transformed early in the nineteenth century at the instigation of McAdam and others, it was not merely the stage-coaches that benefited but also a few dozen vehicles which can best be described as steam buses. The first to be put into regular service, which implied fairly safe road conditions, was Gurney's Steam Coach, which started running between London and Bath in 1827. The return journey was 190 miles and the passengers had to put up with more steam and smoke than was comfortable. Not much better was the Road Steamer, which a certain Walter Hancock put into service between London and Stratford in 1831. In 1833 a London steam-bus service started between Paddington and the City, which was much faster, much more economical and much safer than the horse buses on the same route (although the general public was by no means convinced of its safety: the passengers sat in fear and trembling, for the rival horse-bus owners had confidently predicted that the boiler would explode).

From 1902 onwards the Road Car Company in London used steam buses built by Thorneycrofts, the Paris fire-service employed steam fire-engines, and a number of different versions of the so-called locomobile—mobile steam-engines—were introduced in various parts of Europe. For more than half a century all kinds of vehicles had been travelling under steam on normal roads (and not merely on rails), when Meyer's *Lexicon* came to this rather startling conclusion: 'All experiments so far suggest that it is quite hopeless to consider transporting passengers by road locomotive in the form of steam coaches, steam carriages, steam buses or steam cabs, as is demonstrated by the Bollée steam car and the so-called petrol car, which is fitted with a petrol engine [sic]' (1896 Vol. XI, p. 464).

Ten years *before* this epitaph was printed, Gottlieb Daimler had made the first trial runs with an internal combustion engine developed on new principles, and Karl Benz had experimented successfully with a three-wheeled motor. Five years later, still well ahead of the dictionary, a Peugot car with a Daimler engine ran in the 750-mile (cycle) race, Paris–Brest–Paris, and maintained an average speed of 8·5 miles an hour.

In 1901, ten years after this race, Mercedes racing cars designed by Maybach achieved an average speed of over 50 m.p.h. at Nice.

At a moment when they were acquiring new importance the condition of the roads was depressing enough, but it would have been still worse if cycling clubs, particularly in the Western countries, had not demanded an improvement. From the eighteen-sixties onwards bicycles were being produced in every industrial county in Europe and the so-called safety bicycle mass-produced by Neumann around 1890 was essentially the same as the average model of today—with two wheels of equal size, a fairly low-slung frame and a total weight of 20 to 30 lb., it was well on the way to becoming a 'people's' machine.

It was, of course, expecting a great deal of any State that it should help to reinstate its roads merely for bicycles and cycle clubs. But in England and America clubs as such had become so much an accepted part of life that a public hearing was given even to those people who had banded together in a somewhat eccentric and not altogether gentlemanly form of exercise. The Cyclists' Touring Club and the National Cyclists' Union (which was more interested in the sporting side) had already joined forces to set up an important institution, the Roads Improvement Association, before the first motor-cars appeared on the English roads. The Association concentrated in the beginning on improving existing roads and on making technical recommendations to the Government. It met with considerably less opposition than the first motorists, for the bicycle was obviously much more dangerous to the cyclist himself than to other road-users.

The first motor-cars, on the other hand, aroused widespread prejudice due largely to the occasional boiler explosions and other mishaps that had befallen the steam-driven vehicles, and they were also handicapped by a harsh law requiring that every motor vehicle must be preceded by a man with a red flag. It may have been a pleasing sight to the early Socialists, but to the pioneer motorist it was an intolerable state of affairs. After years of heated controversy the law was eventually repealed and in 1896 the admission of the motor-car to full membership of the fraternity of the road was celebrated with the first London to Brighton run.

If France, Germany and England had once again taken the lead, the United States showed the greatest interest in the internal combustion engine from the outset, and Italy, by inaugurating the famous Targa Floria road race in Sicily, established herself as the leading country in motor racing.

From our own reactions to dust, potholes and awkward bends we can imagine how those early motorists must have felt. As a rule their machines were more robustly built than many present-day models, but they were nothing like so safe to drive. The motorist, in fact, had to fight on three fronts simultaneously: against the poor roads, against a general public that was almost universally hostile, and against the defects of his machine.

Gradually, however, in all the countries concerned, the sentence of death (which had really been pronounced on the roads) was lifted and they were given a new lease of life. And not before time, for otherwise not only would the roads have been condemned to play the part of mere accessories to the railways, but the motor-car would almost certainly have been killed in infancy. Why? Simply because costs were too high. By modern standards the purchase price of cars was astronomical; and driving these luxury vehicles was also a costly business, for even on a reasonably good road there was heavy wear and tear on tyres. In fact, some authorities maintain that the main reason why the inventions by the Germans Daimler and Benz and the Austrian Siegfried Marcus were not developed in their own countries was the state of the roads. The Daimler invention had to be exploited by the French firm Panhard-Levasseur, for only France had the long, straight roads with a surface that showed these new vehicles to advantage and enabled them to be used in good conditions.

To be quite fair one must admit that, while the motorists were dissatisfied with the roads, the roads had no reason to be satisfied with the motorists. The explanation was simple: speed. The propulsion through the wheels of the motor vehicle imposed a strain on the road surface which it had never experienced from a horse-drawn cart—a strain which was greatest with acceleration and braking. Moreover, the early models were so constructed that the danger of skidding was much greater than it is today. Experiments were made with various combinations of strip steel and rubber in an attempt to produce skid-free tyres, but the only effect was to increase the damage to the roads. The clouds of dust of which drivers and passengers complained were nothing more than pulverized road, and each cloud that settled helped to undermine the surface still further. And the damage done to a soft, wet road by these early motor vehicles can be imagined by anyone who has driven a heavy truck on rough country roads.

Then, as now, speed restrictions were soon devised, and in the Swiss canton of Graubünden motor vehicles were even forbidden altogether. But the hotel-keepers of Graubünden soon had reason to regret this hasty decision which robbed them of valuable tourist traffic, and elsewhere both motorists and not a few city fathers realized that imposing a speed limit was not the best answer.

A much better solution was found. In the 1880s a process had been invented by a French engineer, Girardeau, and an Italian, Rimini, which consisted in coating the surface of the road with tar. This eliminated dust and made the road more resistant. In the early stages the process was applied somewhat crudely. A few men with brooms swept the road clean, then a roller went over it, and the men returned with large cans of liquid tar which they sprayed over the road. A layer of soft sand on top, and after a few days the road was reopened to traffic.

The first State to adopt this method officially was the Principality of Monaco. The whole of its roads put together only covered a few dozen miles, but around the turn of the century they were amongst the busiest in Europe. At that time cars were only driven for pleasure. None revelled in this new sport more than the wealthy inhabitants of the Riviera, for, quite apart from the fact that they could afford such a luxury, the weather, the beautiful landscape, and the relatively short distances between Alassio and St. Tropez were all conducive to motoring. So in the year 1900 about 500 horse-carriages, the same number of motor-cars, 200 motor-cycles and several hundred local carts were passing every day along the Grande Corniche—the Roman road which Napoleon had reconstructed.

Guglielminetti, the Swiss engineer, who had written a number of articles in support of tarred roads, was commissioned in 1901 to apply the process to all the roads in Monaco. The lead, once given, was soon followed by Belgium, Germany, Switzerland, Austria and Italy.

The way was now clear for experiments with other binding materials. Local peculiarities had an important bearing: in California, for example, petroleum proved to have stronger binding qualities and was more plentiful than in Europe; in Canada a large gas company made experiments with impregnation, and on a particularly busy road, where most of the traffic was heavy commercial vehicles, tar was not merely spread over the surface but poured into the underlayers, thus producing the first tar macadam road.

Most people, however, still regarded the motor-car as a completely useless invention and motoring as a form of sport reserved for the leisured classes—like polo or golf, only much less agreeable for the bystander. Two things happened—apart from a series of sporting events—to make people realize that 'there might be something to the motor-car after all'. The first was the long-distance drive from Peking to Paris, which has since become almost legend and which was deliberately proposed by the French newspaper *Le Matin* in order to put a stop once and for all to the endless discussions about the pros and cons of the motor-car. The second important development was the First World War. . . .

Today it may be difficult to understand why *Le Matin* chose the Peking–Paris route in particular, but Peking, though in the Orient, still lay in the Old World; it was as much a part of it then as Russia; the tarred road had just been forestalled by the Trans-Siberian Railway, which had brought East Asia and Europe closer together than anyone could have foreseen. The old metropolis Peking and the old metropolis Paris regarded themselves as the Eastern and Western centres of a common sphere of culture which was bound together internally by countless ancient trade routes.

The makes of cars which took part in this unique rally can only be found today in the catalogues of certain museums: two De-Dion-Boutons (as a works team); a Spyker (from Holland); an Itala, driven by Prince Scipione Borghese and a co-driver named Guizzardi and carrying as passenger the famous Italian journalist Luigi Barzini; and finally a three-wheeled Contal, which was driven by August Pons, father of the famous singer Lily Pons. The advance report on this contest in *Le Matin* had a simplicity that is lacking in the conditions laid down for many modern events:

> There are neither formalities to be observed nor any regulations which might impede the competitors. All that is required is to drive off from Peking and to arrive at Paris . . .

In spite of all the publicity given to it, the contest was a triumph of sportsmanship. Prince Borghese spent vast sums on his preparations, on reconnaissance trips along the route and particularly in the mountains of China. Supplies of fuel, oil and water were provided at prearranged points (or at least they were brought with this in mind) and on June 10th 1907, the small convoy set off bravely on its journey.

Monsieur Pons was the first to fall out: his three-wheeled machine was quite unsuited to roads which in places were almost impassable. After undergoing incredible hardships in the mountains, the others crossed the Gobi desert. In the sand, however, these old machines with their large wheels stood up better than camels. Borghese and Barzini were the first to reach the Russian frontier at Kiachta, the old tea centre, after taking only four days to cross the desert—a journey that took at least fourteen days by caravan. The two De-Dion-Boutons were close on the Itala's heels, but the Spyker had fallen far behind. It looked as if the race was more or less over, for Siberia, unlike China, was well supplied with roads. But then something happened that any motorist in Russia must dread: it rained.

After driving three thousand miles through mud and overcoming the most fantastic hazards, even the indomitable Prince Borghese nearly gave in, but in fact the only one to capitulate was the courageous driver of the small Dutch car, who was forced through illness to stop at Berlin—only a day's journey from his goal. On August 10th, after sixty days on the road, Borghese arrived in Paris, covered in dust but in excellent spirits. The two De-Dion-Boutons followed twenty days later.

Had Sven Hedin this pioneering expedition in mind when he put forward his plan for a Trans-Asiatic Motorway? We do not know. No one thought, after this successful experiment, of abandoning the Trans-Siberian Railway in favour of a Eurasian highway. Nothing was changed. Anyone who seriously suggested using this route today would be unlikely to interest any motor-car firm sufficiently even to obtain a production model. But the whole enterprise was symptomatic of the enormous optimism and enthusiasm which fired the devotees of motoring at the beginning of our century. It was no fault of theirs, or indeed of the motor-cars, if there is still no trans-Asiatic motor traffic.

Then came the First World War, in which the Uhlans rode once more with penons and lances as they had done in 1870, but this time they met their end to the clatter of caterpillar wheels and the drone of aeroplanes. By the time the war was over, it had consumed more motor vehicles than all the countries in the world had possessed up to 1914, but, for all the lives and machines it had destroyed, it had at least proved the worth of the motor-car.

The generals had managed to hold up the electrification of the railways, because if one single power-station was put out of action, they argued, then a whole traffic network would be immobilized. So they were all for steam. But the war showed how vulnerable railways and stations were, whereas a strongly-built motor vehicle could drive round shell-holes, was not too heavy for pontoon bridges, and could even reach forward positions. After the First World War it was clear that the next war would be waged with gasoline engines and, especially in submarines, with diesel engines. This grim certainty did more than anything else to stimulate road-building in Europe. At long last the road-builders had an argument which, unfortunately, is most likely to attract funds.

Once again it was not before time. During the war years no one had been prepared to spend money on roads or even shown interest in them. But suddenly the overgrown and dilapidated roads were crowded with surplus army vehicles. Badly sprung, their tires worn, they went for a song. Trucks and lorries soon proved much more convenient for short journeys, and particularly for door-to-door deliveries, than the railways.

more convenient for short journeys, and particularly for door-to-door deliveries, than the railways.

By 1925 there were more than two million commercial vehicles in the United States, in Britain more than 200,000, in Germany 65,000, in Italy 35,000 and in France as many as a quarter of a million—and all this at a time when the modern highway was still unknown!

In 1923 an International Road Congress was held at Seville, a beautiful town which also gave delegates who arrived by car an opportunity of studying at first hand and in advance some of the more pressing problems they were going to discuss.

The recommendations made by this Congress nearly forty years ago have remained so topical that one can safely say the Seville Congress marked the beginning of modern road-building throughout the world. Had these recommendations been put into practice, many later congresses would have been superfluous. At Seville, the road-builders and traffic experts (among others) called for crossing-free roads, or crossings with a clear view ahead of at least a hundred yards; for roads that would be confined to motorists only; for a uniform system of road-signals and traffic-signs; and for bends with a minimum view ahead of a hundred yards. Most important, however, was the demand that roads should be built specially to carry heavy motor vehicles—that a new technique should be evolved for both surface and foundations, which should make allowance for rapid acceleration and the steadily increasing weight of vehicles. Special recommendations were also made concerning gradients and curves. In general, it was made abundantly clear that this new mode of transport—the automobile—had developed to the point where all existing roads, which had hitherto been regarded as adequate, were quite unusable. A vast web of grey and black highways began to spread across the face of the earth, and a new era in the history of world traffic had dawned.

BIBLIOGRAPHY

Albrecht, I. *Die Zunahme des Strassenverkehrs als Folge Wirtschaftsstruktureller*, Veränderungen, Bielefeld, 1957 (Kirschbaum).

Association pour la Diffusion de la Pensée Française, *Les routes de France depuis les Origines jusqu' à nos jours*, Colloques Cahiers de Civilisation, Paris, 1959.

Barthold, V. V. *La Découverte de l'Asie* (translated from the Russian), Paris, 1947 (Payot).

Baudin, L. *La Vie Quotidienne au Temps des Derniers Incas*, Paris, 1955 (Hachette).

Baudin, L. *L'Empire socialiste des Inka*, Paris, 1928 (Travaux et Memoires de l'Institut d'ethnologie No. 5).

Bibby, G. *The Testimony of the Spade*, New York, 1956 (A. Knopf).

Birk, A. *Die Strasse*. Karlsbad-Drahowity, 1934 (Adam Kraft Verlag).

Buchner, E. *Das Neueste von Gestern*, 5 vols., Munich, 1911–13 (Langen).

Burckhardt, J. *Die Zeit Konstantins des Grossen*, Leipzig, first published 1853, modern edition, 1935 (Kröner).

Cambridge Ancient History. Published by Cambridge University Press.

Cavaillès, H. *La Route Française*, Paris, 1946 (Librairie Armand Colin).

Coquand, R. *La Planification et la Construction des Autoroutes Françaises*. La Route Editions Science et Industrie, 1956, issued as a supplement to 'Travaux'. See also, *Routes*, 2 volumes, Paris, 1957 (Editions Eyrolles).

Disselhoff, H. D. *Geschichte der Altamenhanischen Kulturen*, Munich, 1953 (Oldenbourg).

East, G. and Spate, O. H. K. *Changing Map of Asia*, 3rd ed. revised 1958 (Methuen).

East, G. *An Historical Geography of Europe*, London, 1949 (Methuen).

Ferdinandy, M. de. *Tschingis Khan*, Hamburg, 1958 (Rowohlt).

Friedländer, L. *Roman Life and Manners under the Early Empire*, 4 vols., London, 1908–13 (Geo. Routledge and Sons).

Gerster, G. *Sahara*, London, 1960 (Barrie and Rockliff).
Grousset, R. *L'homme et son Histoire*, Paris, 1953 (Plon).
Hagen, V. W. von. *Highway of the Sun*, London, 1956 (Victor Gollancz).
Hedin, S. *Silk Road*, 1938 (Routledge).
Hedin, S. *Wandering Lake*, 1940 (Routledge).
Hennig, R. *Terrae Incognitae*, 4 vols., Leiden, 1956 (E. J. Brill).
Hering, E. *Wege und Strassen der Welt*, Dr. Hans Riegler Verlag, Berlin, 1938.
Herrmann, A. *Die Alten Seidenstrassen Zwischen China und Syrien*, Julius Springer, Berlin-Wien, 1939.
Karais, K. von. *Deutsche Strassenfibel*, Leipzig, 1937 (Staackmann).
Kastl, J. *Entwicklung der Strassenbautechnik*, Berlin, 1953 (Verlag Technick).
Kees, H. *Das alte Agypten*, Berlin, 1955 (Akademie-Verlag).
Kunde, H. *Lehren aus dern Strassenbau in den U.S.A.*, Faschngsgesellschaft für das Strassenwesen, Neue Folge, Part 24, Bielefeld, 1956 (Kirschbaum Verlag).
Krüger, K. *Strassen der Erde*, Berlin, 1949 (Verlag Klasing and Co. G.m.b.H.).
Leeming, E. L. *Road Engineering*, London, 1952 (Constable and Company).
Li Chih-ch'ang. *Travels of an Alchemist*, translated by Arthur Waley, 1931 (Routledge).
Marchal, L. *La Chute du Grand Chimu*, Paris, 1955 (Plon).
Margary, I. D. *Roman Roads in Britain*, 2 vols., London, 1957 (Phoenix House Ltd).
Marseille, P. von. *Uber das Weltmeer Weimar*, 1959 (Böhlan).
Moule, A. C., and Pelliot P. *Marco Polo, the Description of the World*, 2 vols., London, 1938 (Routledge).
Neumann, E. *Neuzeitlicher Strassenbau*, 6th edition, 1959, Berlin, Göttingen Heidelberg (Springer Verlag).
Ortelius, A. *Theatrum Orbis Terranum* (contains the 'Catalogus Cartographo-rum'), Gotha, 1928–30 (Petermanns Mitteilungen).
Otremba, E. *Allgemeine Geographie des Welthandels und des Weltverkehrs*, Stuttgart, 1957 (Franckp).
Panikkar, K. K. (pseu. Kerala Putra). *India and China*, Asia publications, London, 1957 (Luzac).
Percheron, M. *Les Conquérants d'Asie*, Paris, 1951 (Payot).
Przevalskij, N. M. *Hanhai-von Kuldscha uber die Tianshan und zum Lob-nor*, Leipzig, 1952 (Bibliographic Institute, collection Volk und Buch).
Roeder, G. *Altägyptische Erzählungen und Märchen*, Jena, 1927 (Die Märchen dre-Welt-literatur).
Rose., A C. *Public Roads of the past: 3500 B.C. to A.D. 1800*, undated (American Association of State Highway Officials).
Roussel, R. *Les pélérinages à Travers les Siècles*, Paris, 1954 (Payot).
Savill, A. *Alexander the Great and His Time*, London, 1960 (Barrie and Rockliff).
Schreiber, H. and G. *Vanished Cities* (translated from the German), New York, 1957 (Knopf), London, 1958 (Weidenfeld).
Scurla, H. *Reisetagebuch des Forschers*, Hermann Schlagintweit, Berlin, 1959 (Verlag der Nation).
Smith, I. *Windmill Hill and Avebury*, London, 1959 (Barrie and Rockliff).
Speck, A. *Der Kunststrassenbau*, Berlin, 1950 (W. Ernst and Sohn).
Speck, E. *Handelsgeschichte des Altertums*, 3 vols., Leipzig, 1901–6 (Friedrich Brandstetter).
Spuler, B. *Die Mongolen in Iran*, Berlin, 1948 (Akademie-Verlag).

Stein, Sir M. A. *On Ancient Central Asian Tracks*, London, 1933 (Macmillan).

Strong, L. A. G. *The Rolling Road*, London, 1956 (Hutchinson).

Sykes, Sir P. *The Quest for Cathay*, London, 1936 (Macmillan).

Syme, R. *The Story of Britain's Highways*, London, 1952 (Sir Isaac Pitman and Sons Ltd.).

Tarn, W. W. *Alexander the Great* (2 vols.), 1948, Toronto, Cambridge (Macmillan).

Tolstow, S. P. *Auf den Spuren der Altchores-mischen Kultur*, Berlin, 1953 (Kutlur und Fortschritt).

Vacano, O. W. von. *Die Etrusker in der Welt der Antike*, Hamburg, 1957 (Rowohlt).

Wallack, F. *Die Grossglockner-Hochalpenstrasse*, Vienna, 1949 (Springer-Verlag).

Webb, S. and Beatrice Webb. *English Local Government: the Study of the Kings Highway*, London, 1913 (Longmans).

INDEX

Note. Where more than one version of a place-name is given, the place will usually be found under the modern one.

4.50L   3-62

388.1 - S378   cop.1

Schreiber

Merchants, pilgrims, and highwaymen.

 TWO WEEK BOOK

oad   DISCARD